cut here

Essential Education about Home Networking

Source	URL	Topic
2MN8, Inc.	www.2mn8.com	Tutorials and product reviews on home networking
ZDNet	www.pcmag.com	General PC info and product reviews
ZDNet	www.pcweek.com	General PC industry news
Small Office	www.smalloffice.com	Information for the small office or home office

Essential Software for Home Networking

Software	Manufacturer	URL
Internet music	Nullsoft	www.winamp.com
Internet music and video	Real Networks	www.real.com
Online games and animation	Macromedia	www.shockwave.com
Compression utility	WinZip	www.winzip.com
Online video	Apple	www.quicktime.com
Acrobat Reader	Adobe	www.adobe.com/prodindex/acrobat/readstep.html
Chat tools	Mirabilis	www.icq.com
Anti-virus	McAfee	www.mcafee.com

Useful Search Engines

Engine	URL	Description
Lycos	www.lycos.com	General search engine
AltaVista	www.altavista.com	General search engine
Excite	www.excite.com	General search engine
Yahoo!	www.yahoo.com	General search engine
Tucows	www.tucows.com	Windows software
Download.com	www.download.com	PC and Mac software
Lycos	mp3.lycos.com	MP3 music search engine

Optional Hardware for Home Networking

Hardware	Manufacturer	URL
Ethernet hubs	3Com	www.3com.com
Camera balls	Logitech	www.logitech.com
Home automation modules	X-10, Inc.	www.x-10.com
Digital cameras	Kodak	www.kodak.com
Wireless networks	Proxim	www.proxim.com
DVD player	Creative Labs	www.creative.com
Multimedia speakers	Cambridge Soundworks	www.cambridgesoundworks.com
Phone line networks	Tut Systems	www.tutsys.com
Power line networks	Intelogis, Inc.	www.intelogis.com
Wireless keyboard	Logitech	www.logitech.com
Portable MP3 player	Diamond Multimedia	www.diamondmm.com

Essential Content for the Home Network

Site	URL	Description
Macromedia	www.shockwave.com	Games and animations
CNN	www.cnn.com	Audio and video news clips
Broadcast.com	www.broadcast.com	Music, news, and talk radio
The Rio Port	www.rioport.com	Online music
MP3.com	www.mp3.com	Online music
Disney	www.disney.com	Kids games and activities
Discjockey.com	www.discjockey.com	Online music
MTV Online	www.mtv.com	Music videos
National Geographic	www.nationalgeographic.com	Education, culture, and history

Optional Services for the Home Network

Service	URL	Description
Hotmail	www.hotmail.com	Free email site
Hotoffice	www.hotoffice.com	Email, file sharing, groupware
Quicken	www.quicken.com	Online financial services and information
Etrade	www.etrade.com	Online stock broker and financial services
Mplayer	www.mplayer.com	Multiplayer game service
Bonus.com	www.bonus.com	Kids game site
Encyclopedia Britannica	www.eb.com	Online encyclopedia
Merriam Webster	www.m-w.com	Online dictionary
Ebay	www.ebay.com	Auction house

THE COMPLETE IDIOT'S GUIDE® TO

Networking Your Home

Mark Speaker

Mark Thompson

que®

A Division of Macmillan Computer Publishing
201 West 103rd Street, Indianapolis, Indiana 46290

The Complete Idiot's Guide to Networking Your Home

Copyright © 1999 by Que

International Standard Book Number: 0-7897-1963-0

Library of Congress Catalog Card Number: 98-89193

Printed in the United States of America

First Printing: April 1999

02 01 00 99   4 3 2 1

Trademarks

Warning and Disclaimer

Associate Publisher
Greg Wiegand

Executive Editor
Christopher A. Will

Acquisitions Editor
Tracy Williams

Development Editor
Kate Shoup Welsh

Managing Editor
Lisa Wilson

Project Editor
Carol Bowers

Copy Editor
Geneil Breeze

Indexer
Erika Millen

Proofreader
Gene Redding

Illustrator
Judd Winnick

Technical Editor
Jim Cooper

Cover Designer
Mike Freeland

Interior Designer
Nathan Clement

Production
Brandon Allen
Stacey Richwine-DeRome
Timothy Osborn
Staci Somers

Contents at a Glance

Table of Contents

Foreword

The personal computer has become a powerful platform in the home for work, communication, education, and entertainment. Almost overnight, the Internet has exploded into an essential means of information access. Many new digital appliances are on the horizon that will exploit communication of voice and video across digital networks. Just as there is a critical need for high-speed connections to information and broadband entertainment sources *outside* the home, there is a growing need to rapidly move this digital data between devices *within* the home.

The driving force behind the need for home connectivity products is the growth of online households and the growing number of homes with two or more PCs. More than 47 percent of U.S. households are likely to have Internet access devices by 2002, with some 20 percent of this subset owning multiple devices that need to share access to the Internet as well as each other.

Mark Carpenter

Vice President, Home Phoneline Networking Alliance

About the Authors

Mark Speaker is currently the president of 2MN8, Inc., a company focused on delivering home networking education. He was previously responsible for the implementation of a leading-edge system that modeled the communications network of the first local exchange carrier in Canada, Metronet Communications. Mark has editorial responsibility for the tutorials at www.2MN8.com.

Mark Thompson began his career at the University of Lethbridge, working five years in a variety of academic, systems management, and network management positions. While at the university, Mark instructed numerous courses in Information Systems and Networking Technology. He is currently the senior network planner for western Canada with Metronet Communications.

Mark has eight years experience in planning and designing networks ranging in size from small home networks to regional and national networks with thousands of users. He has written dozens of manuals on personal computing and networking and delivered hundreds of lectures and seminars on networking technology.

Acknowledgments

We would like to take this opportunity to extend special thanks to someone who has helped us immensely, George Lermer. As the Dean of the Faculty of Management at the University of Lethbridge, George employed and mentored both of us over the years. His trust and guidance taught us to reach for the top shelf, opening up opportunities for which we are forever grateful.

Mark Speaker

There were many late nights between the day I heard the exciting, yet somewhat humbling, words, "We think what you have to say is perfect for *The Complete Idiot*," and the day we finished writing. I wouldn't have been able to spend so many of them away from close friends without their unending support. Thanks a ton!

I would also like to take this chance to thank my parents, Ray and Ingrid. I don't think I could have coauthored a book like this if I hadn't spent all those hours answering your computer questions. Thank you for everything you've done for me and for encouraging me to do the things I want to do in life.

Mark Thompson

I'd like to thank my father, Neil Thompson, who more than anybody else made me who I am today. I'd also like to thank my two daughters, Jesse and Kyra, for hanging in there and supporting me, especially when they were the ones being affected the most.

Finally, I'd like to thank everybody who tolerated my own special brand of insanity while writing this book.

What a wild ride it has been. I can't imagine going through it again—and I can't wait 'til next time!

Tell Us What You Think!

As the reader of this book, *you* are our most important critic and commentator. We value your opinion and want to know what we're doing right, what we could do better, what areas you'd like to see us publish in, and any other words of wisdom you're willing to pass our way.

As the Executive Editor for the Web development team at Macmillan Computer Publishing, I welcome your comments. You can fax, email, or write me directly to let me know what you did or didn't like about this book—as well as what we can do to make our books stronger.

Please note that I cannot help you with technical problems related to the topic of this book, and that due to the high volume of mail I receive, I might not be able to reply to every message.

When you write, please be sure to include this book's title and author, as well as your name and phone or fax number. I will carefully review your comments and share them with the author and editors who worked on the book.

Fax: 317-581-4666

Email: consumer@mcp.com

Mail: Executive Editor
          Consumer Publishing
          Macmillan Computer Publishing
          201 West 103rd Street
          Indianapolis, IN 46290 USA

Introduction

Welcome to the *Complete Idiot's Guide to Networking Your Home*. By buying this book, you are starting out on an exciting journey: the journey to a networked home. A networked home means different things to different people but, first and foremost for everyone, the journey to home networking begins by connecting two or more computers together.

Although we are going to explore many great reasons to network your computers, the three most compelling reasons for networking are

> ➤ **Sharing files and printers between your computers**   Sharing files between computers can make your life much easier, almost eliminating the need to shuttle diskettes from computer to computer. Sharing can also provide a safe, simple method of backing up files, allowing you to copy files from one computer to another for safe storage.
>
> Printer sharing is not only incredibly convenient, it can also save you money by eliminating the need to buy more than one printer for the home.
>
> ➤ **Sharing an Internet connection so that both computers can be on the Internet at the same time**   Many people will find a shared Internet connection to be the biggest advantage to a home network. There is nothing worse than having to use a specific computer when you want to use the Internet, except maybe having to wait for somebody else to finish checking his email before you can.
>
> ➤ **Playing multiplayer games with your friends**   The number of games that let you play head-to-head against somebody else is growing at an amazing rate. Kids' games, bridge, poker, and digital versions of common board games all have multiplayer versions. Of course, we can't forget to mention the ever popular first person shooter and blow-em-up games.

After the home computer network is in place, the real fun begins! Almost all home devices, from blenders to stereos to doorbells, have computer chips in them already. The overwhelming trend among the creators of these products is to develop a simple, standardized way of connecting every household device to a home network.

Every one of these devices presents a new opportunity to make your life easier or more enjoyable:

> ➤ 1,000 different radio stations can now be accessed directly over the Internet. Oops, make that 1,002. Uh, just a sec—make that 1,005.
> ➤ Watching TV on your computer is cheap and simple to set up.
> ➤ Playing the latest video game on a 36-inch TV is a *much different* experience from playing it on a 15-inch computer monitor.

➤ Wouldn't it be nice to be able to turn off all the lights in your house from a single button on your bed stand, particularly on a cold winter night?

➤ Music lovers will fall in love with the idea of keeping thousands of songs on their computers. Storing and searching for the songs on the home computer is much easier than flipping through 100 compact discs on a bookshelf.

To help you down the road to networking your home, we also want to make sure that you realize that all the products discussed in this book are readily available. With the exception of the look to the future presented in Chapter 20, "Judy Jetson Eat Your Heart Out!: The Home Area Network of the Future," everything you need to network your home can be bought from any well-stocked computer or electronics store. And best of all, incredible advances have been made in making these products easy to install for the average home computer user.

Who Should Buy This Book?

➤ People who have two or more computers in their home

➤ People who are thinking about buying a second computer

➤ Anybody who wants to make her life easier by controlling her home with a computer

➤ Those who want to learn how to play, store, and catalog music on their computers

➤ Anyone who wants to learn how to play computer games against other people

➤ Residents of the states of California and New York or the provinces of Ontario and British Columbia

➤ People who live in a city or town that has running water

➤ Anybody with a pulse

The Lay of the Land: What's in the Book

The Complete Idiot's Guide to Networking Your Home is written in five separate parts. No matter how far down the road to computer or home networking you are, be sure to read Chapter 1, "Beginning at the Beginning: What Is a Home Network?," to see the possibilities behind home area networking. If you already have a network in place, feel free to hop, skip, and jump to the chapters that interest you most.

Part 1: Introduction to Home Area Networking

The first section is a basic introduction to the concept of a networked home—what it is, how it works, and tons of reasons why you'll want to add one to your home.

Part 2: Networking Your Home Computers

The second section explains some of the alternatives for connecting your home computers. Ethernet is discussed in great detail, as are newer products such as phone line, power line, and wireless networks that don't require you to add any new wires or cables to your home.

Part 3: Getting the HAN Up and Running

This section shows you how to share files, printers, and an Internet connection between all the computers on your home network.

Part 4: Mission Control: The Role of the PC

The book's fourth section walks you through the process of finding and installing the most useful software and hardware for your home area network. On the software side, you find out how to get the most out of your Internet browser and email program, as well as new and exciting ways to videoconference, teleconference, and listen to music over the Internet. On the hardware side, we show you the latest home networking products for viewing, scanning, and backing up your digital home.

Part 5: Enhancing the Digital Home

Using the home computer network as a base, this section shows all the major highlights in the world of home area networking. First we show you how to get the most out of your home office and then we let you blow off a little steam by showing you how to play computer games across your network or the Internet. If you need to relax, the chapters on audio and video will astound you with how easy it is to add audio and video to your home area network. If you want to automate simple household tasks in a safer and more secure environment, then you'll love the chapters on home automation and security.

The final chapter shows you some exciting products and technologies that companies are working to bring you in the near future.

Part 6: Appendixes

The book closes with three appendixes. Appendix A presents a glossary of terms related to home computers and home area networking. Appendix B provides a complete list of the most useful Web sites for people interested in home networking. Appendix C is a list of Internet service providers that specialize in high-speed connections to the Internet.

Part 1

Introduction to Home Area Networking

Welcome to the world of home area networking. This section is a quick and dirty introduction designed to show you the top reasons why and how people network their homes. Whether you're brand new to the world of networking or you spend your nights at home trying to shave three seconds off your PC's startup time, you've come to the right place.

Chapter 1

Beginning at the Beginning: What Is a Home Network?

In This Chapter

➤ Building a network with the computers you already have

➤ Why you need a networked home

➤ How to lower costs with a home network

➤ Enhancing your home office with a network

Try as you might, it's becoming more difficult to get by with only one computer in the home. That isn't to say that you can't survive without a computer, let alone three; it's just that it's getting difficult to keep those additional computers from sneaking in.

If you find yourself with more than one computer, most likely you'll admit to it having happened by accident. You got your first computer a few years back to play games or to do some bookkeeping with. Later, you upgraded and neglected to throw the first one away. Whether it was roommates or kids, some time after that, a dependent or two came along. They ended up with a computer on their desk as well. Boom! Three computers, and you weren't even trying.

Even if it were by accident, this would have been a pricey proposition for a household in 1997. Increased competition among computer manufacturers and increased demand from consumers caused computer prices to plummet in 1998. 1999 will see that price fall even farther. Now you can build a two- or three-computer home *on purpose* for less than $2,000. After you've gone that far, there are many great reasons for tying them together in a home area network (HAN).

Here, Share, Everywhere

One of the greatest benefits of a home network is its capability to share the information and equipment on one computer with another computer. The Internet has shown us that the value of a network increases when it is used to share ideas and information. The value of sharing is the same whether it's down the hallway or around the world.

Fortunately, you don't have to look far to find some household examples of the power of sharing:

➤ Much like the way your keys are always in your other jacket, your resume is never on the computer with the attached printer. Wouldn't it be nice to be able to print to that printer from any computer in the house?

➤ How about installing the latest version of Quake on your computer using the CD-ROM in your dad's computer (and then, after it's installed, challenging him to a multiplayer Death Match)?

➤ If Dad doesn't want to take you on, you'll need to find a worthy opponent on the Internet. With some shareware and a few cables, you can always get to the Net through the modem on his computer. Thankfully, you won't have to leave the comfort of your own room to do it.

➤ Do you struggle to keep your kids from using *your* email account to contact *their* friends, but don't know how to get around the problem? No problem! Many Internet service providers (ISPs) will let you have more than one email account on their systems. To help you out, many email programs and Internet browsers will let you set them up for more than one user.

Sharing Equals Saving

Although your kids may enjoy blowing away bad guys, they don't need a CD-ROM on their computer to do it. Each copy of their favorite game can be loaded from your CD-ROM drive. This idea holds for most devices plugged into a networked computer. Sharing hard drives, modems, printers, and tape backups across the home network can save you both money and time:

➤ Does the idea of having to buy two black and white printers—one for each of your two computers—bother you? With a home network, you can share one color printer between them for the same price.

➤ With all the video and audio files that the Internet has to offer, your hard drives may be getting a little bit crowded. Why not add one large hard drive to the computer of your choice and share that space with everyone else?

➤ Do you really need more than one modem? Not if you have one connected to your home network. Sharing one fast modem between a few computers will always be cheaper and easier than outfitting each computer with its own modem and phone line.

Every Gadget Is a Networked Gadget

Computer users have spent the last 10 years figuring out what software makes their lives easier and more enjoyable. Owners of home networks will spend the next 10 years watching their home network grow in ways they never imagined! Consider the following:

➤ Why pay your phone company for voice mail when your computer can answer the phone and take messages for you?

➤ Does the idea of paying long-distance charges make you queasy? Maybe you want to talk to your sister in the next state more often. Why not talk to her over the Internet and use the money you save to buy her a Christmas card? And maybe her smiling face would add to the conversation. Try adding video to the call for good measure.

➤ Why restrict Web surfing to your computer when you can surf from your television?

The Networked Home Office

You get up early every weekday morning. You shower, have breakfast, and get dressed. You open your front door and pick up the morning paper; your neighbor waves as he drives by on the way to work. He's going to spend the next hour on the freeway. You're not. You are an "at home" worker.

Whether you work at home all week long or just every second Wednesday, having a home network is very worthwhile. Here's why:

➤ In today's digital world, there's no reason why your home Internet connection can't be as fast or faster than the one you have at work.

➤ Being in your own space will let you take full advantage of the sights and sounds that your multimedia PC has to offer—without your officemate throwing a temper tantrum every time you turn up the volume on your favorite Internet radio station.

➤ You can cut down your office expenses by using the Internet to send faxes, track your packages, and make long-distance calls.

➤ Does the idea of organizing all those work files on your home PC make you cringe? Why not connect to the corporate network and synchronize your files online?

➤ Do you feel isolated from the people at work? Use videoconferencing for that face-to-face feeling.

Security and Your Networked Home

You may already know someone who has a motion sensor that turns on the porch light when someone approaches her home. Some people may even have a fully integrated security system that can call the police, set off sirens, and notify the neighbors.

You may be able to use your home network to perform many of functions that you would expect from a high-priced home security system:

➤ Does your house need that lived-in look while you're away on vacation? You could have your neighbor come over and turn some lights on and off every few days, but maybe you want all the food in your fridge to be there when you get back. Why not schedule your PC to turn your lights on and off every few hours?

➤ Are you worried that there might be intruders in your house while you're not there, or that the babysitter's locked the kids out of the house? Put your camcorder to good use while you're at work. Attach it to your home network and check in on your babysitter to make sure that everything is okay.

➤ Are you concerned about your summer cottage? After all, it's been in the family for years. Well, relief is on the way! With a remote control video camera, you can look in on your Colorado hideaway whenever you feel the need.

Put Your House on a Short Leash: The Automated Home

When people think of home automation, they usually think of a multimillion-dollar home that only Bill Gates would have. Although a dog door with retinal scanners might be nice, it's more than most people need. Automating a few simple devices can make life easier and save you a few dollars at the same time:

➤ I'm sure that Thomas Edison never thought you would have 37 lights in your home—or if he did, he probably wouldn't have imagined your children leaving all of them on. If Edison were around today, I'm sure he'd be the first guy on his block to control all his lights with the touch of a button. Now you can, too!

➤ Did you forget to turn off that light in the garage before turning in for the night? Don't worry, there's no need to get dressed again; just turn it off with the remote control light switch on your key chain.

➤ Don't you hate coming home to a cold house in the middle of the winter? Fear not! Call home just as you're leaving the ski hill and ask your computer to crank up the temperature and turn on the coffee pot.

It's Just Plain Fun!

Although there are many practical uses for home networking, we can't ignore the fact that there is a fun side to it as well. Ever since Alexander Graham Bell made his first crank call, people have been trying to combine their work with their play:

➤ One of the glories of telecommuting is its nontraditional work setting. With a wireless home network, you can sit on the deck and catch some rays while scouring the Internet for that next big takeover target.

➤ The dedicated armchair athlete has always been a multifaceted personality. First, he needs to see the game in full color and bone-crunching surround sound. On the other hand, his mind must be filled with up-to-the-minute stats on his favorite players.

How can this be done, you ask? A TV tuner card can connect your TV to an Internet-enabled computer so that you can check out espn.com for the latest stats while watching *Monday Night Football* on the same big screen.

Some people appreciate a quick game of Doom between journal entries. On the other hand, watching trailer park trials and tribulations on *The Jerry Springer Show* may be just what you need to get through the last three pages of that big report. A few cables and a TV tuner card are all you need to bring television to your computer's desktop!

The Least You Need to Know

➤ There are as many ways to benefit from the use of a home network as there are homes.

➤ All the ideas discussed in this chapter, from simple file sharing to wireless networks on your deck, are possible with hardware and software available today.

Chapter 2

From the Bottom Up: The Foundation of Your Networked Home

> ### In This Chapter
>
> ➤ How networks work
>
> ➤ Different ways to network your home
>
> ➤ To wire or not to wire, that is the question

On your way to work, while desperately trying to avoid thinking of the workday ahead of you, you ponder the question, "What actually *gets* me to work?" Most people would answer, "The car." But is this right? After all, how useful would a car be if there were no roads to drive it on? On a slightly more frustrating note, what if you had perfectly good roads upon which to drive your perfectly good car but had no idea how to drive? With this philosophical impasse blocking the way, you and your daydreams bounce off a telephone pole.

Even though this type of thinking is dangerous for the daily commuter, it goes a long way toward helping you get started on your home network. In truth, many things can help you get to work in the morning. Your garage door, the road, the car, as well as you—the driver. All the pieces work together with a set of rules to get you to work in one piece every day. If any one of them is on the fritz, *wham!* Telephone pole patrol all over again.

The same holds true for networks. Many pieces work together to provide network communication. If any piece fails, the network fails to pass information.

This chapter covers two fundamental pieces of all networks; let's use the "ride to work" analogy to introduce them:

➤ **The road** The road is the foundation upon which all other things operate. Similarly, your network has a physical "layer" that lets all those little bits and bytes travel from device to device. We discuss wireless networks in this chapter and wired networks in the next.

➤ **The car** The car provides a means for driving across the road. Similarly, every network has a method of *interfacing*—or passing information to—the physical network (the road). This interface is usually a network card that goes into a slot inside your computer. As with cars, some of these are fast, sleek, and expensive. Others don't look quite as sexy but, like the old truck in the driveway, are still great at getting you to work in the morning.

The Open Systems Interconnection Model

Studying the Open Systems Interconnection (OSI) model is truly one of The Mysteries of Networking. If you went in search of a guru on a mountaintop, you'd just as likely be asked to explain the importance of the OSI model as you would be asked to describe the sound of one hand clapping. In some ways, the second question is easier to answer than the first.

The OSI model states that networks should be built in small, discrete layers that fit together in a standard fashion. In the same way that building, electrical, and plumbing codes describe how a house should fit together, the OSI model provides a theoretical framework for building networks.

But this is where most of the weirdness starts: The OSI model is exactly that, a model. It's not the real thing. Rather, it's a way of thinking about how the real thing should work. There are no networks in use in the real world that work exactly the way the OSI model says they should. But every network resembles it closely enough that the OSI model can be a blessing when trying to understand both how networks work and how to fix them when they break.

Planning Your Network: Cul de Sac or Interstate?

Believe it or not, there are several ways in which you can network your home:

➤ **Dorm Net: Everything in One Room** Although this type of network is usually built by two students who share a dormitory room while going to college, don't count yourself out if you're not a student. The same principles apply if you happen to have two computers in one room in your home. A dorm net is the cheapest and simplest type of network to set up.

Clean Up or the Chihuahua Gets It!

Managing the cables and wires snaking all over the floor is the biggest challenge to building a one-room network. There is a tendency to promise yourself that you'll clean up those cables later, but pithy little promises won't bring your pet Chihuahua back from the place that mess of cables in the corner took him.

➤ **Condo Net: Between Rooms** You may have some usable space below the carpets, behind a wall, or through a drop ceiling that you can use to run cable from room to room. Unless you have serious issues with steel walls and concrete floors, this network can be put together by most people with a screwdriver, an Exacto-knife (don't forget some Band-Aids), and a few purchases from the folks at your local hardware store.

➤ **The Whole House** Prenetworked homes are becoming more popular in urban centers, so if you're buying a new house, talk to your builder about networking it beforehand. Even if your builder doesn't offer a networking package, you should be able to find a contractor who can work with your builder

Shocking!

Be very careful to avoid electrical cables or heating spaces when trying to build a network like this. Computer cables are susceptible to electrical interference and heat damage. As well, your body tends to be susceptible to heat and electrical damage if you happen to touch the wrong wire at the wrong time. Ouch!!

to prewire the house before the walls go up. Prewiring is usually preferred because it is often cheaper to do it while the house is being built rather than later. It also tends to result in less drywall dust in your toothpaste during the construction.

If you're already in the house, things get a little bit more complicated but by no means insurmountable. At the very least, you may want to give Barney (your electrician brother-in-law) a call to see whether he can give you a hand. A more expensive option, but one that will keep Barney from emptying out your fridge in the process, is to check your Yellow Pages for networking or electrical contractors who specialize in this sort of work.

Aside from determining how much of your house will be networked, you'll need to decide what type of network architecture to implement. There are more than a few types, including

➤ Point-to-point networks

➤ Bus networks

➤ Star networks

Point-to-Point Networks

A point-to-point network is one where every device on the network is directly connected to every other device on the network. Useful only in the simplest of networks, point-to-point networks tend to be extremely difficult (and expensive!) to manage if they grow beyond two devices.

To illustrate this, consider how your computer connects with your modem. If you're set up like most people, your computer/modem network is a small point-to-point network. Using this same network layout, try to imagine adding a second computer to the network. Two modems and two Internet connections is the result. Now add a third.

A cheap and simple point-to-point network.

A not-so-cheap and not-so-simple point-to-point network.

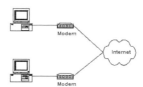

Bus Networks

It's easy to see how the point-to-point network layout breaks down as the number of computers connected to it grows. The solution to this problem is to leave behind the idea that each device needs to be connected to every other device on the network.

Rather, all the devices should share a common network connection. To this end, imagine one long wire pulled around a room or down a hallway. To this wire, or *bus*, you connect all devices that need to be networked.

But just as the point-to-point network outgrows its usefulness as the number of network connections grows, so does the bus network. On larger networks, problems arise when somebody accidentally cuts or disconnects a cable on the network. Because the bus is merely one long cable, it tends to disrupt the whole network when something goes wrong on one little part of it.

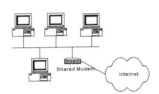

A bus network.

Star Networks

In response to the problems that arise in large bus networks, star networks have all but replaced them. A star network is defined by the use of a device that sits at the center of the star, known as the *hub*. It serves to isolate each of the devices on the network from all the others. This helps ensure that somebody with clumsy feet in the next room won't accidentally interrupt the Internet surfing session going on in your room.

Because star networks are easy to expand and maintain, this layout should be your first choice if you use a wired network. The number of "for home" products available in this category has really taken off in the last few years. Some of these products are from young companies trying to make a break into this hot new market, but many are from experienced networking companies who are scaling down their industrial-strength products to fit the needs of the home network. Check Appendix B, "Online References for Home Area Networking," for a list of products that fall into this category and for links that you can follow to learn more about them.

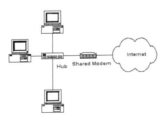

A simple star network.

Laying the Pavement: Wiring

After you've decided how large your network will be, you'll be able to start making some decisions about whether your network will be wired or wireless. How large your network is going to be will help you decide whether a wired network is right for you.

Going Wireless

Wireless networks aren't as different from wired networks as you might think. Both types of networks have some sort of interface card that connects your computer to the network, and both communicate over that network in a similar manner.

The most significant difference (I know, this one's a real stretch) is that there are *no wires* in a wireless network. Depending on the size of your network, this may or may not be a big deal. The next major difference is that wireless networks use *base stations*, which are small antennae connected to your computer that transmit and receive information destined for other base stations on your home network.

A basic wireless network.

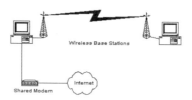

Network Interface Cards

All networks require your computer to connect to them somehow. This is typically accomplished with a *network interface card* (NIC). This card takes up a slot in your computer's motherboard and assumes the role of carrying the information destined for another place on your network to the network itself. Likewise, it also passes along information from the network destined for your computer.

The Least You Need to Know

➤ Think about the ideal configuration before you buy home networking products. Having a design in mind before tackling a project saves you a great deal of time and money.

➤ The basis of a home network can be looked at in two broad categories: wired and wireless. Done properly, wired networks provide a reliable network that is usually simple to expand.

➤ A wireless network is relatively simple to install when compared with a new wired network installation. It should be considered if you want a network up and running fast, particularly if the idea of making holes in walls gives you the heebie jeebies.

Part 2

Networking Your Home Computers

Congratulations, you made it! Now that you've seen all that a home network can do for you, the next step is connecting the computers in your home. This section's claim to fame is explaining the various alternatives for making the home computer connection. You need to seriously consider this decision because the computer network is a core component of your home network.

As the most common type of network, ethernet is discussed first. Although ethernet is reliable, it does have one serious drawback: It requires all the computers in your house to be connected by computer cables. You can install phone line, power line, and wireless networks in your house without having to add any new wires. Which one you eventually select depends on the size and type of home you have, as well as how much time (and money) you have on your hands.

Hop
Hop·

Chapter 3

Tried and True: Networking the Ethernet Way

In This Chapter

➤ How an ethernet network works

➤ Choosing the right pieces

➤ Installing your network

➤ Ethernet options: With or without a hub

The most popular type of network in existence today is *ethernet*, which is a standard way of connecting two or more computers. Because it is the prevailing standard for computer networking, ethernet products are *interoperable*. (This is just a geeky way of saying that ethernet products you buy from one manufacturer tend to play nicely with ones that you buy from another manufacturer.)

Because you are setting up a new home network, this isn't such a big deal. As a rule, people starting something from scratch tend to buy everything from the same manufacturer. But, like the hula-hoop and the Rubik's cube, networking manufacturers come and go. That ethernet card you buy today may not be available in a few years—worse yet, neither will the company that manufactured it!

Another big benefit of ethernet is its *scalability*, or the measure of its capacity to continue to meet your needs as the network grows. Ethernet is a highly scalable network technology in terms of both the size and speed of networks that it can support. For example, networks with 100 ethernet-attached computers are common.

Probably the single largest drawback to ethernet—particularly in a home network—is the fact that every device on the network must have a cable that plugs into it. For the semi-serious home network enthusiast, this usually means a basement office that ends up looking like the snake pit scene from *Raiders of the Lost Ark*. You can overcome this downside with some planning and, depending on the size of your network, a few strategically placed holes in your walls.

Shopping for Your Ethernet Network

Like all shopping trips, the best place to start is with a good grocery list. Take a look at the following list for a rough overview of the pieces that you need to buy to get started with your home network:

➤ **Computers**   Although there are many reasons for wanting an ethernet network in your house, none is as compelling as the fact that you have two *or more* computers to share information and resources between.

➤ **Ethernet card**   This little guy acts as the middleman between your computer and your home area network. It plugs into an unused slot on your computer's motherboard. After the ethernet card is properly installed in your computer, you need to plug an *ethernet cable* into it from outside the computer. You'll need to buy one ethernet card for every computer that you want to put on your network.

Ethernet cards connect a computer to the home network.

➤ **Ethernet driver**   This is a small piece of software that your computer needs to be able to talk to your ethernet card. Unless you have a very old card, your operating system probably has a driver for it. If not, you'll have to use the disk supplied with the ethernet card you bought to install it yourself. More on this process later.

➤ **Ethernet cable**   Just like your VCR must connect to your TV so that you can watch taped reruns of *Gilligan's Island*, every computer on your network must have some way of connecting with the rest of the network. Ethernet cable is that connector.

➤ **An ethernet hub**   As mentioned, each ethernet card has a matching ethernet cable. Each ethernet cable plugs into a computer on one end and the ethernet hub on the other. In this way, your ethernet hub forms the center of your network, passing information from each device to all other devices. By sitting in the center of your network, the hub also serves to protect and isolate each of the cables and cards on your network from one another.

Cables

The two most common types of ethernet cables are Category 5 Unshielded Twisted Pair and 10BASE-T coaxial cable. These are more commonly referred to as Cat 5 and coax. Cat 5 cable is used to create star networks with an ethernet hub (see the following figure). Coaxial cable, on the other hand, does not require a hub.

Because Cat 5 networks are easier to install and maintain, most network kits use Cat 5 cables and ethernet hubs. For a simple network, such as one that has two computers connected in the same room, coax is a cheap and easy solution.

Ethernet hubs are compact and easy to use.

Buying a Hub

Count up how many ethernet cables you are going to have in your network and make sure that the hub you buy has at least as many connectors as you have cables. Better yet, make sure that you have a few left over in case you add more computers next year. That idea might make you laugh now, but if somebody had told you five years ago you'd be reading a book on how to network your house, you probably would've told him or her to have another drink.

➤ **Other ethernet devices**   Computers aren't the only devices that can plug into an ethernet network. Many types of printers can be connected directly to a network as well, enabling you to print to them without having to rely on a computer to drive your printer for you. Another network device growing in popularity provides a high-speed connection to the Internet. If you're lucky enough to

Check This Out

We'll talk more about cable and ADSL modems in Chapter 7, "You've Got the Whole World in Your HAN: Connecting to the Internet."

Save Some Cash: The Home Network Kit

If you want to save a few bucks, check out the all-in-one network starter kits. The most basic models typically include two ethernet cards and a four-port ethernet hub. These will run you $120 to $150. If you need a little more room to grow, an eight-port hub with three ethernet cards will set you back about $225.

live in an area that has them, cable modems and their telephone-company cousins ADSL modems both come ready to connect directly to your ethernet network.

Pick a Card, Any Card: Which Network Card Is Right for You?

With a gazillion network cards on the market, it's sometimes difficult to figure out which one is right for you. Here are a few things to consider:

➤ **Plug and Play**   Plug and Play is a Windows 95/98 capability that makes it easy for you to add new hardware to your computer. If you plan to run a Windows network and the ethernet card you are considering purchasing does not support Plug and Play, do yourself a favor and reconsider.

➤ **Cost**   Ethernet cards are, for the most part, quite cheap—about $50 to $70 per computer.

➤ **Speed**   Ethernet can transmit up to 10 megabits per second (Mbps) across your network. This is generally fast enough for home networking. If you are going to be moving large files on a regular basis, or if you are considering testing videoconferencing or other high-capacity network services across your network, consider fast ethernet, which operates at 100Mbps. Watch out for the price, though; a fast ethernet home networking kit will cost you about twice as much money as a comparable ethernet kit.

Using the Card You Already Have

As networking has grown in popularity, many computer manufacturers have started shipping models with ethernet capability already installed. Although manufacturers might not include an actual ethernet card in the computer, they may have one built in as a part of the computer's motherboard. Talk to a representative at your computer store, or check your computer's documentation if you're not sure.

If you are considering buying a new computer and you know for sure that you want to use it on a network, ask your computer store about its options for built-in ethernet. You may find that it saves you a few dollars (and a few fiddly moments with a screwdriver) over buying and installing a card yourself.

Installing Your Ethernet Card

You knew it was going to come to this. Sooner or later, you were going to have to roll up your sleeves and crack the box on your computer. Every computer is a little different, but the general idea is the same. Here's what you do:

1. First things first, ***turn the computer off***. There's no use turning your computer into a planter by zapping it with an electric shock while trying to open it. In addition, leave the computer plugged in to keep it grounded. If you have to unplug it to bring it to a place where you can work on it, that's no sweat—just make sure that you put it down in a relatively static-free environment. In other words, leave the wool sweater in your closet and avoid letting your cat crawl around inside the box after you have it open.

2. Take a look at the screws on the back (or, depending on what type of computer you have, on the side or the front) and pick an appropriate screwdriver from your collection for the task. The most common screw used to hold computers together is a Phillips, otherwise known as "that funky star-shaped one."

3. After you get the screws out, the cover should slide off slick as a whistle. Of course, pigs fly, chickens have lips, and Bill Gates still balances his own checkbook. If you're still having trouble breaking in, make sure to check your computer manual. It'll help you identify that one nasty screw hiding beneath the *Intel Inside* sticker on the front of the case.

4. After you manage to wrestle the cover off the case, take a look around inside for empty slots that look like they match your card. If you're not sure, close your eyes and let The Force guide you. Alternatively, you could use the cards already installed in your computer as a guide.

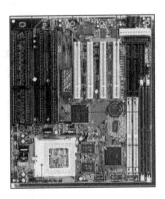

This diagram of a motherboard shows how an NIC fits into a slot.

5. Before trying to insert your ethernet card into the slot, make sure that you remove the little protective plate that's screwed into the computer behind it. The plate looks like an aluminum tongue depressor with a screw hole in it.

6. Being careful not to accidentally unplug any of the cables snaking around inside your computer, gently insert the ethernet card into the slot until you are sure that it's lined up right. Then, push a little harder until you feel a reassuring *ssh-hunk!!* as the card slides into place.

7. Don't forget to screw the ethernet card's back plate on, because cards have a tendency to work themselves out of the slot over time if you forget.

8. Firmly close your eyes and try to picture the place where you left the screws for the computer's case (that place where you told yourself you surely wouldn't forget). Got it? Good! Go get the screws and put the case back together.

9. Turn your computer back on.

When Plug and Play Doesn't Play Nice

Plug and Play is a feature of Windows 95/98 (and soon to be Windows 2000) that helps you install new hardware into your computer with minimal pain and aggravation. Although it occasionally makes mistakes, Plug and Play can be your best friend when you first start adding new cards to your computer.

If you used a plug-and-play ethernet card and everything goes the way it should, your computer will detect that the new hardware has been added to the computer when you turn it on. After detection, the computer will install the appropriate driver for your ethernet card and return you to the Windows desktop. If this happens, you're ready to move on; if not...Plug and Play isn't playing nice. There are a few things that could be wrong:

➤ You have an older ethernet card that doesn't support plug-and-play installation. If this is the case, after you have installed the card in the slot, you will have to configure the card manually.

➤ Plug and Play has let you down and failed to detect the card. Although this is a heinous crime worthy of jail time for a Microsoft programmer, it's not unheard of. In such a case, you'll need to configure the card manually.

Manually Configuring Your New Ethernet Card

If Plug and Play lets you down, meaning that you have to configure your network card yourself, do the following:

1. Select **Start**, **Settings**, **Control Panel**, **Add New Hardware**.

2. Read the instructions on the screen and click **Next**.

3. Read some more instructions and click **Next**. Windows searches through all available hardware to see whether any new plug-and-play devices can be detected. As per the instructions, you should let Windows see whether it can find your new ethernet card, even though it's not Plug and Play.

4. Windows should find your new ethernet card and allow you to install a driver.

5. Use the disk that came with your ethernet card if you have one; this is because the driver that came with your ethernet card is most likely more current than the driver that came with Windows.

Device Not Found

If for some reason your computer does not select your ethernet card, consult your ethernet card manual for instructions specific to your card.

IRQs and You

IRQ is an acronym that strikes fear into the hearts of many computer users, novice and professional alike. The confusion starts with the name itself. IRQ is an acronym for *Interrupt ReQuest line*; the way the acronym is derived should convince you that this particular computer concept was thought up at a time when drug use was rampant in the computer industry.

IRQs are like little traffic cops in your computer. They give the right to each of 16 different devices in your computer to hold up their hand and say to the CPU, "Hey, it's my turn to talk." Each device is assigned its own IRQ, which your CPU uses to refer to it. Things go haywire when two devices in your computer both try to use the same IRQ to interrupt the CPU. The CPU doesn't know which one to listen to, and it keels over. At best, the two devices will stop working; at worst, your computer decides to take a siesta until you resolve the conflict.

Resolving the conflict means figuring out which devices in your computer aren't playing nice. The easiest way to see which devices are using which IRQ is to click **Start**, **Settings**, **Control Panel**, **System**, and then select the **Devices** tab. Finally, double-click the **Computer** icon in the upper-left corner.

Make sure that the **IRQ** button is selected; you should see a list of all the IRQs from 00 to 15. (Don't you just love computer geeks! Who would have thought that you could count to 16 by going from 00 to 15?)

If you find yourself in a position where you have to change IRQs or other settings on existing equipment to get your ethernet card to work, congratulations. You have officially exceeded the scope of this book. Although not extremely difficult to do, this is one place where you may want to call in your nephew Phil, the computer geek, to come and give you a hand. This is because incorrectly configured IRQs can keep your computer from rebooting, making it difficult to troubleshoot problems that you accidentally generate while trying to fix your problem. If you don't have a Phil at your disposal, the store where you bought the ethernet card may be able to help you with the installation.

To Hub or Not to Hub...

As discussed in detail in Chapter 2, "From the Bottom Up: The Foundation of Your Networked Home," there are several different possible network layouts. Point-to-point and star networks are the two that you will find most useful for the home. Either one can be used, but one will be better than the other, depending on the size of your network.

Networking Without a Hub

A point-to-point network is useful if you plan to have only two computers on your network. This type of connection requires a special ethernet cable that you can pick up from your local computer store called a *crossover cable*. The crossover cable allows you to connect your two computers from the ethernet port on one computer directly to the ethernet port on the other. Cheap? Yes. Easy? Yes. Limited? Absolutely!

By going from ethernet card to ethernet card, you have created a *hubless network*. It will be difficult—if not impossible—to add a third computer to the network. If you think you'll ever grow beyond two computers, consider adding a *hub* to the center of your network.

Networking with a Hub

Every ethernet cable on your network should plug into the hub. Positioned at the center of the network, the hub's job is to pass information from every networked device to every other networked device.

This diagram shows a four-port ethernet hub plugged into two computers.

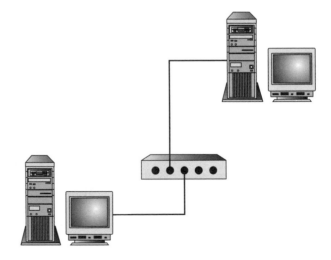

Selecting a Hub

The most important thing to remember about selecting a hub is that it must match the speed of the ethernet cards you want to use. There are several different types of ethernet, ranging in speed from 10Mbps to 1000Mbps:

➤ Ethernet, often called 10BASE-T, operates at 10Mbps. It is the oldest form of Ethernet and is, therefore, very reliable. The speed of this network should be enough for most home users, but if you transfer huge files across your network, you might want to consider fast ethernet.

➤ Fast ethernet, often called 100BASE-T, operates at 100Mbps. Although newer than ethernet, fast ethernet has been in use for a few years now and is stable enough for use in your home network. You'll have to work long and hard to think of something to do on your network that will push fast ethernet to its limits.

➤ You've decided that you just can't survive without the latest, greatest, and fastest. Never fear! Gigabit ethernet is here! Operating at a whopping 1Gbps (that's 1000Mb, folks), gigabit ethernet has more speed than you'll ever need. Beware, though: As a cutting-edge technology, gigabit ethernet comes with a cutting-edge price as well as a few cutting-edge problems. Only bite into gigabit ethernet if you have the time and the money to do it right.

KISS: Keep it Simple, Silly

Although it is possible to mix different-speed ethernet cards on the same network, it is easier (and cheaper) if you choose which speed you want and purchase the hub and ethernet cards to match.

Integrated Modems and Ethernet Hubs

Recently, ethernet hubs have begun to appear with modems built right in. This frees the modem from being connected to a specific computer—in effect, putting the modem directly on the network. Although there are other ways to do it (hint: check out Chapter 7), these devices offer a quick and painless solution for connecting every PC in the house to the Internet with a single modem.

The Wiring Closet

The place where you choose to put your ethernet hub should be easy to get at and relatively free of clutter. In your closet underneath the clothes hamper is not recommended.

Note

If you decide at a later date to connect to the Internet with another type of connection (such as a cable modem, ISDN, and so on), you're not going to be able to do it with the modem built into your new hub. If you use one of these alternative methods to connect to the Internet, you should forego the built-in modem and stick with a plain ethernet hub.

The Least You Need to Know

➤ Ethernet is a mature, scalable form of networking that is well suited to the home.

➤ On the downside, depending on the size of your network, a few strategically placed holes in your walls will be required.

➤ You should now be comfy with the hardware and software that you will need to get your ethernet network up and running. Even better, you should now be ready to try to do it yourself!

Chapter 4

No New Wires: Home Networking Using Phone Lines, Power Lines, and Wireless Technologies

In This Chapter

➤ When ethernet is *not* the best solution

➤ How to use your phone lines to build a home area network

➤ Building an (almost) wireless network

➤ Using your household power lines to connect your PCs

As discussed in Chapter 3, "Tried and True: Networking the Ethernet Way," ethernet networking provides a speedy, low-maintenance network. Because category 5 wiring can be used to connect your network at 10, 100, or 1000Mbps, you should also feel comfortable with an ethernet network's capability to grow with your networking needs. But ethernet's speed and flexibility come at a price.

The problem with ethernet is that you'll have to install it. Although there is a growing trend toward offering ethernet wiring as a cost-plus option in new homes, the home that you move into will probably not have an ethernet network in place.

Connectivity

The underlying concept in all networking is *connectivity*. There must be some way to get information and commands from every networked device to every other networked device. Adding a new set of wires to achieve these connections is common in a business setting. The physical size of corporate networks and the number of computers that they need to support require specific capabilities. These capabilities can only be met with the installation of new wires.

The physical requirements for your networked home, however, are much different. First, your home is smaller. Most homes are smaller than 2,000 to 3,000 square feet. Second, your networked home doesn't need to support as many different devices. Even die-hard computer users would have difficulty imagining needing more than five or ten (well, okay, maybe 20) networked devices.

When you consider the hassle and cost associated with hiring an electrical contractor to put in new wires and balance that against the distinct nature of a home network, you've got to wonder if there is a way to network your house without poking holes in your walls. Well, there is!

Spectral Compatibility

No, this isn't how to build a network Shirley MacLaine will like.

The basis for phone line networking is the fact that phones communicate with each other over specific frequencies, or *spectrum*. The trick to running a computer network over a phone line is to find a frequency that won't interfere with other devices already on the phone line, such as regular phones or ADSL equipment that might be used for Internet connectivity.

Telephones talk to each other at between 20Hz and 3.4KHz in North America. ADSL and other DSL flavors communicate at between 25KHz and 1.1MHz. This leaves the area above 1.1MHz unused. Tut Systems chose to use the frequencies above 2MHz for its phone line network equipment.

Phone Line Networking

Truth be told, phone lines have been used for computer networking for more than a decade. Early corporate networks tried to save money by taking advantage of unused phone lines pulled into office walls to create ethernet networks.

These early networks ran ethernet over one set of wires, while the office's phone connection ran over a separate set of wires. This practice was eventually stopped because the quality of cable used for telephone communication wasn't high enough to create reliable computer networks.

The new crop of home network products takes this concept one step further. Rather than require a separate set of wires, the phone line networking products use the same set of wires.

At first glance, this doesn't seem like a tremendously earth-shattering idea. After all, people have been using modems to connect to the Internet for years, right? But similar to the way most people use their brains, phones and modems use only a small portion of the capacity of the phone line network. Fortunately, some smart folks figured out a way to use up that excess capacity (in the phone lines, not your brain) so that your home network could share the phone line with your phone.

Because phone line networks operate at a different *frequency* than your phone, you can use your home network without worrying about whether it's going to interfere with your phone.

Phone Line Products

A few products enable you to use your phone line to connect your home network:

➤ **Tut Systems' HomeRun** www.tutsys.com

➤ **Diamond Multimedia Homefree** www.diamondmm.com

➤ **ActionTec ActionLink** www.actiontec.com

Although any of these products will work, the strength and simplicity of Tut's approach to the complex problem of networking homes made it the reference technology used by the Home Phoneline Networking Alliance (HomePNA).

Tut Systems designed its innovative HomeRun technology to work with a standard ethernet card. This stroke of genius lets your computer use the phone lines in exactly the same way it would use a standard ethernet network, thus ensuring compatibility with the extensive array of ethernet devices already on the market. The HomeRun adapters plug directly into your telephone jack and have pass-through jacks for telephones (so you won't have to worry about using up all the available phone jacks for your network).

HomeRun currently operates at 1.6Mbps, more than enough for high-speed Internet surfing and standard file and print sharing. Of course, if there is one truism in networking, it's this: If you provide people with speed, they'll use it. Tut Systems and the rest of the HomePNA members anticipated this need and plan to have a specification ready for 10Mbps operation over phone lines by summer, 1999.

Power Line Networking

Much like phone line networking uses the excess capacity of phone lines for computer networking, power line networking takes advantage of unused spectrum (see the Techno Talk titled "Spectral Compatibility" earlier in this chapter) in the wires that send power to your various household appliances.

One big advantage of power line networking is connection availability. There probably isn't a room in your home that doesn't have at least one power outlet. Compare this to phone jacks for phone line networking, which aren't nearly as common.

Power line networks are currently available in the 350Kbps range, with plans announced into the 10Mbps range. Intelogis Passport Plug-in (www.intelogis.com) is one product that enables you to take advantage of your power lines for networking.

On Power Line Networking

Even though several companies are hard at work developing technology for power line networking, few have brought product to market at this time. Power line networking remains a relatively immature technology compared to phone line and wireless networking.

Check This Out

Catch 22: Almost Wireless Networking

Even though you won't have wires snaking through your walls or across the floor between computers, the truly wireless network is still a long way away. By adding a wireless adapter to your computer, you are not only adding a new wire (the one connecting your base station to the computer), but you are also adding the wireless base station itself. Although most base stations aren't that big, if you're the kind of person who has to fight to find a piece of desk big enough to roll your mouse on, every little bit counts.

Wireless Home Area Networking

Wireless technology is the ultimate in no-new-wires networking. Using radio technology, home wireless solutions transmit their signals through the air, virtually eliminating the need to install new wires or interconnect with existing wiring systems in your home.

In addition to freeing your home of many of its wires (see the section titled "Catch 22: Almost Wireless Networking"), wireless home networking has one other major advantage: mobility. If you're lucky enough to own your own laptop or unlucky enough to have to haul one home from work every night, you are well aware of the benefits of mobility.

Consider how valuable your laptop would be to you if it could be connected to your home network (and through it, to the Internet) while roaming around the house. Forget the house, how about checking www.nasdaq.com while sitting on a sunlit balcony with a tall glass of lemonade? Ahh, the power of mobile networking!

Even though wireless networks have many advantages to wired networks, there is one major shortcoming: speed. Most wireless products claim to have speeds in excess of 1Mbps, but independent testing shows that wireless networks tend to operate at speeds more like 300Kbps. For Internet connectivity, nobody would ever notice the difference. Large file transfers or print jobs, however, will be noticeably slower than similar operations done with ethernet.

Wireless networks require two pieces of hardware to connect a computer to the network:

➤ **A network interface card**   Similar to an ethernet card, this is a card that goes into your computer and is used to connect it to a wireless base station.

➤ **Wireless base station**   The base station is a wireless transmitter/receiver module that communicates with all the other base stations on the network. Each computer on the network requires its own base station.

You can purchase wireless home networking products from the following manufacturers:

➤ **Proxim Symphony**   www.proxim.com

➤ **Diamond Multimedia's Homefree**   www.diamondmm.com

➤ **Webgear Aviator**   www.webgear.com

Wireless LAN technology has been used in corporate networks for five years or more, but has only recently begun to move into the world of home networking. Although only a few home wireless products are available, the Home Radio Frequency Working Group (HomeRF) is hard at work developing standards for home wireless technology, ensuring compatibility between different products.

The HomeRF membership roster reads like a who's who of networking. With the likes of 3Com, Cisco, Hewlett-Packard, IBM, Motorola, and Texas Instruments on board, home wireless has a bright future.

Niche Networking: Infrared

Infrared technology is another wireless option that deserves mention but not for its capability to network computers. Unlike the other types of wireless networks talked about so far, infrared requires that all the devices communicating be able to "see" each other. This limitation has pigeonholed infrared into a few specific applications for which it is particularly well suited.

➤ **Laptop/desktop file synchronization**   Infrared can be used to copy or synchronize files back and forth between your laptop and your desktop computer. That means that you don't have to shut down your computer and crawl around on the floor with a parallel or serial cable.

➤ **Laptop printing**   Infrared's capability to connect with any printer that it points to makes printing one-page memos quick and easy. (Note that both the laptop and the printer must have infrared ports on them for this to work.)

➤ **Remote control devices**   The short distance (5 or 6 meters) limitation of infrared works just fine for remote control devices. For example, infrared mice and keyboards are all the rage this year, freeing typists from the confines of their office desks. As more household devices become controllable via computers, this type of remote control will become increasingly important.

The Least You Need to Know

➤ Ethernet is the fastest and most stable technology for creating a home network. Unfortunately, because you must install ethernet cable, setting up an ethernet network in your home can become more complex than setting up a wireless network or a network that runs over your power or phone lines. Which network is the least expensive to install depends on the size of your house and the number and locations of the computers that you want to connect.

➤ The cheapest and easiest way to wire your house with ethernet cable is while the house is being built.

➤ Although they currently don't operate at speeds as fast as ethernet, several options exist for setting up a home network that does not require any new wires.

➤ Phone line networking is an inexpensive and easy way to connect your PCs together over the existing home phone network.

➤ Power line networks use excess capacity in your household power system to connect PCs together into a network.

➤ Wireless networking lets you set up a network with no wires at all.

Part 3

Getting the HAN Up and Running

With Part 2 behind you, the physical pieces of your computer network should now be in place. Whether you chose to add new wires or used one of the no-new-wires solutions, the end result is the same: You are now ready to share resources over your network.

This section shows you in clear, simple steps how to share the three most common network resources. First, file sharing cuts down on the need to use a specific computer to reach an important file. Next, printer sharing enables you to save money and space by letting every computer in your home print to the same printer. Finally, you learn how to share the most important resource of all, information. Connecting a household computer to the Internet opens up a world of knowledge and fun for you and your family. Connecting all your computers to the Internet over the same connection makes the Internet more accessible and cost effective.

Chapter 5

Windows of Opportunity: Windows Networking

In This Chapter

➤ Assign names to your computers

➤ Customize Windows for use by more than one person

➤ Log on to your computer

➤ Configure Windows 98 for home networking

The preceding three chapters laid the underlying foundation for networked communication. But there are still a few more steps before you can leave the nuts and bolts of networking behind. In this chapter, you'll use the adapter that you've already installed and give it the tools that it needs to communicate with Windows. These tools are known as *clients* and *protocols*.

First, though, let's go through how Windows will keep track of all the computers on your home network, as well as the people in your family who want to use those computers.

Name Your Computer

The most fundamental piece of Windows networking—okay, in all networking—is *addressing*. Just as with the postal system, everybody who wants to receive mail has to have a mailing address. In the world of networking, each computer on a network needs its own unique name.

The unique name used to describe a computer on a Windows network is a *computer name*. To give your computer a name, do the following:

1. Click **Start**, **Settings**, **Control Panel**, and then double-click the **Network** icon.

2. Choose the **Identification** tab.

3. In the **Computer name** space, type the name you want to give your computer.

4. In the **Workgroup** space, type the workgroup name. Don't forget the name you type in here because you'll have to use the same workgroup name on all the other computers on your network.

5. Optionally, fill in the **Computer Description** space. This description will appear in the *comment column* in Network Neighborhood. The Network Neighborhood is discussed later in this chapter.

Computer Names

Although you can name your computer anything you want, choose a name that will be easy to remember. The important thing is that each computer on your network must have a *unique name*. Calling your computer Mark's Computer is fine as long as no one else in your workgroup uses a computer by the same name.

Workshop Names

Your workgroup name has to match the workgroup name of all the other computers on your network. Most people choose a workgroup name that describes something about everybody on the network. For example, if your family name is Smith, you could use the workgroup name **Casa del Smith**.

On a small network, the workgroup name is almost useless because everybody will probably use the same workgroup. Nonetheless, it's a vital tool on larger networks for isolating different workgroups from each other.

Tips On Naming

Computer names and workgroup names are similar to first and last names for people. All the people in a family go by the same surname, which is similar to the workgroup name. Within the workgroup (or family), though, everybody has his or her own unique name. This is like the computer name.

Computer names and workgroup names identify your computer to other users on the network.

Personalizing Windows for More than One User

Whenever you have more people than you have computers, it's a recipe for disaster. Consider that everybody who uses a computer wants to have his or her own customized Windows desktop. Anybody who has shared a computer with others knows how frustrating it can be to wade through somebody else's applications, browser bookmarks, or that little ducky wallpaper he or she likes so much.

By creating multiple *users* within windows, you can let everybody who uses the computer have his or her own custom desktop. This includes screen resolution, Favorites folder, My Documents directory and, of course, little ducky wallpaper.

Creating Users

1. Click **Start**, **Settings**, **Control Panel**, and then double-click the **Users** icon.

2. Click **Next**.

3. Type the name of one of the people who will use this computer in the **User Name** text box, and then click **Next**.

User profiles let you customize Windows for each user of a computer.

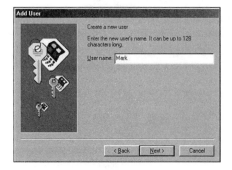

4. Type a password, and then retype it in the **Password Confirm** box. Leave the Password field blank if you don't want to have to enter it every time you log on.

You will use your user name to log on to Windows.

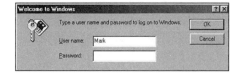

5. Click the **Next** button to proceed.

Select which items you want individualized for this profile.

6. Select the items you want to personalize by checking the appropriate boxes. You would typically check all the boxes. In typical fashion, Windows gives you many personalization options:

   ➤ **Desktop folder and Documents menu**   Selecting this option gives each person control over how his or her desktop will look and which programs and shortcuts will be displayed on it. Further, it gives each user a personalized Documents menu (located in the Start menu) to track recently opened documents.

   ➤ **Start menu**   By having your own Start menu, you can have complete control over which programs will appear when you click the Windows **Start** button. This not only lets other users have easy access to your own programs, it will also let you avoid the clutter of wading through everybody else's to get to them.

   ➤ **Favorites folder**   With your own Favorites folder, you can keep a personal list of your favorite Web sites. By keeping it individualized, you don't have to worry about your son's Marilyn Manson Web sites getting mixed up with your husband's golf sites.

   ➤ **Downloaded Web pages**   Every time you visit a Web site, your computer keeps a record of that visit. This record, called a *cache*, gives your browser a snapshot of the pages you have visited. Using this snapshot, subsequent visits to the Web site show up much faster in your browser. Although individual folders for this item will make multiple visits to Web sites faster for everybody, you may want to avoid it if you are short on disk space.

   ➤ **My Documents folder**   All Microsoft Windows applications use the My Documents folder as the default location for storing files. The creation of separate My Documents folders will allow each family member to keep his or her files separate from everybody else's.

7. Select **Create new items to save disk space** and click **Next** to create this user.

8. Repeat the steps for creating a new user profile for everyone who will use this computer.

Remember, this process only applies to the computer on which you create the profile. If you want to have personalized logons on other computers, you will have to create profiles on them as well.

User Templates

In step 7 of the preceding section, we used the Create New Items to Save Disk Space option when creating new user profiles. This option uses Microsoft's default user profile, giving each new user a basic profile upon which he or she can build. Alternatively, you could make a profile that provides a common starting point for everybody in your household. For instance, applications such as Microsoft Word or Netscape Navigator probably need to be in everybody's profile.

Using the Create Copies of the Current Items and Their Content option when creating a new profile takes a snapshot of the current profile as the basis for the creation of the new one. Doing this for everyone in the home makes a consistent yet customized starting point for every profile that you create.

Choosing the Client That's Right for You

People tend to get wrapped up in concepts like "little computers" and "big computers" when talking about clients and servers. For instance, the server must be the big computer in the corner over there, right? Wrong!

A *server* is just a piece of software that runs on a computer that allows it to provide network services to a client. Some common examples of servers are *print servers* and *file servers*. A *client* is a program that runs on a computer that enables it to use one of those servers. Windows 95/98 comes with two different clients:

➤ **Microsoft Family Logon**   This is the most basic client and will enable all the users you create to log in and work within their own Windows desktops. However, it does not allow you to share files or printers. Use this client if you have only one computer but several people who want to use it.

➤ **Client for Microsoft Networks**   Client for Microsoft Networks picks up where Microsoft Family Logon leaves off. In addition to allowing several different people to manage their own destinies on each computer, it also allows you to install the network software necessary to share files, folders, disk drives, and printers across your network. Now we're talking networking.

To install Microsoft Family Logon, do the following:

1. Select **Start**, **Settings**, **Control Panel**, **Networks**, and then click the **Add** button.

Selecting the client is the first step in setting up your Windows network.

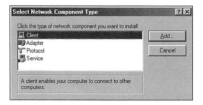

2. Double-click the **Client** option, and then select **Microsoft** in the left pane and **Microsoft Family Logon** in the right pane.

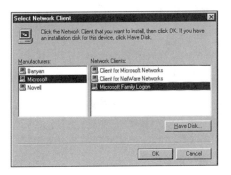

Microsoft Family Logon provides basic Windows logon capability.

3. Reboot your computer. After you reboot, you should see a list of the users that you created during the "Add User" exercise. Log on using one of these users, and you will have your own customized desktop. Yahoo!

Because the Microsoft Family Logon client applies to users with only one computer, we'll focus here on Client for Microsoft Networks. To install Client for Microsoft Networks, do the following:

1. Select **Start**, **Settings**, **Control Panel**, **Networks**, and then click the **Add** button.

2. Double-click the **Client** option, and then select **Microsoft** in the left pane and **Client for Microsoft Networks** in the right pane. Click **OK**.

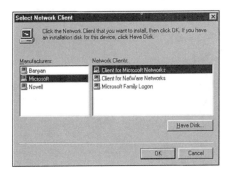

Client for Microsoft Networks is an important step in configuring file and printer sharing.

3. Reboot your computer.
4. When your computer starts, you should see a dialog box asking for your username and password.
5. Microsoft Client for Windows requires that you type the entire username (and password if you created one) before logging in. Type them, and then click **OK**.

45

If you find that Windows is starting with the incorrect Welcome to Windows window, do the following:

1. Select **Start**, **Settings**, **Control Panel**, **Network**, and then click the **Primary Network Logon** drop-down menu.

You can change your Primary Network Logon any time you want.

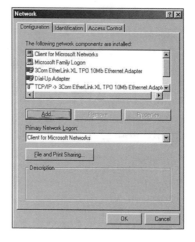

Don't Forget

You won't be able to use file and printer sharing in the next chapter if you select anything other than Client for Microsoft Networks here.

2. Select the client you want to use to log on to Windows.

Pick a Protocol, Any Protocol

After selecting your client software, your next step is to choose a protocol. Protocols are the language that your computers use to communicate with each other. Different protocols are good at different kinds of networking. There is a variety of protocols to choose from, including

➤ TCP/IP

➤ NetBEUI

TCP/IP

TCP/IP (Transmission Control Protocol/Internet Protocol) is the standard protocol used for networking over the Internet. TCP/IP's greatest strength is its capability to communicate over vast distances through complex networks. Accordingly, TCP/IP itself is moderately complex and has many configurable components.

You already have TCP/IP installed if

➤ **You use Windows 98**   Windows 98 installs TCP/IP by default.

➤ **You have an Internet connection**   If you have a properly functioning Internet connection, you must have TCP/IP installed.

Your Internet service provider will provide detailed instructions for configuring TCP/IP for its network, so we'll save the detailed discussion of TCP/IP networking for Chapter 7, "You've Got the Whole World in Your HAN: Connecting to the Internet."

NetBEUI

NetBEUI is everything that TCP/IP is not:

➤ **Simple**   Configuring a TCP/IP connection should only take 5 or 10 minutes. NetBEUI is even easier. By installing NetBEUI after the adapter and clients are installed, no configuration will be required. There are no addresses, names, or networks to configure—it just works!

➤ **Focused on small networks**   TCP/IP is designed with large networks in mind. NetBEUI, on the other hand, assumes that it will work only on small networks. Given this, NetBEUI is the perfect protocol for the home area network.

Installing NetBEUI

If you're lucky, you'll already have NetBEUI installed. To see whether this is the case, select **Start**, **Settings**, **Control Panel**, **Networks**,

TCP/IP

If you want your computer to communicate over the Internet, you must use the TCP/IP suite of protocols. TCP/IP does many things to make your Internet connection work, including providing a unique address for every computer on the Internet. Using this address, you can email messages and surf Web sites on any part of the Internet from anywhere in the world. In addition, TCP/IP can use different routes to get to the same place. By using different routes, TCP/IP can recover from failures on one part of the Internet and make sure that your message gets through on another part of the Internet.

Note

Although there are several different protocols you can use on your network, all computers that will communicate on the network must have at least one protocol in common.

and look in the center dialog box for mention of the word NetBEUI. If it's there, you're already done. If not, do the following:

1. Click **Start**, **Settings**, **Control Panel**, and then double-click the **Network** icon.

2. Select the **Configuration** tab and click **Add**.

3. In the Select Network Component Type box, select **Protocol** and then click **Add**.

Network protocols allow one computer to speak to another.

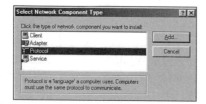

4. In the left-hand pane, select **Microsoft**. Then select **NetBEUI** in the right-hand pane. Click **OK**.

NetBEUI is used for sharing files and printers on a Microsoft network.

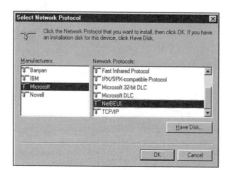

Getting to Know Your Windows Network: A Quick Tour of the Network Neighborhood

Network Neighborhood is your network tour guide. Much like a real tour guide, Network Neighborhood shows you the highlights of your network in an organized fashion. To see what other devices are on the network, double-click the **Network Neighborhood** icon on your Windows desktop. As shown here, our test network has two computers with Client for Microsoft Networks installed on them: Mark's computer and Jeff's computer.

Network Neighborhood shows all available resources on your network.

The Least You Need to Know

➤ All the computers on your network should have names and workgroups assigned to them so that you can find them in Network Neighborhood.

➤ User profiles can be created on your computer to provide a customized look and feel for each person who uses it.

➤ Installing NetBEUI, Client for Microsoft Networks, and File and Print Sharing for Microsoft Networks will let you share files and printers in a snap!

➤ TCP/IP is the protocol used to connect your computer to the Internet. Installing takes only a few minutes; surfing the Net will take a lifetime.

Chapter 6

Sunny and Share: Sharing Files, Printers, and Other Resources

In This Chapter

➤ Using a printer attached to any computer in the home

➤ Sharing folders and files among home computers

➤ Sharing hard drives and CD-ROM drives

If you've ever had to share a computer with a sister or brother the night before a big report is due, then this chapter is for you. Picture the two of you, each on your own computer, accessing the CD-ROM encyclopedia in Dad's computer. Six hours, three bags of nachos, and two rewrites later, you both print your reports on the printer attached to your sister's computer.

This chapter is about sharing files, folders, and printers between two or more computers. It's about doing the things we take for granted in the office environment without having to be at the office to do them. With a little forethought, you can do more with your home computers in less time for less money.

Sharing files or printers takes three separate steps:

➤ Installing the software that will allow the two computers to communicate with each other. This software, called a *driver*, comes as part of Windows 95 or Windows 98. The drivers must be installed on every computer that will either share or access shared files and printers on your network.

➤ Configuring resources for sharing. An example could be a printer, a single file, a whole folder, or an entire hard drive.

➤ Configuring the computer from which you want to access the shared resources.

Print Sharing

To share files or printers from your computer, you must first install file and printer sharing for Microsoft networks. Let's assume that you want to use the printer attached to your sister's computer to print your reports. At your sister's computer, do the following:

1. Select **Start**, **Settings**, **Control Panel**, and then double-click the **Network** icon.

2. On the Configuration tab, click **Add**.

3. In the dialog box shown next, select **Service**, and then click **Add**.

This dialog box is used frequently when setting up your network.

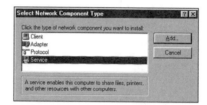

4. Click **File and printer sharing for Microsoft Networks**, and then click **OK**.

Use the Select Network Service dialog box to find a service.

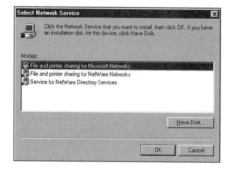

5. Click **OK** to close the Network window.

6. Click **Yes** to reboot Windows.

Access Control: Who Gets What?

Now that file and printer sharing for Microsoft networks is installed, you're only a few clicks away from being able to print from your computer to your sister's printer. While still at your sister's computer, do the following:

1. Click **Start**, **Settings**, **Control Panel**, and then double-click the **Network** icon.

2. Click the **File and Print Sharing** button in the lower half of the dialog box shown here.

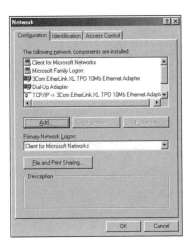

Choose File and Print Sharing in this dialog box.

3. Select the check box for the sharing options you want (file sharing and print sharing can each be selected independently), and then click **OK**.

This dialog box allows you to share your files, your printer, or both.

Setting Up Shared Access to Your Printer

Now that you've installed and enabled Microsoft File and Print Services, you're ready to share a printer. While still at your sister's printer, do the following:

1. Click **Start**, **Settings**, **Printers**.

2. Choose the printer you want to share with others by single-clicking its icon.

3. Choose **File**, **Properties**.

4. Click the **Sharing** tab, and then click the **Shared As** option.

Your printer has a share name that can be any name you want.

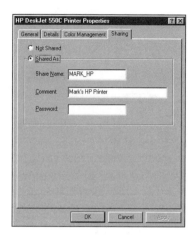

5. In the Share Name field, enter the name that you want the printer to be known as. This is the name you will use to refer to this network printer from other computers on your network.

Don't Forget

You can only share out a printer that is directly connected to your computer.

Using a Shared Network Printer

Your sister's printer is now available to your home network. To print to it, perform the following steps from your computer:

1. From the Windows desktop, double-click the **Network Neighborhood** icon, and then double-click the name of the computer attached to the printer. (In this example, this is the name of your sister's computer.)

A Reminder

All the computers on your network were given names in Chapter 5, "Windows of Opportunity: Windows Networking."

2. Even though the printer is attached to your sister's computer, you must have the printer driver installed on your computer as well. To install the printer driver, double-click the printer icon.

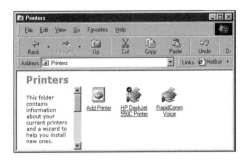

All printers are displayed in this Printers dialog box.

3. Each printer type has its own unique set of instructions. Follow the onscreen instructions for installing the printer driver.

After the driver is installed, you should see it in the Printers window, along with any other printers available to your computer.

Disabling Print Sharing

One of the best things about networked printing is that somebody can print her report on your printer any time she wants. And conversely, one of the worst things about networked printing is that somebody can print her report on your printer whenever you don't want her to—for instance, when you need to print or when you need to sleep. To disable print sharing, do the following:

1. Click **Start**, **Settings**, **Printers**.
2. Select the icon for the printer you want to stop sharing.
3. Choose **File**, **Properties**.
4. Select the **Sharing** tab, and then click **Not Shared**.

File Sharing

Long gone are the days when computer programs came on a single diskette—or even 10 diskettes, for that matter. Some games now take more than one CD! Just in case you really want to scratch your brain, that's about 450 diskettes worth of space. To make things worse, the availability of files for downloading from the Internet is threatening to overrun every spare megabyte that you have on your hard drive.

But fear not. Rather than buy new hard disks for every computer in your home, you can

➤ Use some of the space left over on another computer to store the files you download from the Internet.

➤ Load up one of your computers with lots of disk space and use it as the main file storage area for the network.

Files When You Need Them, Where You Need Them

Remember when you needed to borrow the car and your brother was already out with it on a date? When your brother had the car, there wasn't much you could do about it.

Well, sooner or later, you'll need to get at a file when somebody else is using the computer. It'll be "Déja vu all over again." But with a home area network, you can share the files on one computer with another computer. That way, you never have to worry about any particular computer being tied up. Using file sharing, you can get to the files when you need them, where you need them.

Just think: If Ward and June Cleaver were around today, they could have saved the family to-do list in a household activities directory, which anybody in the family, including the Beav, could access from any computer on the network. Here's how you can share your own family to-do list:

1. Open a program—such as Microsoft Excel—by selecting **Start**, **Programs**, **Microsoft Excel**.

2. Type **Family To Do List** in the text field.

Many applications can now be shared by the whole family.

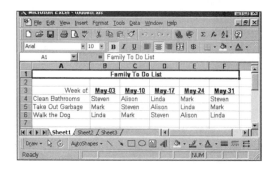

3. Save the file in the shared family folder by choosing **File**, **Save As**. (Creating shared folders is covered in the second half of this chapter.)

After you've taken these steps, users can open and see the file from any networked computer in the home.

Establishing Existing Folders as Shared Folders

Say that you spent last night downloading song files from the Internet (check Chapter 20, "The Song Heard 'Round the World: Adding Your Stereo to the Network," to learn how to do this). Much enamored with your choice in music, your little brother wants to listen to the songs on his computer as well. Unfortunately, his computer doesn't have enough disk space to hold them all. What to do, what to do? You decide to share out your Songs folder for his listening enjoyment.

1. At your computer, select **Start**, **Programs**, **Windows Explorer**, and then single click the **Songs** folder.

2. Choose **File**, **Properties**.

3. Click the **Sharing** tab, and then select **Shared As**. By default, the share name of the folder is the name of the folder as it appears in Windows Explorer. You can change this if you want.

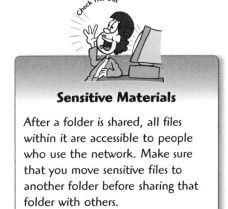

Sensitive Materials

After a folder is shared, all files within it are accessible to people who use the network. Make sure that you move sensitive files to another folder before sharing that folder with others.

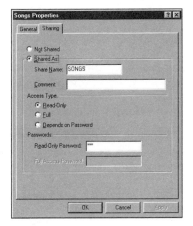

Use the Comment box for pertinent information regarding this directory.

4. Click the access type you want and, if you think it's necessary, enter a password. (If you enter a password, you'll need to remember it to access this shared folder from another computer.)

Beware What You Share

If you want to make a folder available for sharing but want to make sure that nobody changes anything in that folder, select **Read-Only** as the access type in step 4.

In some cases, you may want certain people to have read-only access and others (such as yourself) to have full access. If this is the case, select the **Depends on Password** option under Access Type. Then enter passwords to be used for both read-only and full access. One of these passwords must be used when someone tries to access the shared folder; which password the person uses determines what level of access he has in that folder.

Here you can see how the Songs folder appears from the computer that is sharing it. Notice the little hand on the Songs folder's icon. This indicates that the folder is accessible to others on the network.

The open hand signifies a shared directory.

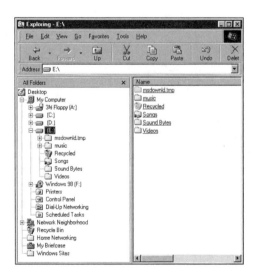

Accessing Shared Folders

Now that you've made the folder available for sharing, head over to your brother's computer and help him access the Songs folder on your computer:

1. At your brother's computer, select **Start**, **Programs**, **Windows Explorer**.

2. In the All Folders pane, double-click **Network Neighborhood**. Notice in this figure that the Mark's computer folder has the Songs folder available for sharing.

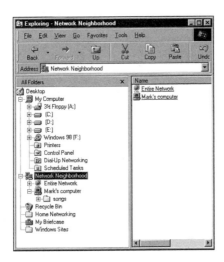

Network Neighborhood is found below the local drives.

3. Select the **Songs** folder by clicking it once.

4. You should see all the song files in the right-hand pane. They are now available for your brother's listening enjoyment.

Tidy Up the Neighborhood: Mapping Shared Folders

If there is a shared folder that you *always* use, it can be a real pain to find it in Network Neighborhood whenever you need it. Instead of hunting for it, you can *map* it to a drive' letter for quick and easy access. To map a shared folder to a drive letter, do the following:

1. In Network Neighborhood, right-click the folder you want to map.

2. Select **Map Network Drive**. Windows assigns the next available drive letter to this shared folder. In the following example, the next available drive letter is G.

Choosing Reconnect at Logon automatically reconnects you after you have rebooted.

3. Select the **Reconnect at Logon** check box to make this folder available as a drive letter the next time you start Windows.

4. Click **OK**.

Alternatively, you can move the shared folder to the desktop, providing you with even easier access:

1. In Network Neighborhood, place the pointer over the folder you want to share and hold down the right mouse button.

2. Drag the selected file from Network Neighborhood to a convenient place on your desktop.

3. Release the right mouse button and select **Create Shortcut(s) Here** from the menu.

Sharing Drives

In a few cases, sharing an entire drive may be the best way to set up sharing for your files. For example:

➤ You want to access all the files on a drive from anywhere on the network.

➤ You've installed a large hard disk in one computer and want to use it as the main storage place for files on your network.

➤ You want to share a CD-ROM in your computer with other computers on the network. (Note: Some programs, such as games, cannot run from another computer's CD-ROM.)

To share a drive, do the following:

1. In Windows Explorer, click the icon of the drive you want to share.

2. Choose **File**, **Properties**.

3. Click the **Sharing** tab, and then click **Shared As**.

4. Click the access type you want and, if you feel it's necessary, enter a password.

Because Windows treats a CD-ROM just like any other hard disk, the method for sharing a CD-ROM is similar to the method for sharing drives. To share a CD-ROM, do the following:

1. Insert a CD-ROM into your CD-ROM drive.
2. In Windows Explorer, click the CD-ROM icon.
3. Choose **File**, **Properties**.
4. Click the **Sharing** tab, and then click **Shared As**.
5. Assign a name to the shared CD-ROM, and click **OK**.

The Least You Need to Know

➤ File and printer sharing is the heart of network access.

➤ To use file and printer sharing, you must set up the appropriate network drivers.

➤ Establishing printer sharing and controlling printer access are straightforward procedures.

➤ With Windows, you can easily share folders, drives, and CD-ROMs among the computers on your home network.

Chapter 7

You've Got the Whole World in Your HAN: Connecting to the Internet

In This Chapter

➤ A short history of the Internet

➤ Choosing your Internet service provider

➤ Internet connection options: modems and more

➤ Adding a modem to your PC

Just in case you've been living under a rock for the past 10 years, the Internet has changed the world forever. It has changed how people learn, love, and laugh; how they play, work, and shop. You will have to look hard to find a place where the Internet has not changed some facet of your life, even if you don't use it yourself (yet).

We'll say it quickly and politely once more: It's not a fad, it's not going away, get used to it, the Net is here to stay!

An Oldie but Goodie: How the Net Was Born

Much has been made of the fact that the Internet was born from the needs of the U.S. government. The feds had a twofold need:

➤ First, the bean-counting piece of the Pentagon hated the fact that some computers were overutilized whereas others were underutilized. So, in a manner befitting any good accountant, it was decreed that computing tasks should be shared among the different computing resources. "Neat idea," said the computer scientists, "except how the heck are we supposed to do that?" The accountants didn't like the idea that the computers in use couldn't talk to each other very well and promptly told the computer geeks to go away and figure it out.

➤ Second, the military side of the house thought it would be pretty cool to have a computer network that could survive a direct hit from the bad guys. Up until that point, most networks had some form of *nerve center*. This nerve center controlled how the network worked, as well as how to resolve problems if they arose. This was seen as a major setback by the bomb-chucking crowd because the nerve center made networks vulnerable to attack.

With these two criteria (among others) in mind, the scientists and professors promptly got to work. To take care of the accountants' problem, they needed to build a network that would allow any type of computer to talk over it. To pacify the generals, they needed to install a healthy sense of paranoia in the network itself. This paranoid network would assume that any link could be broken at any time, and so would constantly check each possible path and choose the best one available. *Best* would eventually become some variation on

➤ The most cost-effective route between two points on the network

➤ The shortest route between two points on the network

➤ In the case of a military strike (or a tripped-over power cord), any available link

Webster Update

The word *internet* with a little *i* is the technical term used to describe any interconnecting network of networks. The word *Internet* with a capital *I* is the name for that cool thing with all the Web sites on the other end of your modem.

With the help of a few government dollars, a noteworthy handful of very smart people all smacked their heads together to come up with a technology that provided solutions for these concerns. They used this *interconnecting network of networks*, known as an *internet*, to share computer resources as well as to build a military-grade network.

It Wasn't About Technology; It Was About People

For a few years, it could have gone either way. The Internet was a high-tech play land for students, academics, and researchers. It could have run out of money and died like countless other government projects, but it didn't—something happened outside the technology itself. The academics started to appreciate it for what it did best: *bring people and ideas together*.

True, most of it was technical at the start. But as the number of people using the Internet grew, so did the variety of ideas that those people brought to the table. Even though it was primarily an academic hangout at that point, the flavor of the Internet was shifting from raw academia toward the world at large.

But there was one small hurdle that had to be crossed before things went crazy: The Internet was just plain tough to use. The World Wide Web cleared up this last hitch, and then things *really* started to heat up.

BigBucks.Com

As more people heard about and joined the Internet world, which quickly became synonymous with *the Web*, you could be sure that the business world wouldn't be far behind. Imagine a sandy beach without a hot dog vendor or a sunny wharf without an ice cream stand. Not likely.

While the academic core of the Internet tried to stave off the capitalist intrusion, the growing number of people online and the pressure to make money from such a mass of people were unstoppable. The modern Internet was born.

Selecting an Internet Service Provider

Okay, you're convinced. You've decided that it's time to make the leap to the Internet. The first step is finding an Internet service provider, or an *ISP*. Your ISP will be your on ramp to the Internet.

The first question should always be "What's available in my area?" Although this might sound like a simple question, it can get more complicated if you want to use the same ISP from work, from home, and while you're traveling. Consider all the places where you want to be able to connect to the Internet before selecting a provider. Here are your options:

➤ **Local ISPs** Some ISPs are available in only one location. If you try to connect from anywhere other than that city, you're going to get hit with a long-distance call on top of your regular fees.

Long distance fees will usually dwarf your ISP fees. Be careful to avoid long-distance calls to the Internet whenever possible.

➤ **Regional ISPs** Many phone companies now offer ISP services from anywhere within their calling area. As long as you're in your phone company's territory, it will only be a local call.

➤ **National/international ISPs** If you're a true road warrior, you might want to consider one of the providers that offer local access in major cities worldwide. CompuServe and America Online are the premier providers in this category.

If you're not sure who is available in your area, contact a few of your local computer stores and ask them for the names of the more dependable ISPs.

The following are some of the factors you should consider when selecting from the available providers:

➤ Connection speed

➤ Rates

➤ Extra services

Broadband Connections

Comcast@home operates a site dedicated to serving customers with broadband Internet connections. Comcast uses the term *broadband* as a catchall name to refer to anybody who has an ISDN (128Kbps) or faster link to the Net.

Surf on over to www.onbroadband.com if you have a high-speed connection or if you want to make your modem beg for mercy.

Connection Speed

In general, the faster you want to connect to the Net, the more it's going to cost. You shouldn't go hungry so that you can get a wickedly fast Internet connection, although you wouldn't be the first to do so. On the flip side, just as you can never have too much RAM, too big a hard disk, or too fast a processor, you can never have too fast an Internet connection. This is because a faster connection to the Net doesn't just allow you to do what you would normally do faster; it allows you to do different things.

For instance, someone with a 300 bits per second (bps) modem can surf most of the same Web sites as somebody with a 28,800bps modem. The only difference is that the 300bps Net surfer will avoid highly graphical Web sites due to the amount of time it takes for those pages to download on his system. So even though there is no technical reason that the 300bps surfer can't go to the same sites as the 28,800bps surfer, he probably won't.

Bumping up a level, the 28,800bps surfer may be perfectly happy perusing www.yahoo.com or www.amazon.com, but when she attempts to visit a site with video and audio links on it, such as www.cnn.com, the lengthy download times will likely send her straight for the proverbial hills. Somebody surfing the Net with a cable modem (about 40 times faster than a 28,800 modem), however, might be more inclined to spend a few moments downloading news clips.

The Need for Speed

Most people aren't willing to sit and stare at their monitors for more than a minute at a time. Check out Table 7.1 to see how much information you can download in about one minute using some of the most common connection speeds.

Table 7.1   One Minute Flat

Connection Speed (Kbps)	Technology Options	Data Downloaded
14.4	v.32 modem	105KB
28.8	V.32bis modem	215KB
56	v.90 modem	415KB
128	ISDN	1MB
400	Direct-PC satellite	3.3MB
1,500 download/512 upload	ADSL modem	12MB
4,000 download/64 upload	Cable modem	30MB

Table 7.2 illustrates how quickly various types of Internet connections can download a 10MB file (for the sake of comparison, the current versions of Internet Explorer and Netscape Navigator are both closer to 20MB).

Table 7.2   10MB Flat

Connection Speed (Kbps)	Technology Options	Download Time
14.4	v.32 modem	1.6 hours
28.8	V.32bis modem	48 minutes
56	v.90 modem	25 minutes
128	ISDN	11 minutes
400	Direct-PC satellite	3 minutes
1,500 download/512 upload	ADSL modem	53 seconds
4,000 download/64 upload	Cable modem	20 seconds

Get the Right Rate

Unlike the phone company, which is regulated in what it can charge for telephone service, ISPs suffer no such burden. Accordingly, there are as many different billing plans as there are ISPs:

➤ **Hourly billing**   The longer you spend online, the more you get charged. Surfing on a clock, although better than nothing, usually results in tension in the shoulder and an itchy mouse finger. Avoid it unless you have no other choice.

➤ **Flat rate for *x* hours, plus hourly billing after that**   Much better than hourly billing because it allows you to wander through the Net like you would through an old bookstore, without worrying whether it's going to cost you anything. But, as the clock ticks closer to closing time (when you have to start paying), people usually start heading for the exits.

➤ **Flat-rate billing**   Originally championed by America Online, flat-rate billing has replaced hourly billing as the most common rate for access to the Internet. With this type of billing, some people are tempted to stay online until they get tired or until the boss calls and asks them why they're late for work, whichever comes first.

➤ **Hourly billing during prime time, flat rate during off hours**   A mix of two of the preceding options, but with the ISP trying to get a few more bucks out of the rich while giving the not-so-rich the opportunity to surf the Internet during off hours. Imagine what an ISP run by Robin Hood's merry men might be like and you've got this one figured out.

➤ **Extra cost for extraordinary use of services**   In an attempt to recover the *actual* costs of doing business, some ISPs charge a few extra bucks if you really exercise their networks. For instance, if you decide you're going to spend your life downloading every single video game you can get your hands on, some ISPs might charge you a few extra bucks for every megabyte you download.

➤ **Free? You're kidding, right?**   Some ISPs have an innovative way of charging the customer: *They don't.* As you might expect, *nonprofit* institutions such as universities, colleges, and libraries fall into this category. If you are a student or a member of another not-for-profit institution, look around for these diamonds in the rough.

Extra Services

One final reason for deciding to use a particular provider is because that provider offers services above and beyond a speedy, affordable, and available connection to the Internet.

➤ **Web space**   Not all ISPs will give you access to a Web server on which you can set up your own World Wide Web home page. If this is a big deal for you, check with your prospective providers to make sure that they will.

➤ **Communities of interest**   Although the Internet itself has the built-in capability to do so, some ISPs, such as CompuServe and America Online, go out of their way to make it easy for people with similar interests to get together.

➤ **Net programming**   Some ISPs provide access to information and news services that are available only to their customers. Cable modem ISPs seem to be at the forefront of this curve. (It's not hard to figure out why this is the case when you remember that cable companies are in the business of providing content; having enough bandwidth to deliver innovative audio and video services doesn't hurt either.)

Mastering the Net with a Modem

Every major computer manufacturer offers modems with its computers, and you'd be hard pressed to find a city in North America without a dial-up ISP. These factors combine to make a dial-up connection—that is, one made with a modem—the most common way of accessing the Internet.

Picking a Modem

A trip down the modem aisle at your local Circuit City can be intimidating, but it doesn't need to be. Only a few options for your modem need serious consideration:

➤ **Speed**   All other things being equal, *faster is always better*. The current crème de la crème in modem speeds is 56 kilobits per second (also called 56K or 56 Kbps). Of course, many modems are still on the shelves in the 28K and 33K range. Of equal (or greater) importance to 56K is the *protocol* that the modem uses to achieve that speed. A *protocol* is an agreed upon method for performing some task, in this case, communicating at 56K.

➤ **Protocol**   Although not a particularly snazzy name, the industry standard protocol that 56K modems use to connect with each other is known as *V.90*. If the 56K modem you're looking at doesn't say *V.90* somewhere on the box, do yourself a favor and look at another modem.

Techno Talk

Imagine being sold a car that can travel 560 miles an hour. Sounds great, right? Wrong. First of all, it's against the law to drive a car that fast. Second, most roads can't support a car that *tries* to drive that fast. (Can you say "speed bump" boys and girls?)

You run into exactly the same problems when you buy a 56K modem. Although a V.90 modem is capable of handling information at 56Kbps, telecommunications laws require that standard telephone lines be limited to transmitting information at only 53Kbps. That means you will *never* connect at 56Kbps with your 56K modem. Welcome to the speed limit.

Furthermore, the telecommunications infrastructure in many parts of North America isn't up to the rigors of 56K (or 53K, for that matter) communication. So don't be surprised when you connect at speeds between 33Kbps and 46Kbps.

Don't let this dissuade you from getting a 56K modem, though. Even if you only get a 28.8K connection to your ISP, it's still faster with a 56K modem. This is made possible by the more advanced compression technology built into 56K modems. Every bit per second is worth it when you're downloading the trailer for the new *Star Wars* movie.

Adding a Modem to Your Computer

Adding a new modem in Windows 95/98 is a fairly trivial exercise. If you have an internal modem, the act of installing the card itself is the same as that of installing an ethernet card (refer to Chapter 3, "Tried and True: Networking the Ethernet Way").

If you purchased an external modem, turn off your computer and hook up the cables as indicated in the modem manual. (This assumes, of course, that you bought a modem cable when you bought your modem. As silly as it might seem, most external modems don't come with the cable that you'll need to connect it to your computer. Make sure that the nice little computer geek at the store sells you the cable you need when you buy the modem.) When you turn your computer back on, you should be rewarded with the Add New Hardware Wizard. It will walk you through the process of installing the drivers for your modem. (Microsoft *has* done a few things well....)

Configuring Dial-Up Networking

Before you can make a connection, you will have to configure a *dial-up connection* to use the modem you just installed. Do the following:

1. Select **Start**, **Programs**, **Accessories**, **Communications**, **Dial-Up Networking**.

2. Click the **Make a New Connection** button. This will start the Make a New Connection Wizard.

3. You'll be asked to name the connection you are creating—**My Connection**, for example. If you have more than one modem in your computer (not very likely), select the one you want from the drop-down menu. Click **Next.**

Windows 98 will automatically detect the modems you have installed in your computer.

4. Type the telephone number of your ISP. (The documentation that your ISP gave you when you signed up should include this piece of information.) Click **Next**.

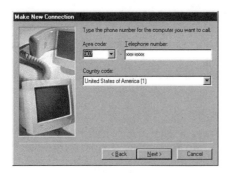

Enter the telephone number for your ISP into the Make New Connection Wizard.

5. Click **Finished**. You have created the Internet connection.

All ISPs will have some specific documentation regarding connecting to their service. There may be a few more steps for you to do manually—or if you're lucky, creating the connection may be as simple as executing a setup program that your ISP provides.

Getting to the Net with ISDN

ISDN, which is the next step up the food chain from a regular modem line, is widely available in the U.S. and Canada. ISDN operates at around 120Kbps, giving you two or three times the speed of the modem you probably have right now. Your ISDN connection will need a new type of line coming into your house, known as a *basic rate interface* or *BRI*.

To use an ISDN line, you will need an ISDN adapter—which can cost between $200 and $300—to connect to your ISP. Expect ISDN service itself to cost you around $100 for installation and about $30 to $40 per month for the line. Don't forget that ISDN service itself doesn't include an ISP—you may need an ISP on top of this, which will likely put you back another $20 or so per month.

BRI

A BRI is made up of three channels: two bearer channels and one delta channel. (Because of the names of the different channels, this type of ISDN line is often called a *2B+D*.) The B channels, each operating at 64Kbps, will carry your information back and forth to your ISP. The D channel is used for signaling information (such as a busy signal) between your ISDN modem and your provider's. Some ISPs will let you use the D channel for low-bandwidth ongoing communications, such as checking email and downloading stock quotes.

71

Adaptable Adapters

Look for ISDN adapters that will allow you to plug a phone into them so that you can make phone calls over your ISDN line as well. Although this will let you make a phone call at the same time you are surfing, the phone call will use up one of the 64Kbps B channels while doing so.

Going Ape with ADSL

Asymmetric digital subscriber line modems, often called *ADSL modems*, are one of the two contenders for high-speed Internet connectivity in the home. With a few rare exceptions, ADSL is the fastest Internet connection you can buy today.

As an *asymmetric* connection, ADSL speeds are different in each direction. The fastest direction is on the download side where, depending on your provider, you can see speeds as high as 7 or 8Mbps. On the upload side, speeds as high as 1Mbps aren't unheard of.

Although you might think that you're getting ripped off with a connection that has a slower speed in one direction than in the other, the way most people use their Internet connection shows it's not that big a problem.

The vast majority of people use the Internet for two things:

➤ **Net surfing**   The act of surfing the Net is an inherently asymmetric activity. First, you click a link. Then the Web server sends the information resulting from the click to your computer. The click sends a trivial amount of traffic toward the Web server, but the Web server could respond with a multimegabyte file, depending on what you're surfing for.

➤ **Email**   When somebody sees that she has an incoming message, even a big incoming message, she wants to read it *now*! But when someone is sending a message, whether large or small, the fact that it gets delivered now or 10 minutes from now isn't a particularly big deal. Again, it's easy to see how an asymmetric connection wouldn't hinder this form of communication.

Making the ADSL Connection

Because it will probably require some wiring work, your ISP or local telephone company will send an installation person to hook up your new ADSL connection. The connection will go into your ADSL modem, which will in turn connect to your network via an ethernet cable. The ADSL modem will probably be provided—at a charge, of course—by your ISP.

If you have an ethernet hub, you would then connect the ADSL modem into your ethernet hub to serve your entire network. If you have only one computer, you should connect the ADSL modem directly to an ethernet card in the PC.

Going the Distance with ADSL

All types of communication have some inherent distance limitation. For example, speaking is a wonderful method of communicating as long as you are within earshot of the person you're trying to talk to. Try to have a meaningful vocal conversation with somebody four miles away and the quality of the exchange is going to be a little on the low side.

ADSL is no different. There is a maximum distance that your house can be from the phone company's office. This distance depends on the particular flavor of ADSL your ISP uses, of which there are many. If your house is beyond this distance, no ADSL for you. So even if ADSL is available in some parts of your city, you'll have to check with your prospective provider to make sure that the neighborhood you live in can be served.

Cranking It Up with Cable

Along with ADSL, cable is the other big contender for your surfing buck. Even though cable modems share the speed of the connection with other cable surfers in your area, the download speed of a cable modem connection is just this side of amazing.

Like ADSL modems, cable modem speeds are asymmetric. Information you upload to the Internet goes about twice as fast as the fastest regular modem you can buy, whereas information you download to your computer goes about 40 times faster than the fastest regular modem you can buy.

In addition to raw speed, cable modem providers have upped the ISP ante in another way: Because they are already old pros at providing television content, they are best positioned to add compelling Internet-based content as well. This usually takes the form of video news clips, movie trailers, and stereo-quality audio from their customer Web site. This Web site will be available only to the cable modem provider's clientele, so don't surf your brains out trying to find one of them if you're not already a paying customer.

How Cable Modems Work

As funny as it sounds, cable modems work exactly the way their name suggests: The cable guy comes to your home and runs a splitter off the existing cable feed going to your TV. This new cable in turn runs into the back of your new cable modem. The cable modem then connects to your network via a standard ethernet cable. Whether this goes directly into your PC or into your ethernet hub depends on the state of your existing home network. If you have two computers that you want to connect to the Internet and you don't have an ethernet hub, quickly dart back to Chapter 3 and see why you should consider getting one.

Are Cable Modems Safe?

Cable modems differ from all other connection technologies in one way: The connection between your cable modem and the cable company is shared with other people in your neighborhood. This differs from all the other connection methods discussed so far, which make a *direct connection* between your home and your ISP. Because your modem connects directly to an ISP, nobody (unless your phone is tapped) can intercept the call. With cable modems, however, the people who share your piece of the cable network could theoretically "listen in" on all your Internet activity, including surfing as well as sending and receiving email. That's bad.

Fortunately, cable modem manufacturers and providers have worked together to provide a solution to this problem. The technology now exists to provide an *encrypted connection* between your cable modem and the cable company equipment. Of course, that doesn't mean someone with above-average network-snooping skills can't spy on your network traffic; however, with an encrypted connection at work, the traffic they see will look a little like a high school term paper with two platefuls of spaghetti poured on it. They'll have to plow through a heck of a mess to get anything out of it.

The Future of High Speed Internet

According to Jupiter Communications, cable modems will be the fastest growing segment of the high-speed Internet access market in the next five years. ADSL will be next, although 80 percent of households will still be using dial-up access in the year 2002.

How Much Cable Modems Cost

Although cable modems are a bit pricey off the shelf (around $400), you can usually persuade your cable modem provider to kick one in free of charge as part of the subscription price for the service. The cost of cable modem service can run you anywhere from $30 to $70 per month, in addition to your television cable charges. And of course, because somebody will have to come to your house to do some cabling, expect to get dinged with a $40 to $100 installation fee.

Enough Already! Where Can I Get One?

Although cable modems are regarded as the technology most likely to replace your modem, they are available in precious few cities to date. This is due largely to the fact that a good portion of the existing cable infrastructure has to be replaced before it will be capable of delivering this service.

Are Two Modems Better Than One? Dual-Modem Technology

A new breed of hardware capable of *bonding* two separate modem connections into a single Internet connection has recently hit the market.

First the good news: By combining two dial-up connections into a single pipe, your Internet connection will appear to be twice as fast as one provided by a single modem. So if you currently have a 56K dial-up provider, you'd be able to surf at around 100K—pretty darn close to the speed of an ISDN connection.

Check This Out

Diamond Multimedia's Shotgun technology is one of the first working examples of dual-modem technology. (You can check out Diamond's Suprasonic dual-line modems at http://www.diamondmm.com/.)

Now comes the bad news: To enjoy your double-speed connection, you will have to have two phone lines and a special modem capable of bonding two telephone lines together. (To make things even worse, your ISP must also support bonding.) If you are an unabashed and well-heeled Net surfer, this is a small price to pay.

Get Psyched with Satellite

There are a few good reasons to consider connecting to the Internet via satellite—the most compelling of which is, of course, speed. Satellite systems are rated at a download speed of around 400Kbps, which is about eight times faster than a good modem connection. The second reason to consider this technology is that it is widely available. City dweller or country cousin, your only requirement for being able to use a satellite connection is a clear view of the sky.

As with all silver linings, satellite has one little cloud that you should be aware of: It takes *asymmetric connection* to a whole new level. Although cable modems and ADSL have different upload and download speeds, at least they use the same *facility* for both. Internet satellite providers, on the other hand, use a modem to send your mouse clicks out to the

Why Do I Still Need a Modem?

The reason for this is simple enough. Anybody who wants to send signals through the air needs a broadcast license from the government. To avoid the technical and financial issues involved with such activity, satellite providers require that you use a modem to send your outgoing traffic and limit the satellite connection to receiving traffic.

Internet and the satellite connection to send the Web page that you requested back to you. So even though you have a satellite connection to the Internet, you will still need a modem.

The Least You Need to Know

➤ A connection to the Internet is an essential component of any home network.

➤ Selecting an ISP, a connection speed, and a connection method are all critical factors in extending the reach of your home network.

➤ Carefully consider the various methods of connecting to the outside world and make your decision based on your particular needs.

Chapter 8

FIRE IT UP, DUDE.

Sharing an Internet Connection Between Two or More Computers

In This Chapter

➤ How to connect a multicomputer home network to the Internet over a modem

➤ How to connect two or more computers to the Internet through a cable modem or ADSL connection

➤ Assess when an Internet proxy will help you connect your computers to the Internet

The advent of the multicomputer home was unavoidable. Inevitably, families grow, applications push existing hardware, or the simple desire for speed compels people to buy a second computer. The multicomputer home comes with challenges, though. Part 2, "Networking Your Home Computers," discusses the challenges and solutions related to sharing resources between computers on your home network; Chapter 7, "You've Got the Whole World in Your HAN: Connecting to the Internet," focuses on the details of connecting a *single* computer to the Internet.

This chapter looks at the ultimate setup for home PCs. By connecting all the computers to each other and to the Internet at the same time, the value of the home network grows by leaps and bounds. No more trying to access the computer with the modem on it; no more fighting over the phone line. If anyone is on the Net, everyone is on the Net.

What You Need

For you to use a single Internet connection for all the computers on your home network, you need the following:

➤ All your PCs must be connected to each other. Whether this connection is via ethernet, phone line, power line, or wireless is immaterial. All that matters is that the computers can communicate with each other over the home network.

➤ Each computer should have its own network interface to connect it to the home network.

➤ You must have an Internet service provider (ISP).

On Internet Service Providers

Some ISPs are better at providing multiple computers access to the Internet than others. The issues requiring special consideration for multicomputer home area networks are as follows:

➤ Speed

➤ Connection type

➤ The capability to issue multiple IP addresses to a single account

➤ The capability to issue multiple mail addresses to a single account

Speed

If a fast connection matters for a single computer, it matters even more for a house with two or more computers. How much it matters depends on how the people on the home network use the Internet:

➤ **Click and read, click and read** If the people on your network use the Net primarily to surf for online information, a standard V.90 56KB modem should work fine. This type of surfing is light on network usage and lends itself well to sharing a 56KB connection. Because the odds of two people clicking links at the same time are small, each user typically will have the modem to herself for the duration of any particular download.

➤ **Multiplayer gaming** Gamers use the Net for the entire time that they are involved in a game. Further, online games are sensitive to network delays. Accordingly, if several people in the house want to play games across the Internet at the same time, seek out the fastest connection you can afford.

➤ **Download and install** With a wide array of high-quality shareware and demos available for the taking, it's easy to get hooked on Internet downloads. Some demos can be as large as 20 or 30MB. Because files of this size take two to three hours to download, the odds of this affecting somebody else's surf session are high. If Junior loves to download a lot of large files, consider getting the fastest connection you can buy.

Connection Type

How you connect to the Internet—whether via a dial-up account or via an always-on connection such as a cable or ADSL modem—has a great impact on your network layout.

Multiple IP Addresses

Whether your ISP lets you have more than one IP address has a major impact on the setup of your home area network. Regular dial-up modems can have only one IP address, period. On the other hand, the answer isn't as clear cut if you have an always-on connection type, such as a cable modem, ADSL, ISDN, or satellite. The only real way to tell for sure is to ask your ISP's technical support desk (via phone or its Web support page).

➤ **Yes, your ISP will let you have more than one IP address**   A network where each computer has its own IP address is fast and simple to set up. Unless it's inordinately expensive to acquire additional addresses, this setup should be your first choice.

➤ **No, your ISP won't let you have extra IP addresses**   If you can't get additional IP addresses, things get a little more complicated but by no means insurmountable. There is software and hardware that you can buy or download to trick the computers on the network into thinking that they have their own IP addresses. For more on these options, see the sections titled "Network Address Translation (NAT)" and "Proxy Servers" later in this chapter.

Multiple Mail Accounts

Although not directly related to getting many computers on the Net, you're going to need several mail accounts for all the people in your home. Support for multiple mail accounts, particularly if they are free, makes an ISP attractive for a multicomputer home network. ISPs that support this feature either let the holder of the primary account call in and request another mail account or (preferably) allow you to create a new one from a Web page.

Don't get too down on ISPs that don't support this feature, though. A number of *free* email services on the Web can take care of this problem if your ISP can't solve it.

A few of the more popular free email services are

➤ **Hotmail**   www.hotmail.com

➤ **Rocket mail**   www.rocketmail.com

➤ **Yahoo mail**   www.yahoo.com

Configuring a Multicomputer Network

There are many different ways that you can lay out your home computer network. This section covers three simple solutions designed to get the network connected to the Net with minimal hassle and expense. The most common home network configurations are

➤ Dial-up connection

➤ Cable modem/ISDN/ADSL modem *with* multiple IP addresses

➤ Cable modem/ISDN/ADSL modem *without* multiple IP addresses

Dial-Up Connections

Almost by definition, dial-up connections can have only one IP address. But if you want every computer on your network to be capable of connecting to the Internet, each computer must have its own IP address. If it sounds like the preceding two sentences are in conflict with each other, you're right!

Because there is only one IP address to go around, the network needs some method of distributing that address among all the computers on the network. The two methods for doing this are network address translation and proxy servers.

Network Address Translation (NAT)

Network address translation (NAT) is one of the methods of sharing an IP address among several computers. Devices that use NAT *listen* to the home network for requests destined for the Internet.

Once received, the NAT device makes note of which home computer made the request and then forwards it along to the Internet using the IP address allotted to it. When the response comes back from the Internet, the NAT device realizes which computer made the request in the first place and returns it to that computer.

Two examples of devices that use NAT to share IP addresses are

➤ **3Com's 56KB LAN modem**   www.3com.com

➤ **Proxim's Symphony cordless modem**   www.proxim.com

3Com's 56KB LAN modem

The 3Com 56KB LAN modem simplifies your home area network by combining an ethernet hub and modem into a single device. Of even greater impact is the fact that it performs network address translation, allowing all computers on the network access to the Internet through a single IP address.

One big advantage to running a LAN modem like 3Com's (or Proxim's, for that matter) is that it removes the need for a computer-based proxy server to translate addresses. Because of this, there is no need for one of your household computers to remain on all the time to translate addresses. Further, because there is no proxy server, there is no need to figure out how to install two ethernet cards in a single computer.

Each computer in the home requires an ethernet card and a connection to the LAN modem with an ethernet cable. The LAN modem then connects to the phone line with a regular phone cable. These connections provide fast, reliable ethernet connectivity for the home.

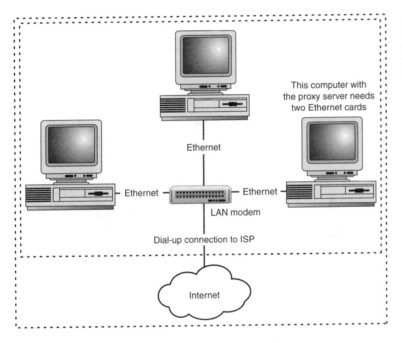

A combined ethernet hub and modem is a simple, cost-effective solution for connecting a home area network to the Internet.

Proxy Servers

Let's get this straight right off the bat: NAT devices and proxy servers do (just about) the same thing. In general, a *proxy* is a process that does something on your behalf. This definition opens up the door for servers that proxy many different types of services, from file transfer to Web browsing to IP address sharing. Because we're talking about Internet access here, the type of proxying in which we're most interested is IP addresses themselves, otherwise known as NAT.

Although several different proxy servers that do NAT are available on the Internet, two of the most popular are

➤ **WinGate** www.wingate.com
➤ **WinProxy** www.winproxy.com

81

A proxy server performs two functions worth mentioning:

➤ **Network address translation (NAT)**   In so doing, the proxy server passes along requests from your home computers to the Internet through the single IP address that your ISP gave you. When these requests are returned from the Internet, it passes the responses back to the computer that made the request.

➤ **Monitor the Internet traffic on your network**   In this way, the proxy server can let you know what Internet sites were visited by each computer on your network.

As shown in the following figure, a proxy server acts as a gateway between two different networks. To act as a gateway, proxy servers require an individual connection to each network—the home network and the Internet. Each of these connections requires its own network card. Although the figure shows the home network being connected via ethernet, it could just as easily be wireless or connected by phone lines or power lines.

The computer running the proxy server must be turned on whenever anybody wants to use the Internet.

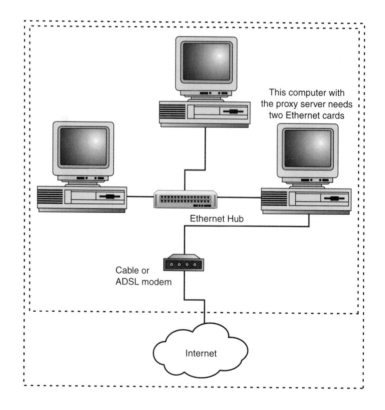

Other Dial-Up Alternatives

Although an ethernet-based home network is an excellent starting point for connecting several computers to the Net, there are other alternatives:

➤ **Proxim cordless modems**   Proxim's Symphony line is good not only for connecting the PCs in your home but also for connecting them all to the Internet through a Symphony cordless modem. Proxim's Symphony line of products can be found at www.proxim.com/symphony.

➤ **Diamond HomeFree PhoneLine**   The HomeFree PhoneLine creates a home network using the phone lines in your home without interrupting your use of the telephone. In addition to connecting your PCs, it can bring them all onto the Net with a single Internet account as well. You can find more information regarding Diamond's HomeFree from http://www.diamondmm.com.

Cable Modem/ISDN/ADSL Modem Without Multiple IP Addresses

Except for the fact that modems are slower, this type of network works similarly to the dial-up solutions described in the previous section.

There is a hub (or wireless network) between all the PCs and, as with the dial-up network, one of the computers must act as an Internet address *proxy* for the others. (Remember, because there is only one IP address to share among all the computers, this computer will forward and receive messages for all the other computers on the network.)

Accordingly, the computer acting as a proxy for the others must be turned on whenever any of the other computers wants to use the Internet. The software that the computer runs to perform this function is known as a *proxy server*.

Cable Modem/ISDN/ADSL Modem with Multiple IP Addresses

A high-speed connection where each computer has its own IP address is a dream network. Because each computer has its own IP address, there is no need to perform NAT or proxy services, making this solution quick and easy to install. Further, the removal of the proxy server also means that none of the computers on the home network needs to rely on any other to access the Internet.

If you have the option, this should be your preferred network.

A high-speed Internet connection is simple and easy to set up when each computer has its own IP address.

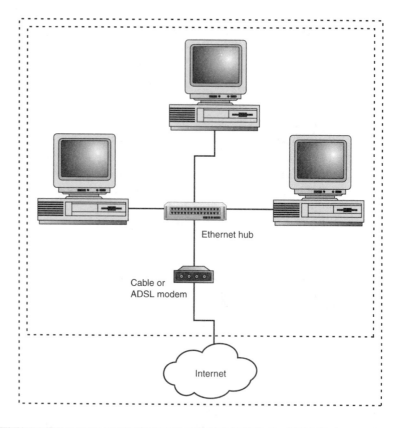

Ethernet hub

Cable or ADSL modem

Internet

The Least You Need to Know

➤ A home with multiple computers doesn't have to have multiple Internet connections. With a properly laid out home network, all the computers in your house can share the same Internet connection.

➤ An Internet connection can be shared regardless of the type of home network, be it ethernet, wireless, phone line, or power line.

➤ A dial-up network can easily share an Internet connection with a combination home network/Internet device such as a LAN modem.

➤ A proxy server is used to send requests to and from the Internet when there is only one IP address to share among several computers.

➤ A computer running a proxy server requires two network cards and must be turned on whenever someone wants access to the Internet.

➤ If every computer on the home network can get its own IP address, there is no need for a proxy server.

Chapter 9

Surf's Up: Configuring Your Internet Browser

In This Chapter

➤ Surfing better with Internet Explorer

➤ Navigating the Net with Netscape Navigator

➤ A look at channels and the Active Desktop

➤ Two browsers together on one desktop

Not surprisingly, new versions of browsers appear more often than new hairstyles. Make sure that you have the latest version for the optimal surfing experience. (The browser, that is.)

This chapter focuses on the two most popular World Wide Web browsers today: Netscape Navigator and Microsoft Internet Explorer. Other browsers are available, although support for them is limited.

Microsoft Internet Explorer

To download the latest version of Microsoft's Internet Explorer:

1. Open your current browser and type **www.microsoft.com** in the address line.
2. Choose **Downloads** and find Internet Explorer.
3. Follow the onscreen instructions.

Installation

Installation routines change as frequently as versions do (very often). If the instructions we've provided are inadequate, check Microsoft's Web site at www.microsoft.com. (You may find that the instructions you receive at www.microsoft.com change periodically as well, because Microsoft constantly improves its site.)

The Active Desktop

Have you ever wished you didn't have to open up your browser and search your Favorites list to get back to that great Web site on home networking? Wouldn't it be nice if that site just lived on your desktop and updated itself every once in awhile? The Active Desktop can give you what you're looking for—it lets you put *active content* on your desktop. Like your television, your desktop can have channels for you to watch. These channels can include any type of content—the most common examples are stock tickers, online newspapers, and up-to-the-minute weather reports.

Of course, you're not limited to accessing the Web from your desktop with channels; you can also access the Web from folders, desktop icons, and your Favorites folder. Your programs can look and feel like Web icons as well.

Setting Up Active Desktop on Your PC

To configure your computer to use the Active Desktop, do the following:

1. Choose **Start, Settings**, **Active Desktop**, **Customize my Desktop**.

2. In the Web tab of the Display Properties dialog box, click the **Folder Options** button, and then click **Yes**.

3. Click **Settings** and then select the settings you want for your desktop. As you can see, you have many choices as to how Web-like you want your desktop to be. Conversely, if you're a little shy of the Web look-and-feel, you can retain the classic Windows desktop that you're probably used to. When you've made your selections, click **OK**.

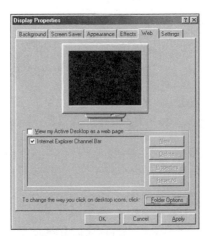

Remember to select
Apply *after selecting the*
IE Channel Bar.

*This dialog enables you to
select many different
"Web-like" options.*

Single Clicking

Even though it seems like a small thing, the option to single-click on files to open them (instead of double-clicking) has been one of the most popular. It takes a little getting used to, but after you do, you'll never go back to the old double-click.

Subscribing to a Channel

Subscribing to a Windows channel is easy:

1. After you've opened an Internet connection, click the **Channels** button in Internet Explorer.

2. In the **Explorer** bar, click the **Channel Guide**.

3. Select one of the channels that interests you, and click **Add Active Channel**.

If you are using the Active Desktop, you can subscribe to a channel directly from your desktop instead of through Internet Explorer:

1. Right-click the desktop and then select **Active Desktop**, **Customize My Desktop**.

2. From the resulting dialog box, select the Web tab, and then make sure that both the **View My Active Desktop as a Web Page** and the **Internet Explorer Channel Bar** options are selected.

If you're not sure what channels are available, check out Microsoft's Active Desktop Items Web site. Do the following:

1. Right-click the desktop, and then click **Properties**.

2. Make sure that the **View My Active Desktop as a Web Page** and the **Internet Explorer Channel Bar** check boxes are checked.

3. Click the **Web** tab, and then click **New**.

4. Select **Yes**. Microsoft's Active Desktop Gallery automatically appears in your Web browser.

High-Speed Surfing with Internet Explorer

There are a few tricks you can use to add some snap to your browsing experience. This section explains how you can

➤ Quickly search pages for the information you need

➤ Reduce your amount of typing

➤ Rename and reorganize Favorites folders for the whole family

➤ Configure your computer's cache

Searching Pages for Information

Do you tire of reading through long, wordy pages, trying to find that gem of information? Here's how you can quickly find what you're looking for:

1. After you have found the page where you think the information you want is located, select **Edit**, **Find** from Internet Explorer's menu.

2. Type the word or phrase you are trying to find, and then click **Find Next**.

This dialog box can greatly reduce your searching time.

3. Continue clicking **Find Next** to search for more instances of the phrase you typed.

Reducing Your Typing

Maybe you're not the touch typist you'd like to be. No worries! Here's how you can surf the Web with less typing:

➤ If you type the middle part of an address (for example, if you type microsoft instead of typing www.microsoft.com) and then press **Enter,** the browser adds the www and the .com for you and tries to find the Web server associated with that address. If it doesn't find one with .com on the end, it looks for one with an .edu extension.

➤ If you want to add the www and the .com yourself, simply press **Ctrl+Enter.**

➤ To edit an address quickly and easily, press **Ctrl+left arrow** or **Ctrl+right arrow** to jump from one dot to the next in the address.

➤ Using AutoComplete, Internet Explorer completes an address that you have used previously after you have typed a few letters.

Renaming and Reorganizing Favorites Folders

In Chapter 5, "Windows of Opportunity: Windows Networking," we used different profiles for different members of the family to log on to Windows. This affects your family's surfing experience in a couple of ways:

➤ Having a separate profile means that you can have your own Favorites folder in Internet Explorer. This can be a blessing, because Dad's favorite news sites are likely to be very different from Junior's.

➤ Downloaded Web pages can be kept in separate directories. Both your temporary Internet files and the helper applications that assist your browser are kept separate from users with different profiles.

If setting up profiles is too much hassle for your family, you can still get by with one profile. But if you want to try using multiple profiles, the key to keeping chaos from your door is organization. One option is to rename your favorites so that it is clear who saved them. Better yet, you could create a folder for each family member.

To rename your favorite shortcuts, do the following:

1. In Internet Explorer, click the **Favorites** button on the toolbar.
2. In the **Favorites bar**, find the shortcut you want to rename.
3. Right-click the shortcut, and then click **Rename**.
4. Type the name you want, and then press **Enter**.

To organize your Favorites folders, do the following:

1. In Internet Explorer, click the **Favorites** button.
2. Choose **Organize Favorites.**
3. To create a new folder for a family member, click the **New Folder** icon in the top-right of the box.

This dialog box resembles Windows Explorer.

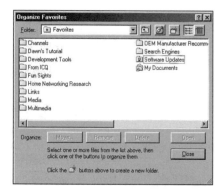

4. Type the name of the family member in the space provided.
5. Move files between folders by dragging and dropping them from one folder to the next.
6. Organize the folders using the buttons provided at the bottom of the window.

Configuring the Cache

Even though you may not have heard of your browser cache before, you've undoubtedly used it. Your cache resides in a folder under the c:\windows folder called Temporary Internet Files. This folder is used to temporarily store Web pages that you view on the Internet. This folder makes your browsing experience faster. How? Well, if you visit a page today that you've visited in the recent past, Internet Explorer opens the page from the cache on your hard disk instead of from the Web—and access to your hard disk is much faster than access to the Web.

Sound great? It can be, but there are a few downsides. For one, even though you are able to view the page more quickly, it may not be the most up-to-date copy of that page. After all, the owners of that page are updating it on the Web, not on your hard drive. All is not lost, however. You can control how often the page is updated with IE 4.0:

1. Select **View**, **Internet Options**.
2. Click the **General** tab.
3. Click the **Temporary Internet Files Settings** button.
4. Select an option in the **Check for Newer Versions of Stored Pages** section.

This dialog box allows you to manage your cache effectively.

How Often Should You Update?

To quickly browse to pages you've already visited, click **Never**. This will give you speed, but you undoubtedly will run into outdated information because calls to Web servers will always be served from your browser cache rather than from the Web itself. This might be fine for viewing the Constitution at www.ourconstitution.com, but not the latest newscasts from www.cnn.com. To make sure that you receive the most recent content, click the **Every visit to the page** option. Although clicking this option makes your browsing slower, it enables you to receive the most up-to-date information the Web has to offer.

In addition to being able to set how frequently items in the cache are updated, you can also specify the amount of space your Temporary Internet Files folder takes up on your hard drive. To change the size of the folder, do the following:

1. Select **View**, **Internet Options**.
2. Click the **General** tab.

3. Click the **Temporary Internet Files Settings** button.

4. Allocate more space for the cache by dragging the slider at the bottom of the Settings dialog box to the right.

Netscape Navigator

To download the latest version of Netscape Navigator, do the following:

1. Open your current browser and type `www.netscape.com` in the address line.

2. Choose **Downloads**, and then choose **Netscape Navigator**.

3. Follow the onscreen instructions.

Using Netcaster to Subscribe to Channels

Similar to the Channel bar in Internet Explorer, Netscape's Netcaster is used to organize and distribute Netscape's channels. To subscribe to channels in Netcaster, do the following:

1. Open Netcaster and click the **Channel Finder** bar.

2. View the list of channels, and preview one by clicking its bar.

3. If you like what you see, add the channel to My Channels by clicking the **Add Channel** button in the preview window.

4. After you finish adding the channel, its link appears on a bar in My Channels. To view the channel, click its bar.

High-Speed Surfing with Netscape Navigator

As with Internet Explorer, Netscape Navigator provides you with a few ways to add some zip to your browsing. For example, you can configure your cache, and you can create profiles for each person who uses Netscape.

Configuring the Cache

Netscape Navigator is similar to Internet Explorer in that it uses a cache to increase the speed of your surfing experience. To adjust the cache in Navigator, do the following:

1. Choose **Edit**, **Preferences**.

2. Select the **Advanced** entry in the **Category** list, and then choose **Cache**.

3. To set the size (in kilobytes) of the memory cache, enter a number in the Memory Cache field. (Windows' default is 1024KB.) If you have more than 32MB of RAM in your computer, you can experiment with the size of your memory cache to see whether you can make your surfing experience faster.

4. To empty the memory cache, click the **Clear Memory Cache** button.

5. To set the size of the disk cache, enter a number in the **Disk Cache** field. (The default is 7680KB.) 10,000KB is a reasonable amount; reduce it if you run out of room on your hard drive.

6. Specify how often Navigator compares the page that is stored in cache with the updated one on the Internet by clicking one of the options at the bottom of the screen:

   ➤ Select **Once per session** to check for page revisions only once between the times you start and quit the application. This is the default selection.

   ➤ Select **Every Time** to repeatedly check for changes when you request a page, at the cost of slower performance.

   ➤ Select **Never** to perform no verifications, but remember that your pages won't be automatically updated in the future.

7. Exit from Navigator; the cache maintenance is performed.

Customizing Netscape Navigator for More than One User

Many users can share Netscape Navigator through the use of profiles. A *profile* allows you to identify yourself to Netscape Navigator, enabling customized bookmarks, preferences, and so on. To add a new profile, do the following:

1. Click **Start**, **Programs**, **User Profile Manager**.

2. Click the **New** button.

3. Enter the full name and email address of the new user.

4. Choose a name for your profile. (Use your full name unless you have more than one profile.)

5. Select a directory to store the files that make up your profile. Unless you have good reason, stay with the recommended directory.

6. Choose **Finish** to complete the profile.

Reloading on the Fly

You can always obtain page revisions by clicking **Reload** in the toolbar.

Exit Wounds?

If you find that exiting takes a long time, reduce the size of the disk cache. Click the **Clear Disk Cache** button to empty the cache immediately.

This dialog box lists all profiles on this computer.

This dialog box is used to identify you.

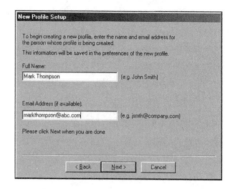

This dialog box captures the profile name.

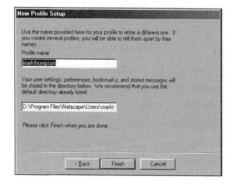

Why Can't We Just All Get Along? Switching from One Browser to the Other

Netscape Navigator and the Microsoft Internet Explorer browser do many of the same things, but much of the terminology is different between the two. Table 9.1 should help you sort out some of these differences.

Table 9.1   Netscape Navigator/Internet Explorer Language Dictionary

Internet Explorer	Netscape Navigator	Purpose or Use
Favorites	Bookmarks	You add Web pages to Favorites/Bookmarks for easy retrieval.
Address bar	Location field	Here you type Web page addresses (URLs) for viewing in the browser.
Refresh	Reload	Selecting **Refresh/Reload** downloads the latest copy of the page you are viewing.
Links bar	Personal toolbar	This is used to add shortcuts to folders and Web sites.

Sharing Bookmarks and Favorites Between Netscape Navigator and Internet Explorer

If you currently use Netscape Navigator and you want to switch to Internet Explorer without losing all your bookmarks, you're in luck. When you install Internet Explorer 4.0, your bookmarks are automatically saved in the Favorites list in Internet Explorer. Viewing them is simple: Choose **Favorites**, **Imported Bookmarks**.

At the time of this writing, neither Netscape Communicator nor Netscape Navigator has a feature that enables you to import favorites into bookmarks. However, a few utilities can help you in this regard. Both WebOBJ Bookmark Importer (www.WebOBJ.com) and Columbine Bookmark Merge (www.clark.net/pub/garyc) enable you to share bookmarks and favorites between the two browsers.

Common Shortcut Keys for Netscape Navigator and Internet Explorer

Table 9.2 lists the shortcut keys that work in both browsers.

Updating Your Favorites with New Bookmarks

Microsoft has reportedly added an Import and Export Bookmarks feature in the not-yet-released Internet Explorer 5. It can update your Internet Explorer favorites with any new bookmarks.

Table 9.2   Shortcut Keys

Key Combination	Action
Ctrl+D	Add the current Web page to Favorites/Bookmarks
Alt+left arrow	Go back to previous page
Alt+right arrow	Go forward to next page
Ctrl+N	Open a new browser window
Esc	Stop loading page

The Least You Need to Know

➤ The Active Desktop can be altered and enhanced in many ways, making your working environment a highly customized place. Your desktop can be highly integrated with the Web, or it can resemble something a little more traditional.

➤ You can add channels to your desktop to get customized information delivered directly to you.

➤ Whether you browse the Web with Internet Explorer or Netscape Navigator, various performance tweaks can improve your surfing experience.

Chapter 10

Talk Amongst Yourselves: Email for One or More

In This Chapter

➤ Outlook Express for several email accounts

➤ Outlook Express for more than one person

➤ Easier email with IMAP

Sending email is second only to Net surfing in terms of its popularity. It has been an ingrained part of communication in the business and academic worlds for several years, and its popularity in these areas has trickled into the realm of personal communications. Many people who would never consider surfing the Net regularly use email to keep in touch with family and friends.

The popularity of email has greatly increased competition among the creators of email software, resulting in wonderful new features designed to make it easy for you to get as much as possible out of your email experience.

Not surprisingly, this popularity has caused a few drawbacks, specifically drawbacks related to your home network. For example, more than one person in your home probably has an email account—some might have more than one.

This chapter shows you how to deal with these issues, as well as a few others that may crop up in installing and configuring one of the most common email clients: Microsoft Outlook Express.

Delivering the Mail

There are two popular ways for you to retrieve email from your ISP:

➤ Post Office Protocol (POP)

➤ Internet Mail Access Protocol (IMAP)

Both of them are "standard," which means that just about every email program you can think of supports them.

Post Office Protocol (POP)

POP is by far the most popular way for individuals to retrieve email from their Internet service provider. POP has been around for years and, for the most part, works great.

Happy POP

POP is happiest when you have a single computer and when you check your mail regularly.

Every time you check your email with a POP email client, it downloads every single message from the server to your computer and (typically) deletes all those downloaded messages from the server. Accordingly, when you read the messages, you're not reading them from the email server—you're actually reading them from your computer's hard drive. If you're using a dial-up connection, this is nice because you can free up the phone to order pizza or to receive helpful calls from friendly tele-marketing firms.

On the surface, POP seems great, but there are some disadvantages:

➤ If you have two or more computers, there may be times when you'll want to check your email from a computer other than your primary one. Say, for example, that you're sitting at your machine, minding your own business, reading your email, when your wife rushes in and insists that she has to use your computer ASAP (after all, yours is the one with all the RAM, right?). You agree, and switch to the laptop you have set up in the dining room. Unfortunately, when you downloaded your email to your computer before your wife booted you from it, the messages were deleted from the server—which means you can't access your mail from the laptop. Darn, bummer, shoot!

➤ Email has entered the era of *attachments*, which are files attached to an email message before it is sent. It's great when you receive a 60KB recipe for peach cobbler from your Aunt Peg, but if Aunt Peg mails you a 4MB scanned picture of her winning the blue ribbon for baking the peach cobbler at the county fair, it's a completely different story. POP drops the ball with this kind of email traffic because it makes you download *every* email message before you can read *any* of them. When Aunt Peg's blue ribbon picture makes you wait half an hour before you can read email from your girlfriend or boyfriend, you'll probably have more than a few words for POP.

The Multicomputer Blues

To solve the multicomputer problem, POP clients have a setting that allows you to get your mail without deleting it from the mail server. That means when your wife boots you from your computer, you'll still be able to check your mail from the laptop in the dining room.

Unfortunately, it creates another problem: Sooner or later, your ISP is going to get upset about you storing all your email on the email server. After grumbling and mumbling to you about how much space you're taking up on the server (via email no less, making the problem even worse), some ISPs will disable your email or your dial-up account entirely.

Internet Mail Access Protocol (IMAP)

Even though many ISPs are still using POP, IMAP will eventually replace POP as the ISPs' protocol of choice. IMAP shores up the shortcomings of POP by keeping email messages on the server, enabling you to see the header information for all messages without having to download them.

The *header information* tells you things like who the message is from, what the subject is, and how big the message is, including any attachments. With all this information at your disposal, you can decide which messages you want to read first, if any. You can even delete messages from the server before reading them (sorry Aunt Peg), or you can choose to skip certain messages and read them when you have more time.

Because IMAP lets you leave your email messages on the server, it clears up the problem of checking email from more than one computer. (This won't relieve you of the problem of storing too many email messages on your ISP's mail server, but it at least makes it easier to clean up your email account when you get a message warning you that the email administrator is about to "drop the hammer.")

It probably will be easy to tell whether your provider supports IMAP mail clients because the provider will be boasting about how progressive it is. But just in case you're not sure whether your provider supports it, don't be afraid to ask.

Upgrading to Internet Explorer 4

If you are running an older version of Internet Explorer, trundle on over to www.microsoft.com and check out the Downloads section of its Web site to pick up the most current version.

Microsoft Outlook Express

One of the most popular email clients is Microsoft Outlook Express, which is an integral part of Internet Explorer 4. If you are running Windows 98, you may already have Outlook Express installed.

The remainder of this chapter shows you how to set up Outlook Express for single users, multiple users, and users with multiple accounts.

Outlook Express for One User

Setting up Outlook Express for one user is a piece of cake. The first time you try to run Outlook Express (by selecting it from the **Start** menu, for example), it automatically displays a Browse for Folder dialog box, which defaults to a directory in your profile directory. Click **OK** in the dialog box to use this directory for all mail for this user.

This dialog box lets you choose the right folder.

High Profile

In Chapter 5, "Windows of Opportunity: Windows Networking," you learned that profiles are how Windows keeps track of different user accounts. These profiles correspond to a subdirectory stored by default in the c:\windows\profiles\profile name folder, where profile name is the name of the current profile. Refer to that chapter for information about creating a new profile.

Before you can send and receive email with Outlook Express, you must fill in the account information provided by your ISP using the Internet Connection Wizard. Do the following:

1. The easiest way to start the Internet Connection Wizard is to click the **Compose Message** button in the upper-left corner of the Outlook Express window.

2. Type the name you want others to see when they receive email from you, and then click **Next**.

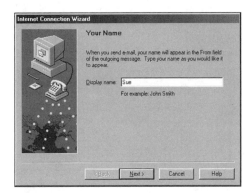

Enter your personalized name here.

3. You are asked to enter the email address that your ISP has created for you. Do so, and click **Next**.

4. Now that you've entered your personal information, Outlook Express needs to know a little about your ISP's mail server. First, specify whether your ISP uses a POP server or an IMAP server by selecting the appropriate entry in the drop-down list.

5. Enter the names for the incoming and outgoing mail servers. They often (but not always) have the same name.

6. Click **Next**.

7. If your ISP's mail server uses Secure Password Authentication (SPA), click the **Log on using Secure Password Authentication (SPA)** button.

Case Sensitivity Training

Email addresses are not case sensitive, so you can mix upper- and lowercase however you want.

8. Enter your account name. In almost all cases, this is the same as the start of your email address. (For instance, Sue's email address is SueBell@Home.com, so her account name is SueBell.)

9. Your provider should have given you a password for your new account; enter it in the space provided, and then click **Next**.

Enter your email address.

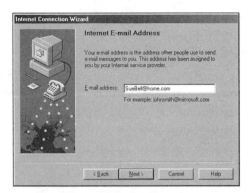

Get from your ISP all the information you need to enter in this screen.

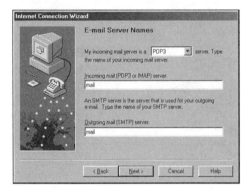

SPA

If your ISP's mail server uses SPA, you are asked for your username and password when you try to check your email. SPA-enabled servers are not common.

10. Here's where Microsoft gets a little touchy feely: Outlook Express asks you to enter a *friendly name*. Entering a friendly name is optional; whether you enter a friendly name or not, click **Next** to continue.

11. Specify the type of Internet connection that Outlook Express should expect. Most likely, you are connecting to the Net with a modem. If this is the case, click the **Connect using my phone line** button. Click **Next** to continue.

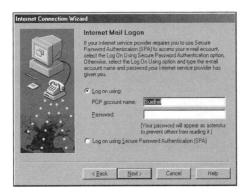

Insert your name and password here.

Friendly Names

The friendly name is used to refer to an account within Outlook Express. It isn't seen by anyone other than those who use your profile to run Outlook Express.

If you are the only person who uses this computer, a friendly name won't do much for you. However, you need to use a friendly name if you have more than one account.

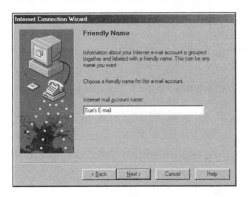

Insert a friendly name if you want.

12. If you created your dial-up connection during Chapter 7, "You've Got the Whole World in Your HAN: Connecting to the Internet," click the **Use an existing dial-up connection** button, and then click the name of the connection on the bottom of the screen. Click **Finish**.

103

Choose the appropriate connection.

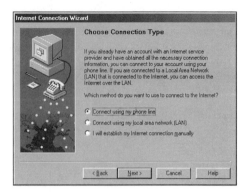

Congratulations! You have successfully created an Outlook Express account.

Outlook Express for Multiple Users

If you're the proud owner of a home area network, you're probably only half (or less) done. You still need to:

> ➤ **Create user profiles for everyone on the network**   If you haven't already done so, you'll need to create Windows profiles for each user of your system. Flip back to Chapter 5 for instructions on creating user profiles.

Check This Out

Creating a Dial-Up Account

If you haven't created your dial-up connection yet, select the **Create a new dial-up connection** button, and then flip back to Chapter 7 for instructions on creating dial-up connections.

> ➤ **Get email accounts for everybody who wants one**   Most ISPs let you have more than one email account per dial-in account. Check your ISP's Web site to see what services it offers. If you're lucky, it's free. If not, you might have to shell out a few extra bucks per month for the accounts.

> ➤ **Configure Windows and Outlook Express for each person's account**   So you don't have to pore through each other's email, you'll want to configure Windows 98 and Outlook Express to keep everybody's mail separate.

To configure Windows and Outlook Express for another user's account, do the following:

1. Log out of the current user profile by clicking **Start**, **Log Off**.

2. In the Shut Down Windows dialog box, select the **Close all programs and log on as a different user** button, and click **Yes**.

104

3. Windows presents you with a logon screen. Depending on which primary network logon you selected in the Control Panel, you either have to type in the profile name or select it from a list of available profiles.

4. After you have logged on to a new profile, start Outlook Express and follow the directions in the preceding section.

5. Repeat steps 1–4 for every user on your network.

Outlook Express for People with More than One Account

For a variety of reasons, it may be in your best interest to have more than one email account. For example, although many people hand out their work email address to their friends, some employers frown on the use of corporate email for personal messages. Nonetheless, that shouldn't keep you from being able to read email from both accounts in the privacy of your own home. Microsoft gives you two different ways to use Outlook Express if you have multiple email accounts:

➤ Multiple profiles

➤ Multiple accounts in a single profile

Multiple Profiles

If you want to use multiple profiles for yourself, you can set up this in exactly the same way as if you were creating separate profiles for multiple people (refer to the section "Outlook Express for Multiple Users"). For example, you could create a work profile called Jesse at Work, and a home profile called Jesse at Home. Then you would set up separate Outlook Express accounts in each of the profiles. If you were using your home account and wanted to check the email on your work account, you would log out and log back on to the appropriate account.

This setup is nice because it separates the messages in one account from the messages in the other account. On the other hand, it's a pain to have to log out and log back in every time you want to check the email in the *other* account. Remember, every time you log out, you have to close all the applications you're working in.

Multiple Accounts in a Single Profile

Outlook Express can check email accounts from multiple servers and display all messages from those accounts in the same inbox. So instead of creating multiple profiles to handle your email at home and your email at work, you can establish two accounts in one profile. This can be a real timesaver compared to the log out/log on/log out/log on routine described previously.

To set up multiple accounts in a single profile, do the following:

1. Open Outlook Express and select **Tools, Accounts**.

2 Select the **Mail** tab. Notice the account we set up earlier, **Sue's E-mail**.

Selecting the Mail tab lets you view the mail accounts.

3. Click the **Add** button and select the **Mail** option.

4. The Internet Connection Wizard starts. Complete it as described earlier in this chapter, filling it in with the information for your *other* account (in this case, we've created an account with the friendly name Sue at work).

A second email account is created.

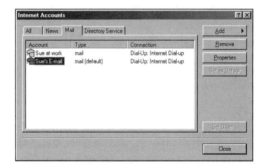

Sending and Receiving Email with Multiple Accounts

After Outlook Express is configured to access multiple accounts, there are a few tricks you can use to make your life easier:

➤ The biggest time-saving feature of using multiple accounts within Outlook Express is that you can check the email from all your accounts at once. To do this, select **Tools, Send and Receive, All Accounts**.

➤ If you're interested in sending and receiving email from only one of your accounts, select **Tools, Send and Receive**, and then select the friendly name associated with the account you want to check.

Changing the Account from Which Email Is Sent

Outlook Express enables you to specify the account from which mail is sent by default, as well as to overrule the default to send mail from a different account. To set the default account, do the following:

1. Select **Tools**, **Account** and then select the **Mail** tab.

2. Select the account you want to use as the default, and then click the **Set as Default** button.

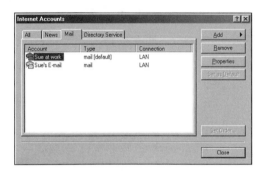

Notice that the Sue at work account now shows its type as `mail` *(default).*

To change the default account for a single message, do the following:

1. Start a new email message by clicking the **Compose message** button in the upper-left corner of the Outlook Express window.

2. Choose **File**, **Send Message Using**.

3. Choose the account from which you want the message to appear to have originated in the resulting fly-out menu.

Notice that both email accounts are available.

107

The Least You Need to Know

➤ All Internet email clients must use either the POP or the IMAP protocol to retrieve email messages. POP is best for people who check their email from only a single computer, whereas IMAP is best suited for roaming users.

➤ Many email programs can be set up for multiple users. Outlook Express lets you set up multiple users using Windows User Profiles and also lets you set up multiple accounts per user from within Outlook Express itself.

Part 4

Mission Control: The Role of the PC

This section walks you through the process of finding and installing the most useful software and hardware for a home network.

On the software side, you find out how to get the most out of your Internet browser and email programs. To improve your personal communication, we show you new and exciting ways to videoconference and teleconference.

On the hardware side, we show you the latest products you can add to your home network. You will be able to use them to see and talk with friends and family no matter how far away they are. You can further enhance the conversation by sending them scanned family photos. To keep from losing all your newly scanned pictures, add a backup device to your network for safe storage of those memories.

Finally, we give you solid direction on how to protect your home network from viruses, hackers, and unwanted Internet sites.

Chapter 11

Hardware for the Truly Digital Home

In This Chapter

➤ Why your PC is so important

➤ Hardware to capture pictures, video, and sound

➤ Using scanners and printers

➤ Personal digital assistants

➤ Devices that make your network safer

The Heart of Your Network

In most homes, one computer is newer and more powerful than the rest. It's often the computer with the fastest CD-ROM, the largest hard drive, or maybe the best printer. Depending on your needs, you might configure the other computers on your network to peripherals through this machine. Even your TV or your stereo may come to rely on this computer, as well (see Chapter 19, "Get the Picture?: Adding Your TV to the Network," and Chapter 20, "The Song Heard 'Round the World: Adding Your Stereo to the Network").

A computer should have three important characteristics if it is going to be used as the centerpiece of a networked home:

➤ **It should be expandable** Getting more use out of a computer inevitably means putting more into it. Make sure that any new computer you buy has a lot of room for additional memory and at least a few extra slots for interface cards.

USB

In the past, computers primarily used two types of connections for peripherals such as printers and scanners: serial and parallel. Serial ports, which could be used to connect mice, modems, and joysticks, were very slow. Parallel ports, which were used originally only for printers but later expanded for use with cameras and scanners, were only a bit faster than serial ports.

Until recently, most computers had only one or two serial ports and one parallel port, which meant that only a few peripherals could be connected to each computer. After you had hooked up your mouse, printer, and a joystick for your favorite game, you were out of luck.

Fortunately, the universal serial bus (USB) was developed to solve this problem. Not only is USB very fast, supporting transfer rates of 12Mbps, it allows you to connect many more devices than either serial or parallel ports ever could. A single USB port can be used to connect up to 127 peripherals, such as cameras, mice, and keyboards.

A few computer manufacturers included USB as early as 1996, but it has now become standard equipment on new computers. It will most likely replace serial and parallel ports altogether.

➤ **It should be reliable**   Computers that share directories, drives, and printers need to be more reliable than ever. If the computer with the printer attached decides to take a nap, then, well, nobody gets to print. Any computer that shares resources with other machines should have a good surge protector, power supply, and cooling system.

➤ **It should be compatible with the other machines on the network** Although hardware compatibility is not absolutely necessary, the number of hardware and software headaches you have will be greatly reduced.

IEEE1394 and FireWire

IEEE1394 is a standard that supports data transfer rates of up to 400Mbps (that's more than 33 times faster than USB). Apple created the technology and used the name FireWire to describe its implementation of it; many other companies have products that meet the IEEE1394 standard.

Like USB, 1394 supports plug-and-play and hot plugging and provides power to peripheral devices. Unfortunately, 1394 is much more expensive than USB. For this reason, it is expected to be used mostly for devices that require large throughputs, such as video cameras, whereas USB will be used to connect most other peripheral devices.

Get the Picture: Digital Cameras Capture the Moment

Film cameras have been great for capturing those family moments to share with friends and family. Nonetheless, they have not been without their drawbacks:

Equipment Reviews

The review section of www.pcmag.com is a great place to look for hardware or software reviews for anything running on Intel PCs.

➤ Film processing is costly. After you're set up with your digital camera, the only expenses you incur are for batteries and maybe some extra disk space on your home computer.

➤ It takes some time to get your film processed. Digital pictures, however, are instantly displayed in color LCD on many digital cameras. Alternatively, you can quickly see how the picture looks by connecting to your computer and transferring your pictures to your PC.

➤ You need to scan your pictures to email them to friends and family. As much as you'd like it if all of your friends lived in the neighborhood, they probably don't. Digital cameras eliminate the need to scan pictures before you can email them to friends and family.

113

Challenging Yourself

Of course, you can create your home network using Linux or Windows NT, but most of the applications built for home networking won't be made specifically for your setup. This means that you'll have to do a little extra searching for drivers and other software. But then, what would life be like without those little challenges?

➤ A lot of pictures don't look quite right and, consequently, are thrown away. Those highly artistic close-ups of the front of your index finger no longer need to make the trip to the photo-mat followed by the journey to your kitchen garbage. Tossing out a digital photograph is as easy as deleting a file.

Digital cameras have had drawbacks that, until recently, have kept the average photo hobbyist from using them. Fortunately, the manufacturers of digital cameras have addressed many of these problems:

➤ Until recently, a $500 digital camera could get you resolution of only 640 by 480 pixels. This wasn't sharp enough for most people, who were used to film cameras that delivered shots of much higher quality. Now, spending $500 on a digital camera gets you quality that is good enough for most household users; you can get a resolution of 1280 by 1024 pixels (usually called MegaPixel), creating a much sharper image.

➤ Spending $1000 or more can get you out of the realm of the hobbyist and into the realm of the professional photographer. This wasn't the case in 1998.

➤ The first digital cameras required you to download directly to a computer, using a serial cable. Today's digital cameras have removable storage devices such as flash memory cards or floppy disks, making transfer and storage much easier. Many also have USB connectivity, allowing you to easily connect them to your PCs without rebooting.

Buying a Digital Camera

Eastman Kodak and Olympus have been leaders in the digital camera field in the past. When looking to purchase a digital camera, try reading product reviews on the Internet or in magazines. Check out *PCWeek* (www.pcweek.com), *Computer Shopper* (www.computershopper.com), and *CNet* (www.cnet.com).

Standalone Cameras That Send You Pictures

Have you ever found yourself wishing you could have taken a picture of someone or something, but you just weren't around to take it? Like when someone is breaking into your cabin in Vermont, for example? You're in luck. These days, a camera doesn't have to be in your hands to get you the pictures you need. Now you can get a portable digital camera that sits in your cabin and sends you pictures when you call it (or, say, when your motion sensor is set off).

Products like the FoneCam from Moonlight Products (www.fonecam.com) are just what you need. You can use any computer on your home network that has access to an unoccupied phone line to call your camera and upload the pictures. And, just in case you want to hear what that burglar has to say about that mouse trap by the door, you can have a listen as well.

Seeing Is Believing: Network-Attached Video Cameras

Projects you previously did with only speech or text can now be enhanced with still or video images:

➤ Including a video clip can enhance presentations or reports.

➤ As the bandwidth available to the average user increases, attaching video to email messages is becoming more popular.

➤ The quality of desktop videoconferencing is now good enough for it to become a mainstream application.

You can obtain your video images in one of two ways:

➤ Using a camera device (sometimes called a *camera ball*) that sits atop your computer monitor.

➤ Using your existing video camera and connecting it to your computer.

Camera Balls

Camera balls have grown increasingly popular because they allow computer users to send real-time video to correspondents as they chat online. When purchasing a camera ball, try to find one that uses USB if your PC supports it. (Intel, Connectix, and Logitech all make USB camera balls.)

Camcorders

With the help of a video capture card and some software, you can convert that video of your kid in the third grade Christmas concert from an analog signal to a digital format, compress it, save it to your hard drive, and send it over email to your in-laws in Dubuque.

Card Compatibility

The video capture card usually works with any device using an RCA or SVHS jack for video input.

Of course, trying to handle video on your computer has its drawbacks:

➤ Storing digital video can consume massive amounts of storage space. You can expect one minute of video to consume anywhere from 1MB to 50MB of storage space, depending on the quality desired.

➤ Some video capture systems have a proprietary format that requires viewers to download special software.

Buying Your Video Capture System

Creative Labs, Core Dynamics, and Alaris are three companies that currently sell video capture systems.

A standard camcorder attached to a PC.

Your Word Is My Command: Putting Microphones on Your Network

You may never have felt the need to own or use a microphone, but these days there are plenty of good reasons to have one:

➤ You can use your computer to send a voice message to a friend. Simply record your message with Windows Sound Recorder, save that sound file to your hard drive, and attach that file to an email!

➤ Chat programs are starting to support voice. Programs that formerly allowed only text-based dialog with others now allow the use of your PC's voice capabilities.

➤ Voice recognition utilities are taking off. Being able to tell your computer to start running Netscape Navigator with your voice and not your keyboard used to

116

be an expensive endeavor, requiring software that could cost upward of $1000. Nowadays, however, you can use your vocal chords to navigate your desktop and programs with the help of inexpensive software.

Dictation has been a more difficult challenge for personal computers, although voice-recognition capabilities have dramatically improved over the last few years. Microsoft, IBM, and Dragon Systems are well-known creators of voice-recognition software.

➤ Internet telephony is becoming more available. Is your long-distance bill getting a little high? You might want to try talking to a friend using the Internet. You can use your microphone and speakers to create your own phone. For details, see Chapter 14, "HAN SOHO: Networking Your Home Office."

Carrying Your Network in Your Pocket: Personal Digital Assistants

It seems that everyone is traveling more these days. And even though you can't take the office with you, you're still expected to keep up to date with all your key information. Personal digital assistants (PDAs) are awesome devices for storing and retrieving all those hard-to-remember things such as email addresses, phone numbers, contact names, and key appointments, as well as for keeping track of expenses and calculating figures. These days, an explosion of applications for PDAs means you can use them for

➤ **Internet browsing** Whether your PDA is running 3Com's Palm OS or Microsoft's Windows CE, you can use it to browse the Web (you'll need to attach a special modem to your PDA).

➤ **Navigate** Your PDA can enable you to access detailed maps for all major cities, as well as information about the best restaurants and popular locations in each city.

➤ **Browsing email** Email on your home machine can be synchronized with your work email to help ensure that you aren't missing any important messages.

➤ **Tracking expenses** Many popular home financial software programs work well with PDAs.

The Paperless Filing Cabinet: Scanners

These days, instead of cramming your filing cabinet with documents, you can scan them and save them to disk for easy storage and retrieval. Alternatively, you can scan your favorite photographs, save them to disk, and email them to relatives. Whatever your reason, having a scanner on one of your home computers allows everyone in the family to benefit from scanned images. Scanners come in four different forms:

➤ **Flatbed scanners** These look a lot like squashed photocopy machines. They are the most popular type of scanner and give excellent results. The downside is that you need to find space on your desk for yet another neat toy.

117

➤ **Sheet-fed scanners**   These are similar to flatbed scanners but have a built-in feed tray. They work the same, just faster.

➤ **Convenience scanners**   These come in a variety of sizes and shapes and are often used for specific purposes such as business cards or slides. A handheld scanner would fall into this category.

➤ **Multifunction devices**   These combine a scanner, fax, copier, and printer into one device and are ideal for the home office that's short on space.

A decent scanner can be found for less than $200. Look for a scanner that has a resolution greater than 600 dots per inch (dpi) for good performance. As with any computer hardware, consider reading a review or two from one of the leading PC hardware magazines or Web sites before you purchase.

Backups, Backups, Backups (You Did Make Backups, Didn't You?)

The only thing more tiring than writing an essay on the geopolitical implications of Keynesian economics in the early twentieth century would be *rewriting* an essay on the geopolitical implications of Keynesian economics in the early twentieth century. It just makes sense to back up the data you have on your computer. A few devices can help you back up those precious files:

➤ Large removable floppy drives can be used to store 250MB or more on one disk. These drives can be carried anywhere and used to provide backup services to many machines. The floppy disks can be stored in a safe location, such as your fireproof home safe or a safe deposit box. Iomega's Zip 250 drive can hold 250MB of data for convenient storage (see www.iomega.com).

➤ Write-able CD-ROM drives can be used to store more than 600MB of data and can usually be used to record audio CDs for playback. The drawback to write-able CD-ROM drives is that they are usually not removable, and they cost more than a large removable floppy drive. Sony is a popular manufacturer of write-able CD-ROM drives (see www.sony.com).

➤ Internet backup services are now available for people who want to avoid using Zip drives. By compressing and encrypting your files, you can deliver them to a service provider's site for storage and retrieval (see www.telebackup.com).

The key to making your backups easier is organization. Separate your program files from the data files that are created when you use those programs. That way, you only need to back up your data directories, because you can always just reinstall your programs from their original CD-ROMs if necessary.

A good example of an organized data structure is shown in the following figure. It includes a root directory called Data and another called Programs. Subdirectories of

Data could be named after family members, such as Dion, Liam, Jennifer, and Olivia. Subdirectories of these directories might contain data for particular programs. For example, Household Finances could be a subdirectory of Dion. A directory structure like this allows you to quickly and easily back up the Data directory and all its subdirectories: Simply drag the Data folder in Windows Explorer to a backup storage device on another drive, and you're done.

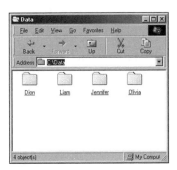

You can have a separate folder for every family member.

Protection from an Electrifying Act of God: Surge Protectors

Sometimes the most shocking events in your life really are more electrical than emotional. For example, a thunderstorm in your area might cause your digitally delicate system to be fried to a crisp. You probably know this, and chances are you have purchased a surge protector or a UPS to protect your investment. Nonetheless, there may be a few things you didn't think of:

➤ A power surge can be delivered through the phone lines as well. So even if your computer is plugged into a standard surge protector, you still could suffer damage. The solution to this problem lies in finding a surge protector that allows you to pass your phone or cable modem line through it. These types of surge protectors are becoming cheaper and easier to find.

➤ One unprotected computer on your home network can expose all the other computers to a power surge. Theoretically, a power surge could travel across your ethernet network and zap a computer that you thought was well protected. You shouldn't expect to stay dry in a rainstorm even though you have only *one* car window open. Protecting your network is no different. Ensure that every computer in the house is equipped with a surge protector that insulates it from all the physical networks it's connected to.

The Least You Need to Know

➤ The PC is the most important piece of hardware on your network. Be careful before buying your next personal computer because it may become the center of your home network.

➤ You can add to your network digital cameras to take both still and video images for a variety of purposes.

➤ Personal digital assistants, scanners, backup media, and surge protectors are only a few of the many hardware devices available to enhance your home network.

Software to Tie
It All Together

We've already covered the basic software that you'll need for an Internet-connected home network. You should now have networked your operating systems, as well as installed and configured your Internet browsers and email clients. Now you need to get the software that lets you do all the neat things you've heard about and really want to try.

A Few Legalities: Software Licenses

You should know a few terms before you start downloading everything you can get your mouse on:

➤ **Freeware/public domain software** This is software that has been designated as free. The owners have either made it available out of pure benevolence or in the hope that you will purchase the next version. Real freeware is fully functional and free forever.

➤ **Shareware** This software has been made available to you on some sort of a limited basis. You may be asked to pay a nominal fee if you like the software, or you may be able to use the software only for a limited time and then be expected to pay for it. The creator of shareware is usually asking you to make a good faith commitment. Try to remember that keeping up your end of the deal allows them to keep making more quality shareware in the future.

➤ **Postcardware** The author of this software would just like to get a postcard from you. Sometimes, creative types just want to know who you are and that they have made your computing experience a little better (or worse, as the case may be).

➤ **Commercial** This is software that you have to pay for. Do it! Paying for the software you use today pays for more research and innovation that creates the useful software of the future. Besides, software piracy is illegal.

First and Foremost: Antivirus Software

Accessing the Internet and sharing files and folders over your home network can increase your exposure to potentially harmful viruses. An infected file on one computer on a network can infect all the computers on that network. Antivirus software should be the first piece of software that you add to each computer on your home network. See Chapter 13, "Keep the Wolves at Bay: Protecting Your Network," for a more complete discussion of antivirus software.

Compression Utilities: WinZip and PKZip

For the next few years at least, the speed at which you can access the Internet (and most any other network) is going to be slow enough to affect how you use it. Thankfully, the size of a file can often be greatly reduced through the use of a compression utility. Two popular shareware compression utilities are WinZip and PKZip.

An *archive* is what WinZip calls a group of compressed files. Many files can be placed in an archive, and that archive can then be password-protected for secure transmission across the Internet. When the archive reaches its destination, it can be decompressed—that is, the files can be extracted—to the specified directory. After the files have been extracted, they are restored to their original, precompression format.

Compression Utilities

A *compression utility* takes a regular file and compresses it using a compression algorithm. A *compression algorithm* is a set of instructions that tells the computer how to pack the file into a smaller space than it originally occupied. After a file is compressed, it can be transported more quickly because it is smaller. However, it must be *decompressed* before it can be used on the other end. The same algorithm used to compress the file is reversed to decompress it.

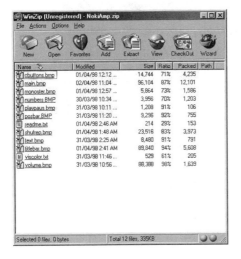

The WinZip dialog box gives you easy one-click access to your files.

Choose the folder to send your uncompressed files to.

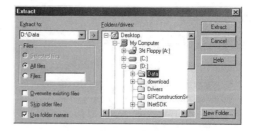

Audio/Video: Media Player and RealPlayer

The Internet is now rife with music and videos for your listening and viewing pleasure. There are many different formats for both audio and video, which used to be a problem because you needed a separate piece of software for every different format. Fortunately, that has changed. You can now play many different audio and video formats with a single utility. Two of the most popular utilities are

➤ **Microsoft Windows Media Player**   This free utility can be found at www.microsoft.com.

Windows Media player plays many music formats.

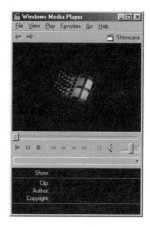

➤ **RealPlayer**   This commercial utility can be downloaded from www.real.com.

Both utilities play the most popular formats of audio and video available. With these two utilities in your toolkit, you should be able to play just about any multimedia file you can find.

The RealPlayer has channels ready for viewing.

Animation and Music: Shockwave

Much of the Web is brought to life through animation and music that is created with Shockwave, a Web browser plug-in from multimedia kingpin Macromedia. To enhance your surfing experience, download the Shockwave plug-in from www.macromedia.com.

After you have the plug-in installed, head to www.shockrave.com to check out its demonstration gallery. Many games, cartoons, and music selections can be found, all created and enhanced using Shockwave technology.

MP3 Players: WinAmp and MusicMatch Jukebox

Multimedia PCs have had sound cards and speakers for years, but until recently, those speakers have been used primarily for games. These days, however, a music revolution is taking place on the Internet, with a new audio format called MPEG-Layer 3—MP3 for short.

WinAmp (www.winamp.com), by far the most popular MP3 player, not only lets you play back MP3 files but also provides a wide array of customization options.

This is just one of WinAmp's "skins" or interfaces.

Many software utilities enable you to record music from your CDs to your computer or vice versa, the most popular being MusicMatch Jukebox (www.musicmatch.com). MusicMatch Jukebox enables you to convert music files from many formats to many others, including WAV and MP3 formats.

MusicMatch keeps your music well organized.

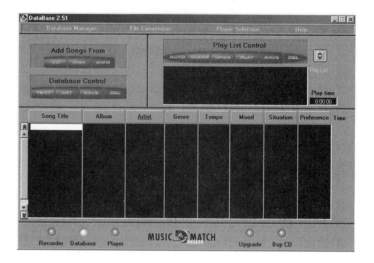

Louis Prima Donna

If playing music on your computer makes you want to jump, jive, and wail, check out Chapter 20, "The Song Heard 'Round the World: Adding Your Stereo to the Network."

Newsreaders: Netscape Collabra and Outlook Express News

The term *newsreader* can be a little misleading because it makes you think of someone reading the *New York Times* or the *Chicago Tribune*. Actually, a newsreader allows you to read Usenet news feeds, which are collections of discussion groups that discuss one of more than 30,000 different topics. Two of the more popular newsreaders are

➤ **Netscape Collabra**   This newsreader is part of the Netscape Communicator suite.

➤ **Outlook Express News**   This newsreader is included with Outlook Express.

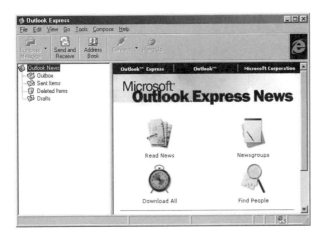

Outlook Express provides a familiar look and feel.

Videoconferencing Software: Microsoft NetMeeting

Until recently, videoconferencing has been relegated to the boardrooms of America. But with the advent of Internet-enabled videoconferencing, affordable desktop video-conferencing has become a reality.

One of the most popular videoconferencing software applications is Microsoft NetMeeting, which enables you to call other people who use NetMeeting and use its audio, video, whiteboard, and chat functions. These functions allow you to not only see and hear your counterparts but to share applications as well.

NetMeeting lets you see yourself and your caller.

On Videoconferencing...

For the complete lowdown on videoconferencing, check out Chapter 17, "HAN SOHO: Networking Your Home Office."

Online Chat Software: Mirabilis ICQ

Online chatting is a bit like email but occurs in real-time. That is, you and your buddy are online at the same time and can see what the other person is typing as he is typing it.

The Mirabilis ICQ (I-seek-you) product is the most popular chat program available today. ICQ users find each other either by exchanging their ICQ numbers or by searching the ICQ Web site (www.mirabilis.com) for another user.

ICQ gives you a compact list of your online friends.

FTP (File Transfer Protocol) Utilities: FTP Serv-U and WS-FTP LE

There may come a time when you need to transfer large files from your computer to someone else's over a network. Luckily, you can use an FTP server to allow others to transfer files directly from their computer to yours or vice versa. The process of transferring files requires both an FTP server (such as FTP Serv-U) and an FTP client. The FTP server allows you to give others access to designated files on your computer. To get a copy of FTP Serv-U, visit www.ftpserv-u.com.

This is the FTP client software you need.

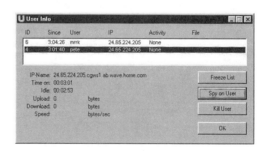

An FTP client, like a World Wide Web browser accessing a Web server, retrieves or places files on an FTP server. One of the most popular FTP clients available is WS-FTP LE, which can be found at www.tucows.com.

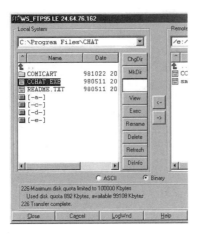

Transfer files by moving them from the left window to the right.

Notice that the directory for the local system is in the left-hand pane, and the remote system has its directory displayed in the right-hand pane. Downloading files from a remote system to your system is simple:

1. Select the files you want to download from the remote system by clicking them in the Remote System pane on the right-hand side.

2. Select the directory where you want the files to reside by clicking the appropriate directory in the Local System pane on the left-hand side.

3. Click the left-arrow button to start the transfer of files.

Uploading files from your system to a remote one is just as easy:

1. Select the files you want to upload to the remote system by clicking them in the Local System pane on the left-hand side.

2. Select the directory where you want the files to reside by clicking the appropriate directory in the Remote System pane on the right-hand side.

3. Click the right-arrow button to start the transfer of files.

Web Server Software: Personal Web Server and Personal Web Manager

There is no doubt about it: The World Wide Web is often the best medium for sharing files. For example, say that you just visited Morocco and have tons of digital photographs that you want to share with your distant relatives. One way you could do this is by having a thumb-nailed Web page with all your photographs. You could then host this Web page on your own Web server. The pictures would be available to all your family members around the world.

First, you'll need some Web server software. For Windows 98 users, an easy-to-find utility is Microsoft Personal Web Server. To install Personal Web Server, do the following:

1. Insert your Windows 98 CD-ROM into your CD-ROM drive.

2. In Windows Explorer, open the `setup.exe` file (navigate to `\add-ons\pws\setup.exe` on your CD-ROM drive).

Find Personal Web Server in the directory.

3. Click **Start**, **Run**. Type `C:\WINDOWS\SYSTEM\inetsrv\pws.exe`, and then press **Enter** twice.

Personal Web Manager, another Microsoft utility, allows you to create a simple home page and then publish it to your Personal Web Server. Others can then access your home page through the Internet.

Personal Web Server is designed for use in small workgroups or as a development environment for larger applications that would be run on Internet Information Server, Personal Web Server's big brother for Windows NT systems. It can also be found bundled with Microsoft FrontPage.

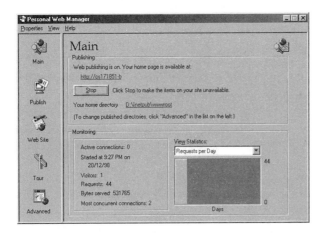

Personal Web Manager is easy to navigate.

The Least You Need to Know

➤ A myriad of software applications is available for the networked home. That software may be licensed for use as freeware, shareware, postcardware, or commercial software. Regardless of its licensing, it's readily accessible to you through the Internet.

➤ Antivirus software is the first piece of software you should add to your network. Used properly, it will keep you safe from nasty viruses.

➤ Compression utilities compact your files for safe and easy transportation across a network.

➤ Enhancing your multimedia experience is easy with multimedia players such as Real's RealPlayer and Microsoft Windows Media Player.

➤ Animation is brought to life with Macromedia's Shockwave.

➤ Songs recorded in a new music format can be played with an MP3 player such as WinAmp. If you want to record and organize MP3s, you can use a program such as MusicMatch Jukebox.

➤ Sharing ideas and information is a snap with the right software. Newsreaders, videoconferencing applications, and online chat software give you the tools you need to communicate with others more effectively. An FTP server enables you to share key files with others, whereas a Web server allows you to share it in a Web-like format.

131

Chapter 13

Keep the Wolves at Bay: Protecting Your Network

In This Chapter

➤ Simple steps for protecting your home network

➤ Guard your network from computer viruses

➤ Safe surfing for your kids with parental control software

The image of pimply-faced teenagers hacking into military computers is an entrancing one. It has captivated news watchers and moviegoers for years. Thankfully, there are some simple things that you can do (or not do) on your home network to protect it from these uber-hackers. This chapter takes a step-by-step approach to configuring computers and software on your network so that they can be as safe and secure as is possible in a networked world. This chapter also covers protection against much more common threats to your computers and the information stored on them: electronic viruses, power surges, and hard disk crashes.

Bad Guys Can't Get in If You Don't Leave the Door Open

Every time you add a new protocol or service to your network, you create a weakness that a hacker or cracker can exploit. This isn't to say that you shouldn't network your computers, just that you should use only those network services that you truly need. Many people install new applications just to try them out and then forget they ever installed them. This leaves a door through which Net nasties can get to your network.

Webster's Update

Remember, a *hacker* is just a smart computer geek, but a *cracker* is a computer geek who uses his or her skills for doing nasty things to others. Sadly, crackers are motivated enough and know enough to make life very uncomfortable for people or companies they dislike.

What Is a Network Application?

If you're concerned that the new video game or word processor that you are about to install this weekend is going to open the door to hackers and crackers worldwide, you shouldn't be. A *network application* usually comes with the capability to listen for requests from the network and respond to the network based on those requests. For example, a Web server sits on the Internet and listens for requests for Web pages. When a request comes in, the Web server figures out which page you, the requester, are looking for and sends it to you across the Web. The danger comes when somebody figures out a way to make your Web server pony up a document that isn't intended for her—such as the contents of your personal finances folder or all the love letters you wrote to your boyfriend last year.

Examples of network applications include

➤ Web (HTTP) servers

➤ File Transfer Protocol (FTP) servers

Port Addresses

All network applications listen for or respond to requests for services at a particular *port*. Port numbers are associated with every type of network service.

For example, you may have seen Web addresses that look like http:\\www.myWebserver.com:8080. The 8080 at the end of the address specifies the port that the request should go to. Some servers listen at specific ports, and some listen at random ports. Web servers, by default, listen on port 80.

When you install a networked application, that application's port address begins listening for requests and is ready to respond to them. Crackers can figure out whether you are running a particular application by scanning your computer for ports that are listening. The process of scanning your IP address for available source ports can take as little as two or three minutes. With this knowledge, crackers can begin to figure out ways to disable or break into your network.

With this in mind, it's pretty obvious that the fewer ports there are available, the fewer there are that can be broken into.

Less Is More

The most basic rule of computer and network security says, "Do only what you need to do, and do those things well." Here are some tips:

➤ Run the applications that you need and only when you need to run them. If you determine that you need to run a specific application, take a hard look at whether you need to run it all the time. For instance, you might have a personal Web server that you use so that your relatives can get pictures of your latest vacation. To reduce your risk of getting hacked by bad guys, you might consider arranging times with your relatives when the Web server will be available.

Securing Your Microsoft System

Microsoft regularly releases security updates for its software on its Web site (check out http://window-supdate.microsoft.com). The Windows update site contains special software that you can use to check the versions of software installed on your computer and that recommend updates of different types of software. Some updates will be fun; some will be functional. Many are related to security vulnerabilities that Microsoft has found with its software. This type of auto-update feature is becoming common for software that must be updated often. For example, antivirus and parental control software is typically updated on a monthly basis.

➤ Follow the directions for the network applications that you install. If you decide to install network services, make sure that you read the instructions. Most network applications come with instructions for their application, many of which include a section on network security. Follow these instructions to make sure that you configure the application appropriately for your needs. Many crackers figure out how to break into networks by reading these types of instructions. Then they look around the Net trying to find somebody who installed his applications wrong.

➤ Keep your software current. Program authors regularly release new versions of their software; these updates often solve security problems that the authors have found. Although keeping your word processor or spreadsheet application up-to-date may not be a big deal for you, keeping your network applications current should be a little higher on your list of priorities.

Hiding in Plain Site

There are a couple of points worth mentioning that should let you sleep better at night. For starters, few Internet users have the skills to do nasty things to your computer from afar. Further, only a small number in that group are warped enough to want to try. Your good night's sleep comes when you remember that *millions and millions* of people use the Internet every day. The chance of somebody taking a run at your computer, one out of millions, is very small. Besides, why would a cracker go after you and your email from Aunt Peg?

The Anatomy of a Sneeze: What Is a Virus?

According to Murphy's Law of Computer Viruses, the only time your computer will be infected with a virus will be the night before you have a career-making report due. This of course changes your career-making report into a career-breaking report.

Whether you run a PC or a Macintosh, there is a virus out there with your name on it. The industrious virus-writing underworld has even come up with a couple of doozies for the UNIX community, which has long prided itself on being invulnerable to viruses.

Like a word processor or a spreadsheet, a virus is just a computer program. However, viruses differ from regular programs in two important ways:

➤ Viruses are designed to replicate. Unlike every other kind of application, viruses are most happy when they are making copies of themselves. As you might expect, this process is known as *infection*.

➤ Viruses don't do anything productive. Although some virus writers might say otherwise, viruses are designed to be a pain in the butt. At best, they make copies of themselves. At worst, they destroy everything on your hard drive.

Antivirus Software

Whether or not your computer is actually connected to the Internet, antivirus software should be the first piece of software that you install after installing the operating system itself. Here are two examples of good antivirus software.

➤ McAfee VirusScan
`http://www.mcafee.com`

➤ Norton Anti-Virus
`http://www.symantec.com`

Check This Out

Share and Share Alike

Both are available as shareware, so they can be downloaded, installed, and evaluated before you choose to buy them.

New strains of computer viruses are constantly appearing, so the job that antivirus software makers are stuck with has three main components:

➤ Keeping abreast of all the new viruses being written

➤ Creating fixes for them

➤ Distributing those fixes to you before you get infected

Sign Your Name

The key to protecting your network is keeping your signature file current. A few antivirus software makers have responded to this challenge by allowing you to update signature files to their software with the click of a button over the Internet. Check the documentation for your antivirus software if you're not sure how to update your signature file.

Whereas the first two jobs are the sole problem of the antivirus companies, you can help with the third. Antivirus authors use a special file called a *signature file* to keep track of all the viruses that they know about. You need only download the signature file (rather than the entire program) when you want protection from the latest viruses.

Regularly scanning your hard drive for infected files allows you to be relatively sure that you aren't infected or about to be infected by a computer virus. Up until a few years ago, viruses could be stored only in *executable files*. Program files and diskettes were the only things that you had to check for viruses to be sure that you were safe.

In this regard, antivirus software has greatly improved. Where scheduled checks used to be standard procedure, many programs now check every file and diskette that you access *as you access them*!

McAfee Vshield scanning a local file as it is opened.

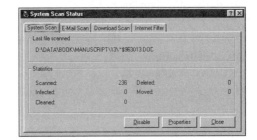

But with the advent of networks and the development of new types of viruses by the bad guys, new methods of virus checking had to be developed. For example, antivirus software now must respond to these types of problems:

➤ **Macro viruses** Microsoft inadvertently changed the virus landscape a few years ago by enhancing the built-in Word and Excel macro programming language known as Visual Basic for Applications. The macro language became powerful enough—and Microsoft Office became common enough—for it to act as an environment for the creation and distribution of viruses.

So-called *macro viruses* now have the power to change files, delete files, send email messages, or just about anything else that a macro can do—all it takes to trigger them is for you to open an infected Word file or Excel file. Infected files can reach you by diskette, via a network, or even by electronic mail.

The current crop of antivirus programs now scans every email message you receive for attachments to make sure that they aren't infected with macro or executable file viruses.

➤ **Programs in Web pages**   Surfing the Web used to be a relatively safe pastime. Recently, though, the use of Java, JavaScript, and ActiveX in Web pages has become common. These programming languages are used to enhance the form and function of Web sites.

To varying degrees, these languages are *supposed* to have security built in to them to protect Net surfers from malicious programming. Unfortunately, programmers make mistakes. Even more unfortunately, there is a crew of hackers and crackers out there whose sole mission in life is to take advantage of those mistakes. Accordingly, Java, JavaScript, and ActiveX have all been used as conduits for bad boys to do nasty things to people's computers.

The most recent versions of antivirus software now scan every Web page that you read to make sure that malicious examples of Internet programs are not lying in wait.

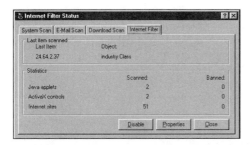

McAfee Vshield scanning an Internet file as it is opened.

Wear a Life Jacket: Safe Surfing

The mere act of Web surfing now comes with its own *personal* perils. Information about people has become a commodity that is being traded among companies for profit. Your name, address, and phone number can be cross-referenced against where you surf to help marketers determine how to sell goods and services directly to you.

Some people think this is a bad thing, some think it's a great thing, and some just don't care. This is a point that can be debated for a long time, but there are a few

Wrong Turn

There are other reasons to supervise your children's forays into the Net. Even if you have taught your children about staying away from the darker side of the Internet, the *click and go* nature of the Web makes it easy for them to accidentally end up at a site you would rather they avoid.

Parental Control

Of course, parental control software is no substitute for spending time with your kids while surfing the Net. It's a big, big Web out there, and having a supportive hand to help them through it is more important than forcing them to skip through a bunch of nasty sites.

things that you should be aware of, regardless of how private you like to keep your personal information.

➤ Never tell somebody your name and address on the Internet unless you would be comfortable having him or her contact you directly. Obviously, if you are buying something online, you're okay because you expect to be able to be contacted by the company. Many sites, however, ask for information merely for marketing purposes. Think twice before you leave your name and address with these sites—you could end up with a deluge of email or paper mail from somebody you were never that interested in.

➤ People online aren't always who they appear to be. Whether you are in a chat room or on what appears to be a reputable Web site, use caution when giving out any personal information on the Net. That nice-sounding 22-year-old woman you bumped into in a chat room could turn out to be a 40-year-old truck driver from Jersey.

➤ Just like you wouldn't let your small children walk down a busy street by themselves, it's a good idea to supervise your children's surf time until you are sure that they understand the rules of the road. A small child surfing or chatting could be easily convinced to divulge personal information such as age, school, or address, which you would definitely not want getting into the wrong hands.

Parental Control Software

As much as the Net is being heralded as the foundation of modern learning, there is a soft underbelly to the Internet that children don't need to see. The Wild, Wild West was a regular juice bar compared to some corners of the Net.

Lucky for you, a genre of software called *parental control software* is designed to protect children from this aspect of the Net. Some adults also use it to avoid accidentally popping into sites with untoward content.

Parental control software uses two different methods for figuring out whether a surfer should be allowed to visit a site:

➤ Predefined lists
➤ User-defined lists

Predefined Lists

Some parental control software companies maintain lists of sites that they deem to be good or bad. Good site filtering is used to restrict surfers to visiting only those Web sites that are suitable for family viewing. Bad site filtering takes the opposite approach, making you skip sites that are known to contain nasty content.

Many people like the use of predefined lists because they are easy to use, and you don't have to spend much time configuring the software. Others criticize them because they don't feel that anybody else should be determining what is good and bad for them.

A Practical Example: Net Nanny

Net Nanny is one of the most popular parental control applications in the predefined list category. In addition to logging and controlling access to the lists provided, Net Nanny also lets you add your own list to determine which sites are allowable for viewing.

Keeping Your Lists Current

Similar to computer viruses, the list of bad sites keeps changing. To make sure that your filtering software blocks the type of sites that you want to block, the lists that control these programs need to be maintained. This means an occasional trip to your software vendor's Web site to download the latest list of sites that should be blocked.

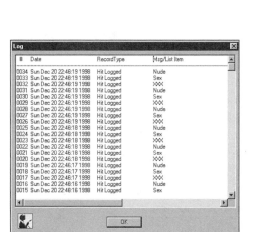

A simple log describes the content of the visited sites.

Net Nanny, available from www.netnanny.com, also lets you control access to some of the resources within Windows to further restrict use. This can be helpful if you don't want your kids (or your roommate, for that matter) running programs or otherwise messing around with your computer.

Net Nanny can be customized to suit your needs.

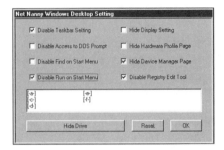

User-Defined Lists

This type of filtering software works on the assumption that you know what you do and don't like. Accordingly, the software companies leave it up to you to define which sites are and aren't allowable for viewing.

The upside of this type of parental control software is that you have absolute control over what you will or won't allow your kids to view on your computer. The downside is that it takes longer to configure because you have to build the lists used by the program.

A Practical Example: Cyber Snoop

Cyber Snoop, available from www.pearlsw.com, is one of the most popular parental control utilities in the user-defined lists category. Cyber Snoop lets you block certain types of traffic—for example, World Wide Web or Usenet traffic—in its entirety. But the real power of Cyber Snoop is in its capability to define lists of allowable or disallowable sites. It does this by letting you fill in spreadsheetlike forms called allow-lists and block-lists. After you have these forms filled in, Cyber Snoop uses an easy-to-read screen to determine which type of sites should be blocked and which type of sites should be allowed.

142

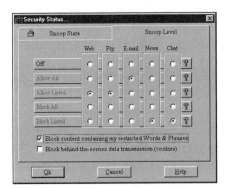

A matrix of selections gives you as much control as you need.

If you use Cyber Snoop as it is configured in the preceding figure, users of your computer can

➤ Only surf the Web or transfer files (via FTP) from the specific sites that you have defined as okay

➤ Send or receive email from anybody

However, users cannot access Usenet news feeds or chat sites defined in your blocklists.

Don't Worry, Surf Happy: Keeping Security in Perspective

The ease with which somebody who is smart enough and determined enough can hack into a Web server, a mail server, or your computer is frightening. No matter how well you configure your computer, there is always somebody who knows how to break into it. That's the bad news. It's the downside. It's the con to the pro.

But remember that there is so much to offer by taking a swim in the vast ocean that is the Internet. The occasional shark sighting will scare some people off, but the majority will head back down to the beach when the sun comes out.

Don't be afraid to read the directions or to follow the few simple precautions laid out in this chapter. You'll sleep better for it, and you'll be safer than the majority of people on the Net. After all, you don't have to be able to swim faster than the shark—just faster than the guy beside you.

The Least You Need to Know

➤ Simplicity is one of the key components of a secure network. The fewer net-work applications or services that you have running on your computer, the more difficult it is for somebody to break into it.

➤ Even though most people fear the wily cracker, viruses account for far more downtime and grief than cracking does. Accordingly, antivirus software should be one of the first pieces of software that you install on your computer. Just having the software installed isn't enough though; it's important to keep the virus signature file current so that you can be safe from new viruses as they appear.

➤ One of the biggest concerns people have with the Internet relates to the safety of children and the information that they are exposed to online. Teach your children the basics of information security. Instruct them that they shouldn't be too free with their personal information with people they don't know on the Internet. You can also protect yourself and your kids by installing parental control software, which can filter out sites that you prefer that they not see.

➤ For most, the benefits of networking outweigh the risks, and a few simple precautions can tip the scales even further in your favor.

Chapter 14

Disaster Prevention: Backing Up

In This Chapter

➤ Understand why you need to back up your computer files.

➤ Learn how to perform simple backups.

➤ Find out what kinds of media are used to back up data.

➤ Learn what goes into creating a backup strategy.

Your computer might be struck by lightning. Your son might mistakenly erase the novel you've been working on for the past three years. Your laptop can fall into the lake...If you've backed up your computer's data, these will be irritations rather than disasters.

As an individual, your data is important to you. To a business, data might be the company's lifeblood. Anyone can back up their personal computer files; to most businesses, however, backing up computer data is a necessity.

If your home computers are on a network, that network is probably the best way to make sure that everyone's files are backed up. Network backups can be more thorough, cost effective, and efficient than backups done individually.

This chapter describes the advantages of backups in general, and on networks in particular. It then describes how to go about planning and performing backups.

Why Back Up?

The reason for backing up your computer files is simple: Your files can be deleted or destroyed when you still need them. There are many ways in which your files can be lost:

➤ **Hard disk crash** A computer's hard disk has elements that are electrical, magnetic, and mechanical. Any of these components can fail, causing the disk to crash in such a way that data is not recoverable.

➤ **Deletions** People delete files all the time, both intentionally and by mistake. If the deleted files existed at a time when the computer's files were backed up, the files can be retrieved later if it is found that they are needed.

➤ **Viruses** A virus can infect the programs and files in a computer. This can result in files being destroyed or infected in such a way that they are no longer useful. A system backup from before the time the virus was introduced can return the computer system (and the data files) to a usable state.

➤ **Computers destroyed** Fires, floods, or other natural—or unnatural—disasters can destroy computers as much as any other kind of property. The backups you created can be used to re-create the computing environment with the new or fixed equipment.

For some people, the information contained on their computers is far more valuable than the cost of computers themselves. Seeing that timely backups are done can save you from a world of grief.

Performing Simple Backups

Generally, a backup consists of copying one or more data files from their permanent location (typically a computer's hard disk) to another location (usually a removable medium, such as a cartridge tape or removable disk). The removable medium can then be stored in a safe place in case it is ever needed.

There are a few simple types of backups that you can do with existing software on your Windows 95/98 computer. Although these procedures do not enable you to perform complex or automated backups, they will help you realize that backups are not so scary.

A Simple Copy-to-Floppy

Perhaps the easiest backup—and the one done by most first-time PC users—is to copy a few important files to floppy disk. Let's say, for example, that you want to back up a folder containing your latest novel (C:\mybook) to floppy disk from Windows 95. The steps for doing so are as follows:

1. Insert a floppy disk into the floppy drive (usually A:).
2. Double-click the My Computer icon.
3. Double-click the C: icon; arrange the My Computer and C: windows on your desktop so you can see them both.
4. Drag-and-drop the mybook icon on to the 3.5 floppy icon.

As long as the floppy disk can hold the amount of data contained in the folder, the files are copied to the floppy disk. At that point, you can pop out the floppy disk and store it in a safe place. That's it!

Using Windows 95 Backup

Although a simple copy-to-floppy technique is okay for a few files, more sophisticated tools need to be used in cases where there are a lot of files that must be backed up on a consistent basis. The Backup utility that comes with Windows 95 is a good tool for setting up a backup that you can run more than once. Here's an example of how to use the Backup utility:

1. Click on **Start, Programs, Accessories, System Tools, Backup.** After a few pop-up windows, the Backup window appears, as shown in the following figure.

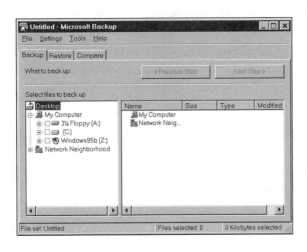

Run simple backups with the Windows 95 Backup utility.

2. From the left frame, select the files and folders you want to back up.
3. Click **Next Step**. The window asks you to enter the location or device to which the files will be backed up.
4. From the left frame, select the backup device (tape drive, floppy drive, and so on) or location (folder).

Check This Out

Hereís your opportunity to back up the files over the network. Any file servers on the network appear in the Network Neighborhood folder. Choose the file server to which you want to back up your files.

Check This Out

During the backup process, you can click **Save As**, then save the backup settings to a file that can be used again. Saving backup settings is helpful because many people save all their data files to the same locations.

5. Click **Start Backup**. A pop-up window asks you to put a label on the backup set. This name will help you identify the backup in case you need to restore the files later.

6. Type the name of the backup set you are creating. At this point, you also have a choice of adding a password to the backup set. If you add a password, the files can't be restored later by anyone who doesn't have the password.

7. Click **OK** to begin the backup. When the backup is complete, you see a message telling you so.

8. Click **OK**.

At this point, you can remove the backup medium and mark it with an appropriate name and date. If at a later time you need to restore the files from this backup, you can do so by using the **Restore** tab in the screen shown in the preceding figure.

Using Iomega 1-Step Backup

Simple backup tools are often delivered with the backup medium itself. For example, Iomega Zip and Jazz drives come with a 1-Step Backup utility. This utility provides a simple way to identify files to back up, run the backup, and save the backup settings for later use.

To start the Iomega 1-Step Backup, select **Start, Programs, Iomega Tools, 1-Step Backup for Zip and Jazz**. The utility assumes you are backing up to your Zip or Jazz drive, but enables you to select the files to back up. You can add password protection to the backup and compress the data (so more fits on the removable disk).

Why Network Backups?

The focus of this chapter is network backups, which entail a lot of issues you might want to consider. Network backups imply that you are dealing with multiple computers and users, so you need to think about

➤ How much data needs to be backed up? If you have a network of three PCs, you might get by with a 100MB Zip drive for all your backups. If the network has 100 PCs, you probably want at least one mass storage device.

➤ How critical is the information? If there is little new data being added to the computers, you might do a backup just once a week. If important data—such as financial or medical records—is being added constantly, you might need to do backups every day or even every few hours.

The more computers and users that are on your network, the more beneficial network backups can be. Many of the advantages you get from sharing other network resources also apply to centralizing your backups. Some of these advantages are

➤ **Shared hardware**   Instead of spending money on a removable drive for each PC, you can have one large backup device, such as a CD tower or tape device, that is shared on the network.

➤ **Central administration**   Because their information is so important, many people set up a schedule about how and when computer files are backed up. Using the network, you can back up all the computers without actually visiting each one.

➤ **Convenient scheduling**   Using some of today's advanced backup tools, backups can be scheduled to run over the network at times when the computers aren't being used much. This can help prevent the performance hits that occur during backups.

Choosing a Backup Type

People who use computers change different amounts of data, add and delete different numbers of files, and place different levels of importance on their files. Each of these issues has an impact on the types of backup you need and how often those backups are run.

Most locations use a combination of backup types. The reason for doing different backups at different points in the backup schedule is to make your backups efficient. For example, if a computer has 1GB of data on it, but only 2MB of data changes between Monday and Tuesday, there is no reason to do a full backup of the computer each day. Therefore, on some days you do a full backup, whereas on other days you do either an incremental or differential backup.

Full Backup

With a full backup, you copy the entire contents of a computer (that is, its whole hard disk) to the backup medium. After a full backup is done, you have the capability to restore that entire hard disk to where it was when the backup was done.

Incremental or Differential Backups

A typical backup schedule backs up the entire contents of a hard disk once a week, then simply backs up the changes that occur on every other day of the week. The backups that are done on those other days are either incremental backups or differential backups.

For an *incremental backup*, the backup program determines which files have been added or changed since the previous (most recent) backup. Only the added or changed files are put on the incremental backup tape. The next backup will again store only those changes made since the previous incremental backup. This continues until the next full backup, at which time the next incremental backup uses the new full backup as the baseline.

For a *differential backup*, all backups that are done after the initial full backup track all changes since the full backup. So, for example, if a full backup is done on Sunday night, a differential backup on Monday contains all files that are new or changed since Sunday. The next differential backup done on Tuesday also contains all files that have changed since Sunday (including files changed on Monday and Tuesday).

The differences between incremental and differential backups include the number of backup media you use and the difficulty in restoring the files if necessary:

➤ **Backup amounts differ**   Incremental backups result in less information being stored each day than with differential backups. Therefore, with incremental you can use fewer media (fewer tapes or disks) and get each backup done faster. Think of Saturday's backup in the preceding example. With incremental, Saturday's backup includes changes between Friday and Saturday. With differential, Saturday's backup contains all changes since last Sunday.

➤ **Restore convenience differs**   With a differential backup you only need two sets of media to restore files from any day: the full backup and the day you want to restore to. Restoring with incremental media requires you to have the full backup (from the week being restored) and the backup media for each day up to the restore day.

Because most backups are done automatically overnight, the differential backup is usually the most convenient. By reducing the restore to two media, one full and one differential, your restore job is much easier.

Some people, particularly those who create or collect large multimedia files, will have enough new files to warrant a differential backup strategy. Most of us, though, will find that an incremental backup strategy is more than enough. In fact, if you can afford to buy a few more tapes, you'll find it easier to do a full backup every time you do backups, thereby making restores easier.

To avoid tying up your computer during prime surfing or working time, you'll want to do full backups at night time or while you're at work.

150

Choosing Backup Media

Remember that a backup means creating a copy of a file or files in some place other than the original medium. Although this typically means a removable medium, a backup can also be done to a hard disk on another computer or to a second hard disk on the same computer. Various types of backup media are available:

➤ Hard disk

➤ Tape

➤ Recordable CD

➤ High-density floppies

➤ Removable disks

Hard Disk

It can be much faster to copy files to another hard disk in your computer—or to another computer on your network—than it is to copy them to tape. This type of backup can be used for backing up data in real-time, where waiting until the night's backup isn't soon enough.

Although hard disks are more expensive than tape devices, prices have decreased significantly in recent years. If the data being protected is critical, ongoing backups can efficiently copy data to another computer's hard disk. That data can then be offloaded to tape when it is convenient.

Check This Out

Although it is possible to back up files onto the same hard disk, that generally defeats the purpose; if the hard disk crashes, you lose both copies.

This type of backup is sometimes referred to as *real-time replication*. Essentially, you are creating a replica of the data on another hard disk.

Tape

Before inexpensive removable disks and writeable CD-ROMs were around, magnetic tape was the backup medium of choice. Although there are still the old 60MB and 120MB cartridge tapes around, much higher capacity tape drives are available today for reasonable prices. These include

➤ **Digital Linear Tape (DLT)**   DLT is considered to be the leading format for high-end tape backup. Although originally created by Digital Equipment Corp., DLT is an open standard for magnetic tapes. DLT is a half-inch tape. Its cartridge is 4.1 square inches and 1 inch high. A DLT 4000 can hold 20GB (or up to 40GB compressed), whereas a DLT 7000 can hold 35GB (or up to 70GB compressed). While DLTs may be appropriate for some high-end home office workers, they tend to be too expensive for most home computer users.

➤ **QIC**   QIC tapes use a 5.25-inch cartridge. The latest versions can hold up to 13GB of data.

➤ **DAT**   DAT holds up to 8GB of compressed data (DDS-2 format) or 24GB compressed data (DDS-3 format). These small cartridges are popular in part because they are compact and are produced by several different vendors.

➤ **8mm**   This type of cartridge tape was created by Exabyte Corporation. Using 2:1 compression, 8mm tapes can hold up to 20GB of data.

DLT is becoming the most popular tape format for high-end operations. DAT is popular for home and home office computers.

Recordable CD

There are two different types of recordable CDs available:

➤ CD-R (compact disk-recordable) enables you to write once to a CD, then read it as many times as you like. This type of media is referred to as *WORM* (write once-read many).

➤ CD-RW (compact disk-rewriteable) enables you to write and erase the CD multiple times.

Although both the media and the drives are more expensive with CD-RW, the ability to rewrite data can make CD-RW more cost effective. However, one drawback to CD-RW is that disks cannot be read by all disk players, whereas CD-R can.

For more information about recordable CDs, refer to the CD-Recordable FAQ (`http://www.fadden.com/cdrfaq`). This FAQ contains a lot of information about the different formats and how you can use them.

High-Density Floppies

The SuperDisk 120MB floppy disk drives can be used to replace standard 1.44MB floppy drives. With the new drives, you can use either the new 120MB floppies or the standard 1.44MB floppies—so you can continue to use your old floppies. For low-volume backups, the 120MB floppy disks can be a good alternative to purchasing another backup medium.

Removable Disks

Like high-density floppies, removable disk cartridges came along to fill the huge hole between floppy disks (holding 1.44MB) and mass storage devices. These drives are fairly inexpensive, can plug into an existing parallel port, and use inexpensive media (under $12 for a cartridge).

152

Iomega is the leader in removable storage devices. An Iomega Zip drive uses 100MB cartridges. The more expensive Jaz drives can handle 1GB and 2GB cartridges. You can find Zip drives today for under $120 and Jaz drives for under $400.

Choosing a Backup Strategy

No single backup strategy fits all cases. Computers that contain constantly changing, critical data need a much more diligent backup schedule than low-use computers containing non-essential data. Large and small amounts of data benefit from different kinds of backup media. This section describes the issues that go into choosing a backup strategy.

What Needs to Be Backed Up?

Determining what data you need to back up is probably the best place to begin. The kind of information you want to back up from computers falls into two basic categories:

➤ **Data files**   These contain the information that users or applications generate and can include word processing files, database records, and spreadsheets.

➤ **System files**   These contain data that is needed to reconstruct your computer system. System files can include information defining user preferences (such as screen layout and colors) and configuration information (such as network addresses).

If a computer is managed in an organized way, data files are fairly easy to back up. If you save your data files in one location on your hard drive, making backups is fast and easy. For example, if you always save your documents to the c:\data folder, it's very simple to perform backups. All backup software will make quick work of your backups if you tell it to backup c:\data and all of the files and folders underneath it.

If, on the other hand, you save some of your documents in c:\my documents, some underneath the c:\program files\office folder, and yet others somewhere underneath c:\windows, you may find it so complicated to perform backups that you won't do it.

Techno Talk

There are a variety of backup utilities available to back up your Windows 95 system files so your computer can be re-created in the case of a disk crash. Safety Net Pro (http://members.aol.com/_ht_a/ron2222/snpro.htm) backs up your Registry, INI files, and startup files to disk. Emergency Recovery System (http://www.mslm.com) can also be used to back up Windows 95 system files.

How Often Is Backup Needed?

Both the kind and the amount of data being created on your computers have an impact on how often you need to back up. Following are a few examples of situations that require data to be backed up at different intervals:

➤ **Personal backups**   Say you have a few computers on a small LAN—perhaps in a home or a school—that are not used for anything critical. In this case, you might choose to back up the computers once a week on a regular basis, with an occasional special backup if someone has just created some important files.

➤ **Daily backups**   Some home businesses put their sales, inventory, scheduling, billing, and all other critical information on a few computers that are connected by a network. Although consistent backups are necessary in this case, once each workday is usually enough. Usually the backup is run after hours so as not to disrupt ongoing work.

When Should Backups Be Run?

Running a backup slows down the performance of the computer being backed up. For that reason, backups are often run late at night. However, for critical data (such as financial data), live backups might need to be run constantly—or at least several times a day.

Backup Tips

The following are some tips to help you perform backups and manage backup media:

➤ **Cycle backup media**   You don't need to use a new tape or disk each time you run a backup. Besides being expensive and difficult to manage, it is also unnecessary. Rewriteable media are designed to be rewritten. So, cycling media is the normal practice.

Have at least two sets of media that you cycle. By alternating them, you always have a good set of media in case the hard disk crashes in the middle of a backup.

Check the manufacturer's specifications for information on how often the medium can be rewritten. Some tapes can handle 100 backup and restore passes and might need to be replaced only once a year.

➤ **Label backup media**   If the day ever comes when you need to restore some or all of a computer's files, you will understand just how important a good label is. The label indicates: when the backup was done, where the data came from, the type of backup (full, incremental or differential), the backup tool used and the number of the medium in the set (such as tape 2 of 3).

➤ **Store the media safely**   It doesn't help to have the backup medium on the desk next to the computer if your house burns down. Media need to be kept in

154

waterproof and fireproof containers. For very important data, media need to be kept at another site.

➤ **Verify the backup media**   Try restoring a few files from your backup medium after the backup is complete. You don't want to find out that the medium was bad when you go to restore the files from a crashed hard disk.

➤ **Clean the drive**   Check the manual that comes with the tape drive for instructions on how and how often the drive needs to be cleaned.

Where to From Here?

Keeping your data safe from disk crashes, fires, and floods can be done using the backup methods described in this chapter. Keeping your data safe from more insidious attacks, such as viruses and hackers, falls under the heading of security. Matters of security, and techniques for improving your security, are described in Chapter 13, "Keep the Wolves at Bay: Protecting Your Network."

The Least You Need to Know

Right now, the least you need to know about backing up data is this:

➤ Computer backups, where data is copied from its permanent source to another medium, can prevent the loss of your vital computer information.

➤ For simple backups, no network is needed. You can simply copy to another medium using drag-and-drop or the Windows 95 Backup utility.

➤ Network backups can make backing up more efficient by allowing many computers to share a backup device.

➤ Backups are typically done with a combination of full backups (perhaps once a week) and incremental or differential backups (perhaps every day).

➤ Backups can be done from one hard disk to another. More often, however, the eventual destination of a backup is a removable medium (such as tape, recordable CD, high-density floppies, or removable disks).

➤ When you create your own backup schedule, you need to determine several things. You must decide what to back up, how often the data needs to be backed up, and when the backups are to be run.

Troubleshooting Your Network

Well, I've got good news and bad news—I'll give you the bad news first. The bad news is that no matter how many networking books you buy, and no matter how careful you are, your network is never going to work perfectly the first time out. Furthermore, over time you're going to encounter dozens of network errors. The good news is that this chapter covers many of the common problems you'll encounter.

Approaches to Troubleshooting

When you're first confronted with a network error, the experience can be pretty daunting. After digesting various error messages, you'll look around the office and see a all of your computers wired up. In that instant, you suddenly realize the worst: The problem could be *anywhere*.

Well, you'll be happy to know that there's a rigid methodology for isolating and fixing errors. It rests on two rules:

➤ Problems can only arise in cabling, hardware, or software.

➤ Most problems are not inherently complex or widespread.

In other words, most problems arise for a single reason, at a single computer. Therefore, when approaching a networking problem assume the simplest and most likely cause first. Only if your suspicions don't check out should you expand your probe to include more complex problems.

The first thing you need to check is whether the problem affects only the one computer or if others are also involved. After you've established that, perform the following steps:

➤ Verify that the network interface card (NIC) is properly installed.

➤ Verify that the network cable is properly attached to the NIC.

➤ Verify that the workstation recognizes the NIC.

➤ Verify that the NIC's driver software is properly loaded.

By taking this approach (working from the inside out), you not only increase your chances of success; you also guard against undertaking unnecessary procedures. Half the time, you'll find simple problems with even simpler solutions, for example, the network cable was accidentally knocked loose.

Because you might be using different network operating systems and disparate hardware, the solutions here are generic (there's a section at this chapter's end that deals with specific network errors). However, you'll find that you can diagnose most network problems with the tools and techniques discussed here.

Troubleshooting Your Cable Paths

Let's start with cabling. Network cable is susceptible to various hardships, including age, abuse, normal wear-and-tear, and so on. Over time, these can damage cable and reduce its capability to transmit a clear, robust signal. Therefore, whenever you perform system upgrades, always take stock of your existing cable—and that includes newer cables.

Believe it or not, even brand-spanking-new cables can sometimes be damaged or faulty. What looks like perfectly a healthy cable might in fact be harboring a short or break. The easiest way to determine if one of your network cables is faulty is to swap it out with another from a computer that you know is working fine. If you don't have another, try borrowing a similar one from a friend.

If worse comes to worst and you can't find a cable, saunter down to a local computer store and see if you can talk somebody into lending you one for a few hours. You may find it helpful to tell them that you are considering launching a worldwide computer business out of your basement and plan to spend millions of dollars there in the next few months. Of course, you could always spring for the $20 and have a spare cable kicking around the house for emergencies (just like this).

Beyond Cables: Diagnosing Hardware, Software, and Protocols

After determining that your cables are trouble free, your next step is to isolate other possible causes, which might include faulty hardware, misconfigured software, user error, and so on. This section covers the tools and techniques used to diagnose network problems.

Ping: Checking for Signs of Life

Ping is a tool for testing whether a computer connected to the Internet is alive and well. Ping's name was derived from submarine lingo. During WWII, submarines found one another by sending sonar waves across the ocean. Whenever those waves struck a submarine, a sonar wave was echoed back to the sender (this noise was the *ping*). This notified the sender that another sub was nearby.

Similarly, Ping sends out a special message to a specified address and waits for a response. Following is an example run from a DOS window:

```
C:\WINDOWS>ping www.microsoft.com

Pinging www.microsoft.com with 32 bytes of data:
Reply from www.microsoft.com: bytes=32 time=183ms TTL=247
Reply from www.microsoft.com: bytes=32 time=164ms TTL=247
Reply from www.microsoft.com: bytes=32 time=168ms TTL=247
Reply from www.microsoft.com: bytes=32 time=156ms TTL=247
```

In this case, you know that www.microsoft.com is alive and well. It took 156 milliseconds to respond with 32 bytes of data. At this point, you're probably thinking, "Well, duh, of course Microsoft is up and working fine." But, if you are pinging www.microsoft.com from a computer that doesn't seem to be working right, and you get a positive response to a ping from it, you know that its network connection is working right, and you should look elsewhere for your problem.

But what happens if you ping a computer from one that isn't working properly? Take a look:

```
C:\WINDOWS>ping www.2mn8.com

Pinging www.2mn8.com with 32 bytes of data:
Reply from www.2mn8.com: Destination host unreachable.
Reply from www.2mn8.com: Destination host unreachable.
Reply from www.2mn8.com: Destination host unreachable.
Reply from www.2mn8.com: Destination host unreachable.
```

From this, you know that something is wrong. www.2mn8.com is not responding and, therefore, either the computer you are pinging from is busted, the network between you www.2mn8.com is bad or the Web server itself is down.

Ping

To use Ping, you must issue the ping command plus your desired address at a command prompt. This is true of both UNIX and Windows.

If you have two computers in your home (a safe bet if you're reading this book) you can also ping one from the other to see if they answer a ping properly. On a windows 95/98 computer, you can run c:\windows\winincfg to figure out what the IP address is that you should be pinging for.

If you ping one of them and get a negative response, check the host's physical connections. Perhaps a wire came loose or the NIC was inserted incorrectly. If these investigations turn up nothing, check to see whether all requisite protocols have been loaded and bound to the NIC.

Traceroute: Checking for Trouble on the Line

Traceroute is a tool for checking the route between two machines. It is used to locate where the problem is. Traceroute performs this task by sending special messages (called packets) to each step of the way between you and another computer on the Internet. In this way, Traceroute builds a network map of the precise route taken between two machines. Because Traceroute "talks" to major network devices (called routers) to build its maps, it is of no real value for diagnosing home network problems, but is helpful if you think that the reason you can't reach a Web server may be somewhere "out there" on the Internet. As an example, I'll trace the route between the Central Intelligence Agency and me. Here's the output:

```
C:\WINDOWS>traceroute www.cia.gov

Tracing route to www.odci.gov [198.81.129.99]
over a maximum of 30 hops:1 140 ms 124 ms 127 ms
tnt1.isdn.jetlink.net [206.72.64.13]
2 214 ms 239 ms 169 ms jl-bb1-ven-fe0.jetlink.net [206.72.64.1]
3 145 ms 134 ms 134 ms ana-3-0-2xT1.sprintlink.net [144.228.79.9]
4 136 ms 141 ms 154 ms 144.232.1.37
5 138 ms 135 ms 136 ms  sl-bb4-ana-4-0-0.sprintlink.net
[144.232.1.30]
6 151 ms 140 ms 39 ms t16-0.Los-Angeles.t3.ans.net [207.25.133.1]
7 199 ms 211 ms 205 ms f2-1.t60-81.Reston.t3.ans.net [140.223.60.142]
8 213 ms 207 ms 205 ms  f0-0.c60-13.Reston.t3.ans.net
 [140.223.60.215]
9 222 ms 215 ms 205 ms  enss3624.t3.ans.net [207.25.139.38]
10 225 ms 219 ms 220 ms  207.27.2.46
11 *           *           *      Request timed out.
12 *           *           *      Request timed out.
13       *           *           *      Request timed out.
14       *           *           *      Request timed out.
```

15	*	*	*	Request timed out.
16	*	*	*	Request timed out.
17	*	*	*	Request timed out.
18	*	*	*	Request timed out.
19	*	*	*	Request timed out.
20	*	*	*	Request timed out.
21	*	*	*	Request timed out.
22	*	*	*	Request timed out.
23	*	*	*	Request timed out.
24	*	*	*	Request timed out.
25	*	*	*	Request timed out.
26	*	*	*	Request timed out.
27	*	*	*	Request timed out.
28	*	*	*	Request timed out.
29	*	*	*	Request timed out.
30	*	*	*	Request timed out.

Hmmm...Something's amiss. Something went wrong at 207.27.2.46. We'll leave it up to the Internet folks that run this router to figure out what it is, but at least you can be safe in the knowledge that it isn't your home network that is broken.

Techno Talk

Traceroute

Traceroute is a command native to UNIX. To use it, you can simply issue the traceroute command followed by the desired address, like this: traceroute 207.171.0.111. On Windows, however, the command is tracert (therefore, the command would be tracert 207.171.0.111). Finally, note that to use tracert on Windows, you need to run it through a DOS or Command Prompt window.

If You Don't Have Traceroute or Ping

If you're not using UNIX or a Windows variant, you might not have Traceroute or Ping. Table 15.1 provides locations of these tools for other operating systems.

161

Table 15.1 Traceroute and Ping Tools for Other Operating Systems

Application	Description/Location
AtcpTraceroute (Amiga)	Traceroute tool for Amiga enthusiasts, located at `ftp://wuarchive.wustl.edu/pub/aminet/comm/tcp/AtcpTraceroute.lha`.
MacTCPWatcher (Macintosh)	Ping/Traceroute utility (with extended TCP/IP debugging) located at `ftp://ftp.tidbits.com/pub/tidbits/tisk/_MacTCP/mactcp-watcher-20.hqx`.
Trumpet TCP (DOS)	A Traceroute tool for DOS, located at `ftp://ftp.trumpet.com.au/tcp-abi/tcp201.zip`.
WhatRoute (Macintosh)	TCP/IP utility that provides Traceroute, available at `http://homepages.ihug.co.nz/~bryanc/beta/whatroute-150b15-fat.hqx`.

The `netstat` Command: Checking the Routing Table and Connections

The netstat command is useful for troubleshooting protocol problems. For example, netstat allows you to examine protocol statistics. Following is a sample report:

```
C:\WINDOWS>netstat -s

IP Statistics
  Packets Received                    = 55
  Received Header Errors              = 0
  Received Address Errors             = 0
  Datagrams Forwarded                 = 0
  Unknown Protocols Received          = 0
  Received Packets Discarded          = 0
  Received Packets Delivered          = 55
  Output Requests                     = 58
  Routing Discards                    = 0
  Discarded Output Packets            = 0
  Output Packet No Route              = 0
  Reassembly Required                 = 0
  Reassembly Successful               = 0
  Reassembly Failures                 = 0
  Datagrams Successfully Fragmented   = 0
  Datagrams Failing Fragmentation     = 0
  Fragments Created                   = 0
```

```
ICMP Statistics
Received     Sent
Messages                    0           0
Errors                      0           0
Destination Unreachable     0           0
Time Exceeded               0           0
Parameter Problems          0           0
Source Quenchs              0           0
Redirects                   0           0
Echos                       0           0
Echo Replies                0           0
Timestamps                  0           0
Timestamp Replies           0           0
Address Masks               0           0
Address Mask Replies        0           0


TCP Statistics
  Active Opens                    = 5
  Passive Opens                   = 0
  Failed Connection Attempts      = 0
  Reset Connections               = 0
  Current Connections             = 0
  Segments Received               = 51
  Segments Sent                   = 54
  Segments Retransmitted          = 0

UDP Statistics
  Datagrams Received      = 4
  No Ports                = 0
  Receive Errors          = 0
  Datagrams Sent          = 4
```

If you pull such a report and find many receive or transmit errors, the local workstation's NIC might be malfunctioning. Another possibility is a faulty network driver.

Troubleshooting in the Trenches: Some Extra Tips

When maintaining your network, you might encounter any of a thousand network problems and errors. Unfortunately, there isn't room to address them all here; however, Table 15.2 lists some common network problems and errors and possible solutions. (Network error messages are italicized.)

Table 15.2   Common Network Problems and Possible Causes

Problem	Likely Cause and Possible Solution
`Cannot find a specific Web server`	You misspelled the server name. Try again.
`Connection reset by peer`	This could be several things. If this occurs while you're connected to the Internet via Dialup Networking, it might be your modem. To cure this, try a different initialization string. For AT&T modems, try `AT&F/Q3/N3`. For Hayes compatibles, try `AT&F&C1&D2&Q5&K3S46=136`. If that doesn't work, it might be a problem on the server side. (Sometimes, servers that set cookies have this problem if the cookie data comes back corrupted.) In this case, simply reload the Web page and continue surfing.
Dialup host keeps dropping you	This happens when you attempt to connect using Dialup Networking in Windows. The actual error message is `You have been disconnected from the computer you dialed. Double-click the connection to try again.` This invariably means that you failed to install TCP/IP. Solution: choose **My Computer, Control Panel, Network, Add, Protocol, Microsoft, TCP/IP**. This installs Microsoft TCP/IP. Next, reboot and try again. Everything should work beautifully. (If not, it's possible that the remote host is expecting an encrypted login. Check with the system administrator at the remote host.)
Excessive packet collisions	If you `netstat` and discover an inordinate number of packet collisions, your cable might be damaged.
`File Creation Error`	This is a security violation message; it means that you attempted to create a file on a network drive to which you had no privileges. Solution: Check to make sure that the share is set up to allow you to write to it.
`FTP Error 57`	This indicates that the FTP server is currently over loaded. Try again later.
`Host name lookup failure`	This error indicates that you're either not connected to the network (or Internet) or that you failed to specify a domain name server. (Without a name server, your system cannot figure out which computer to connect to on the Internet.) Solution: Verify that you're connected. If so, check your DNS setup. As most windows computers will have their DNSs automatically set at the time they connect to an ISP, there isn't much to check. But, if you use a UNIX computer, check `/etc/resolv.conf` for a valid name server address.
`Host or Gateway not Responding`	Check your spelling of the hostname.

Problem	Likely Cause and Possible Solution
Illegal buffer length	This is a NetBIOS error. It means that the system tried to send a unit larger than 512 bytes. This rarely happens and is usually a benign error (you simply resend). However, if you continue to get this error from a particular application, it could be the programmer's fault. If so, discontinue use of the product and notify the vendor.
Memory Errors	Memory errors are rare and usually occur only in DOS or DOS/Windows 3.11 environments. Try commenting out EMM386 in your `c:\config.sys` file.
Network unreachable	This TCP/IP error typically signifies that your ISP's gateway is down, or that there's a routing problem. If this condition persists, contact your ISP to see if they are experiencing problems on their network.
No route to host	This TCP/IP error indicates that your network connection is down. Check your network connection and whether your interface (ethernet, PPP, and so on) is working correctly. On UNIX, you can do this with the `ifconfig` command. In Windows, issue the command `winipcfg` and check that your interface is up. (If you discover your interface is down, activate it or investigate further.)
Session terminated	This indicates that the remote host died, reset, or killed the connection. Check the remote host. (There's nothing wrong at your end.)
Transmission of garbage	If a single computer starts spontaneously transmitting high volumes of garbage or malformed packets, the workstation's cable or NIC has most likely malfunctioned. Solution: Troubleshoot both and replace the offending hardware.
Unable to create directory	This is a security violation message; it means that you attempted to create a directory on a network drive to which you had no privileges. Solution: Get higher privileges.
Workstation(s) often freeze up	First, determine whether the problem is isolated, local, or global. If the problem is isolated, it's almost certainly due to a faulty cable, connection, NIC, or driver on the troubled workstation. Check these first. If the problem is local or global, however, check your hubs, switches, routers, or other networking hardware.
You can't access a network drive	The network drive might not be shared out properly. See Chapter 6, "Sunny and Share: Sharing Files, Printers, and Other Resources," for the section "Files When You Need Them, Where You Need Them" and double-check that all shares are properly assigned. If this doesn't work, verify that the target workstation is currently connected and accessible.

165

HTTP and Web Errors

While surfing the Internet, you might encounter many strange errors. Unfortunately, default Web server clients and server installations seldom have extensive error explanations. Table 15.3 lists a few common errors and the reasons for them.

Table 15.3　Common HTTP and Web Errors and What They Mean

HTTP Error	Reason
Connection Refused by Host	See 403 Forbidden.
Failed DNS Lookup	Either the nameserver couldn't be reached (unlikely) or the site no longer exists.
File Contains no Data	The URL probably calls a script that doesn't currently generate output. Therefore, the server can not return anything. You'll get these errors in the wee hours when folks are fine-tuning their scripts. Try again later.
Invalid Host or Unable to Resolve	The FTP site is down or no longer exists.
NTTP Server Error	The news server is probably down. Try again later.
TCP Error Encountered	Your hardware is malfunctioning. Check your connections. (This can sometimes happen when your connection has been dropped.)
400 Bad Request (Client error)	The server couldn't understand the specified request. This usually arises from a malformed directive (as opposed to a bad URL).
401 Unauthorized (Client error)	This error indicates that you failed to authenticate yourself. This is commonly seen on password-protected Web sites that rely on challenge-response authentication. Solution: Reconnect and enter the proper username/password pair.
403 Forbidden (Client error)	This error indicates that your request is forbidden and there's no further information. You'll get this error if you try to access an off-limits directory. There is no solution.
404 Not Found (Client error)	The document no longer exists. There is no solution. However, if the document was a presentation of some kind and its name was unique, you might try searching for it elsewhere on the Internet.
500 Internal Server Error	This indicates an unspecified server error. Many times this is the result of a malformed server-side script. If you're responsible for debugging the script, check your syntax and ensure that all statements have been closed. Otherwise, notify the party maintaining the site.

HTTP Error	Reason
`501 Not Implemented`	This indicates that the request method is faulty. If you receive this error while testing your own Web pages, check your `method` property in your `form` tag. Following is an example of a fudged request: `<form action="myscript.cgi" method="poist">`. In this case, `poist` should be `post`. If the site isn't yours, notify the maintainer.
`502 Bad Gateway`	This is generally a proxy error. Notify the site administrator.
`503 Service Unavailable`	The server is either busy or down. Try again later.

Where to from Here

In this chapter, you've learned that network troubleshooting is all about the process of elimination. Often the problem is exactly what you expect it to be: simple and easily fixed. In the next chapter, "Upgrading and Expanding Your Home Computer Network," you'll learn how to upgrade and expand your network, as well as glean some tips on saving money and time.

The Least You Need to Know

Right now, the least you need to know about troubleshooting your network is

➤ First, strive to isolate the affected machines. Often this will lead you directly to the problem.

➤ Confine your investigation to the affected machines until you find some evidence to expand your inquiry.

➤ Subject each affected machine to identical diagnostic and repair procedures, and always exhaust testing of each machine before moving on to the next.

➤ If many machines become suddenly affected, check your networking hardware first.

Chapter 16

Upgrading and Expanding Your Home Computer Network

In This Chapter

➤ Assessing your network

➤ Tips and tricks on saving money and time

➤ Expanding and upgrading your home computer

The French have a saying: "Plus ca change, plus c'est la meme chose." It means, "The more things change, the more they stay the same." Is it true? You be the judge.

When we were teenagers, cars were the rage. We would sit around with our friends gawking at hot rod magazines. "Man, when I get some more money, it's all about twin overhead cams and mag wheels!" It didn't even matter if you knew what mag wheels were. You knew they were cool, and that's what counted. I'm happy to report that we've since grown up…Or have we? Today, we sit around looking at computer magazines. "Man, when we decide to upgrade, it's all about twin Pentiums and huge hard drives!" Yes, indeed. Plus ca change, plus c'est la meme chose.

In the computing world, things move fast—so fast that by the time you get your new computer home, it's obsolete. This—coupled with an endless barrage of advertising—probably has you wondering: do you need to upgrade? That's what this chapter is all about.

Taming the Upgrade Monster: Do You Really Need to Upgrade or Expand?

Your local computer hardware dealer has probably told you a dozen times that what you need to increase work production is an upgrade. At first blush, that sounds reasonable; after all, bigger disks, faster processors, and more RAM are bound to improve computing performance.

Before you spend a lot of money, though, there are some things you ought to know. First, unless your existing hardware is hopelessly outdated, it's probably more than sufficient. You can't word process much faster with a 333MHz processor than you can with a 266MHz processor. In fact, unless you're doing high-performance computing—such as compiling, extensive number crunching, or high-end graphics—the difference is negligible.

Moreover, there are many hidden costs to upgrades. For example, upgrades can often be time consuming. Upgrading all of your home computers can take more than a weekend and more than five weeknights if things go wrong. That's not all: If compatibility or reliability issues surface later, a bad upgrade can set you back big time.

I favor upgrading in a gradual fashion, concentrating most of my efforts on the newest and most powerful computer in your home. This newer computer will most likely be attached to the latest peripherals such as your printer or your scanner. If you have two or more newer computers, focus on the computer that's going to be used to run the most powerful applications. For example, computers used for word processing need far fewer resources than those used for graphic design. By wisely and judiciously distributing your processor and memory power where they're most needed, you can save thousands of dollars.

Nonetheless, you'll still inevitably need to upgrade one or more of the following devices or tools:

➤ Hard disk drives
➤ Motherboards and processors
➤ Communication devices
➤ Software

Upgrading to New and Bigger Hard Disks

Having a home PC network allows you to use the extra space on another computer. You may be able to prolong a hard disk upgrade, but with ever larger file sizes, upgrading is inevitable. When upgrading to a new hard disk, you have two choices:

➤ Install the new hard disk as a secondary drive
➤ Install the new hard disk as your primary drive

Most folks decide to upgrade only after their existing hard drive is hopelessly jam packed with software. Therefore, they usually take the first approach—mainly because it's convenient. They designate their new disk as a secondary drive and, in doing so, they quickly and painlessly obtain greater storage capacity. This, of course, leaves their primary disk unchanged. More adventurous users, however, take the high road and designate the new drive as their *primary* disk. This frees up the old drive, which can be used elsewhere. However, this approach demands that you reinstall critical software.

Which approach will you take? That depends on what you're trying to accomplish. If you simply need more storage space, then designate the new drive as a secondary storage device and leave it at that. On the other hand, if you're aiming for high performance (or want to retire or reuse your smaller hard drives) you'll need to undertake the more complicated approach. The next sections cover both techniques.

Adding an IDE Secondary Hard Disk Drive

To add a secondary, internal IDE drive, you must perform four steps:

1. Alter the jumper settings to designate the drive as a slave.
2. Add the drive to the disk drive cable.
3. Set the disk's parameters.
4. Partition and format the disk.

Altering the Jumper Settings

Whenever you use more than one IDE drive, you must specify your *master* or *primary* drive. This tells your machine which disk to use when searching for boot instructions. If you fail to specify your master drive, your system won't boot properly. With few exceptions, IDE drives rely on hardware-based master/slave designations. You set these options using jumpers. *Jumpers* are tiny on/off switches on your hard disk drive's main circuit board (see the following figure).

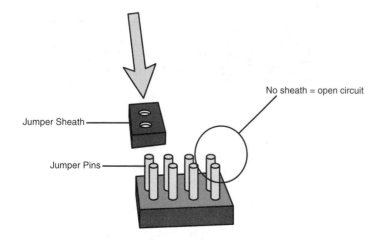

Metal jumper pins jut out from the hard disk drive's main circuit board.

No sheath = open circuit

Jumper Sheath

Jumper Pins

Jumper pins are arranged in pairs; each pair governs a single circuit. While the jumper pin pair is unsheathed, the circuit is open. You can close this circuit by applying a sheath to the specified jumper pin pair (see the following figure).

To close the circuit, cover the jumper pin pair with a sheath.

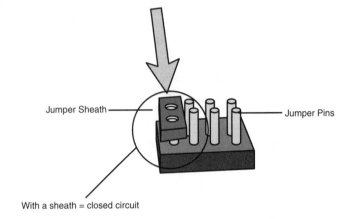

To find the master-slave jumpers on your IDE hard disk drive, turn the drive to reflect a rear view (see the following figure). As illustrated in the following figure, most IDE hard disk drives have the cable connector, power connector, and jumpers at the rear. Typically, there are three clearly marked jumper pairs:

➤ Master (M or C)

➤ Slave (S or D)

➤ Cable Select (CS)

The cable connectors, power connectors, and jumpers are generally located at the rear of the hard disk drive.

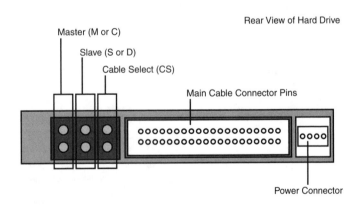

Once you've identified which jumper pin pair you need, set the drive to slave status. You do this by either applying or removing a sheath to the proper jumper pin pair.

Adding the Drive to the Disk Drive Cable

Next, you'll need to connect the drive to your system. For this, you must open your box to expose the disk drive connector cable. Once you remove the cover on the computer, you will see the hard disk drive cable. In older computers, this cable extends from an insertable hard disk controller card (such as the one depicted in the following figure) to the hard drive. In newer systems, however, the hard disk controller is on-board and, therefore, the hard disk cable extends from the motherboard to your existing hard disk.

Check This Out

Not every hard disk manufacturer adheres to these conventions. If you can't immediately make out what each jumper pair does, check the drive's documentation. Also, this information is sometimes printed on the drive's surface (usually on the top, on a peel-off sticker).

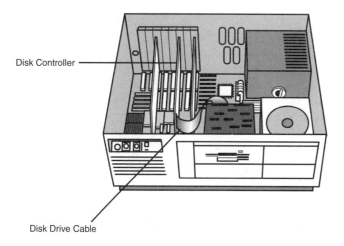

Disk Controller

Disk Drive Cable

Finding the disk drive connector cable.

The hard disk drive cable will look much like the one depicted in the following figure. The cable will have at least three connectors—two for hard drives and one for the controller. Attach your slave hard disk drive to an empty connector on the ribbon cable, plug in the drive, and secure it. You probably don't want to permanently mount the drive yet because you might need to remove it again before installation is complete.

Walking the Thin Red Line

When connecting a ribbon cable, be sure that it goes in right side up. You can quickly determine this by locating the thin red strip on the cable. This strip signifies the location for pin 1 on the drive and motherboard (or card controller). Ensure that you match up the red strip with pin 1; otherwise, the connection will be incorrect—upside-down—and the system won't recognize your drive.

A typical connector ribbon cable with three connection points.

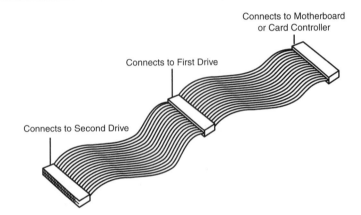

Connects to Motherboard or Card Controller

Connects to First Drive

Connects to Second Drive

Setting the Disk's Parameters

Next, you'll need to set the disk's parameters and geometry, including some—or perhaps all—of the following values:

➤ **The landing zone**   Landing zones are blank spaces on the hard disk drive's surface, reserved for temporarily parking the head or heads. This prevents the head from accidentally writing to recordable portions of the disk.

➤ **The number of cylinders**   Cylinders are collections of associated tracks on a hard disk drive's surface.

➤ **The number of heads**   Heads are tools that read and write data from the disk.

➤ **The number of sectors**   Sectors are small areas of the disk contained within tracks. These sectors house the smallest possible space used to record data. There are usually at least eight sectors per track.

➤ **The number of tracks**   Tracks are similar to grooves in an LP record. They extend completely around the disk's surface. Within each track are several sectors.

Years ago, users had to specify this information manually, a complex and often difficult task. Have no fear, though. Most modern systems collect this information without human intervention.

Once you have the drive connected, restart your machine and enter your system BIOS (or PROM). Depending on your machine's manufacturer, you might have to take different steps to do this. On most PCs, you can strike the **Delete** key anytime before the system actually boots. This brings you to a CMOS screen.

In your CMOS, find the Hard Disk Drive Auto Detection option. On some systems, this is one menu deep, usually in the Advanced Settings section. On other systems, it's immediately available from the main menu. Once you find this option, click it and the machine automatically detects your new disk's parameters (including heads, cylinders, sectors, landing zones, and size). Your machine then asks whether you accept these parameters. Click **Yes**, save your changes, exit, and reboot.

Techno Talk

On older systems, the BIOS might not offer hard disk auto-detection. If you own such a system, you'll have to manually set the drive's parameters. To do so, copy down the parameters from the drive's peel-off sticker (or accompanying documentation). Be sure to have these values ready before entering the BIOS. Once there, enter the values manually, save the configuration, and reboot.

Partitioning and Formatting the Disk

Most new hard disk drives already come with a viable partition. In many cases, therefore, you can format the drive immediately upon reboot. To do so in Microsoft Windows, double-click the **My Computer** icon, right-click your new disk's icon, and choose **Format**. If your new disk does *not* contain a valid partition, you'll need to create one. To do so, go to the Start menu and choose **Programs, MSDOS Prompt**. This opens an MS-DOS window (see the following figure).

The MS-DOS Prompt window.

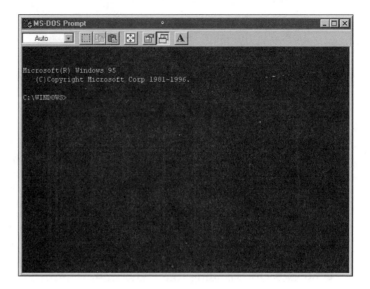

Once you've opened the MS-DOS Prompt window, issue the following command:

```
fdisk
```

This starts FDISK, the disk-partitioning tool that comes with Windows. At this point, if you're using Windows 95, you'll see the following advisory:

> Your computer has a disk larger than 512MB. This version
> of Windows includes improved support for large disks, resulting
> in more efficient use of disk space on large drives, and allowing
> disks over 2GB to be formatted as a single drive.
>
> IMPORTANT: If you enable large disk support and create any new
> drives on this disk, you will not be able to access the new
> drive(s) using other operating systems, including some versions
> of Windows 95 and Windows NT, as well as earlier versions of
> Windows and MS-DOS. In addition, disk utilities that were not
> designed explicitly for the FAT32 file system will not be able
> to work with this disk. If you need to access this disk with
> other operating systems or older disk utilities, do not enable
> large drive support.
>
> Do you wish to enable large disk support (Y/N)...........? [N]

If you see this advisory, choose **Y** (**N** is the default). This takes you into FDISK's main menu. You then see a screen similar to the one in the following figure.

The FDISK main menu.

From here, there are six remaining steps:

1. Choose **Create DOS Partition** or **Logical DOS Drive**.
2. Choose **Create Primary DOS Partition**.
3. Specify that you want the maximum available space.
4. Choose **Yes**.
5. Exit FDISK.
6. Reboot.

If you survived all that, you have installed a new secondary IDE hard disk drive.

Adding a New Primary IDE Drive

The procedure for adding a new primary IDE disk drive is almost identical to the process for adding a secondary one. The only real procedural difference is that you leave the jumpers alone when installing a new primary drive. However, the *preparation* for upgrading your existing primary drive is different.

Next, before upgrading, take stock of your software. Are there irreplaceable software programs on your existing primary drive? If so, are those applications critical to your family? If your answer to both questions is yes, you need to carefully consider upgrading. Here's why: If you designate your existing primary drive as a slave, many of its software programs will not work anymore. Applications have system calls hard-coded into their design that expect certain files to be on certain drives. For example, when you first install a software program, it unpacks its resource files to the primary drive. A record is then made of their location (in this case, C:>). If you later change your drive's logical designation (from drive C to drive D, for instance), important

177

resource files are no longer where they're supposed to be. Therefore, when applications look for those files, their search fails. (Typically, the program throws up a dialog box explaining that files are "Not Found.") This results in a fatal error. So before you replace your existing primary drive, ensure that you have original, installable versions of all critical software.

A Gentle Warning

First, before you do anything, *back up the existing drive*. This is to ensure against potential disaster during the upgrade process. Although the likelihood of disaster is slim, stranger things have happened. You might accidentally drop the drive while removing it, or you might unwittingly expose it to excess static electricity. This can damage or incapacitate components. Once, I was hot–swapping two disks (like a complete idiot) and inadvertently dropped the primary disk into the box. The drive lodged itself between the motherboard and the ethernet card. I reached in to get the drive but quickly recoiled. Before I was able to pull the plug, the drive fused itself to the motherboard and the network card (arc-welding, anyone?). Needless to say, the data on that drive was unrecoverable. To learn about backing up your system, refer to Chapter 14, "Disaster Prevention: Backing Up."

The CD-ROM Problem

It's now time to answer the number one technical support question of all time! Today, most commercial software is distributed on CD-ROM. Therefore, when you install a new drive which has absolutely no software on it, you need to install the CD-ROM drivers. If you don't, you end up with an empty drive and no way to install your applications.

If you have the original CD-ROM software installation disks, you have no worries. After you format the drive, you simply install the CD-ROM software and that's that. From there, you can install Windows, Office, and so on. But what if you only have the CD-ROM drivers, and no installation disks? How do you make a boot disk that catches the CD-ROM? I can't tell you how many times I've been asked that question. The following steps provide an answer:

1. Take a clean, formatted floppy disk and convert it into a system disk. You can do this in one of two ways:

   ➤ **In Windows**   Double-click **My Computer**, right-click your desired floppy disk's icon, and choose **Format, Full, Copy System Files**.

178

➤ **From a prompt**   Issue the following commands:

```
sys a:
cd c:\windows\command
copy *.exe a:
copy *.com a:
```

2. Locate your CD-ROM drivers. If you're uncertain where these reside, check the contents of your CONFIG.DOS file. Typically, it contains a line similar to this:

```
DEVICE=C:\DEV\HIT-IDE.SYS /D:MSCD001
```

In this case, my CD-ROM driver is located in the directory C:\DEV. After you locate your CD-ROM driver, copy it to your floppy disk; for example:

```
copy c:\dev\hit-ide.sys a:
```

3. Create two files on your floppy disk: CONFIG.SYS and AUTOEXEC.BAT. In the CONFIG.SYS file, specify your CD-ROM driver as a device. Using the previous example, your CONFIG.SYS file looks similar to this:

```
DEVICE=HIT-IDE.SYS /D:MSCD001
```

In your AUTOEXEC.BAT file, you'll initiate the MSCDEX.EXE command, which drives CD-ROMs. Hence, your AUTOEXEC.BAT file looks similar to this:

```
MSCDEX.EXE /D:MSCD001 /m:8
```

4. Test the disk. Make certain that the floppy disk is inserted into the floppy drive and reboot. Your system will boot from the floppy and load the CD-ROM driver. From there, you can format and partition the drive and then proceed with a complete software installation.

Notes on SCSI Hard Disk Drives

The process of upgrading to a new SCSI hard disk drive is very similar to the procedure in the preceding section, but with one exception: If you're installing a secondary SCSI drive, you might need to alter the new drive's SCSI ID.

The SCSI interface enables you to daisy chain SCSI devices with ease. A *daisy chain* connects from one to seven SCSI drives to the same computer. In order to keep track of these multiple devices, the SCSI controller relies on *SCSI IDs*—addresses where each device can be found. Typically, most SCSI drives are capable of occupying IDs 0 through 7.

Most PC SCSI controllers attempt to boot from SCSI ID 0, or the first available SCSI device. Many new SCSI drives are set to ID 0 at the factory. Hence, if you're adding a new SCSI drive and want to designate it as a secondary disk, you'll need to change the drive's ID from 0 to any higher number. If you don't, there will be a SCSI conflict because the controller finds two devices registered at ID 0.

To change your new hard disk drive's SCSI ID, you'll need to either apply, relocate, or remove one or more jumpers. To find out which jumper (or jumpers) to remove, check your new drive's documentation.

Manually Determining the New Drive's SCSI ID

If you purchased a SCSI drive without documentation, you can still manually determine the jumper settings. Simply attach the drive, reboot, and watch the error messages from your SCSI adapter. In particular, note the SCSI ID that the adapter automatically detected for the secondary drive. Then, turn off the machine, alter the drive's jumpers, and try again.

If this technique fails, try visiting the Web site of the drive's manufacturer. Most SCSI manufacturers post jumper settings and other schematics for all their current products, and occasionally for their ancient ones. For example, someone recently gave me a SCSI disk that was manufactured in 1991. I had no trouble finding their jumper settings at Seagate's Web site.

Upgrading Motherboards and CPUs

Another common upgrade path is to replace your motherboard, your CPU, or both. This is an economical way to obtain better performance without replacing the entire computer. (These days, you can buy a motherboard/CPU upgrade for as little as $150.)

Upgrading the Motherboard

Your motherboard is your computer's largest and most important circuit card. This board houses the *Central Processing Unit* (*CPU*), the computer's memory, and the important firmware (BIOS) used to perform basic hardware configuration.

In desktop systems, this board is located at the very bottom of the machine, as depicted in the following figure. In tower and mini-tower systems, the motherboard is located on either side.

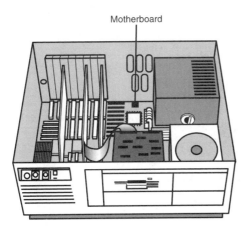

Motherboard

The motherboard is generally fastened to the bottom of the machine.

Often, other devices (including the power supply, disk drives, and so on) obstruct open access to the motherboard. Therefore, you might have to remove these devices to perform the upgrade. Before you do, though, check to see whether access is provided through the bottom or side of the computer's casing.

When you do gain clear access to the motherboard, you'll see that it houses many important slots, bays, and ports. Some of these are identified in the following figure.

The motherboard houses serial ports, parallel ports, on-board disk controllers, memory bays, and so on.

Chances are, your motherboard also houses several expansion cards. These fit into expansion slots (see the following figure).

*Expansion cards (typi-
cally green or dark green)
fit into slots on the
motherboard.*

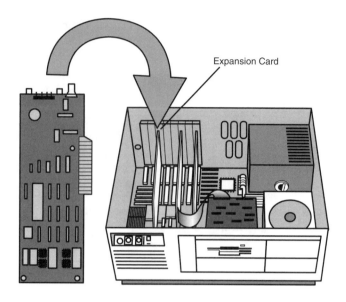

Expansion Card

Before removing the old motherboard, you must first disconnect all expansion cards
and power cables. (To disconnect expansion cards, you'll need a Phillips-head screwdriver.) When removing expansion cards, handle them gently and make every effort
to protect them from excess static electricity.

Once you've disconnected all expansion cards and cables, you're ready to remove the
motherboard. Most motherboards are secured to the computer case with screws or
plastic fasteners. These are generally located at the corners (see the following figure).

*Screws and fasteners are
usually located at the
corners.*

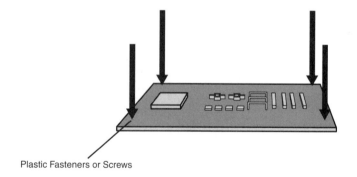

Plastic Fasteners or Screws

Once you've removed all screws and fasteners, you can safely lift out the old motherboard and install the new one.

CPU Upgrades

There are two basic CPU upgrade types:

➤ **Upgrading to an overdrive processor**   Overdrive processors are an inexpensive solution to upgrading very old systems. (A good example is converting a 486DX66 to a 486DX100). While overdrive processors offer only marginal speed gains, they can provide the extra oomph needed to upgrade a system from Windows 3.11 to Windows 95 (barely).

➤ **Upgrading to a new processor**   In contrast, upgrading to a new processor presents a world of possibilities (including any range of speeds, from 133MHz to 450MHz). However, new processors can be expensive.

About Those Overdrive Chips...

Many folks opt for overdrive chips as an inexpensive way to upgrade older boxes, such as 486 systems. Personally, I'd advise against it. I've never seen an overdrive chip that can offer the same performance as a new chip with the same clock speed. For example, installing an 80MHz overdrive chip into a 40MHz Sparc IPX achieves only a moderate speed increase—certainly less than a regular, non-overdrive 80MHz chip. This is equally true of X86 chips. In essence, it's worth the extra $150 or so to really upgrade to 133 or 166.

Several factors influence your choice of CPU upgrade, but none so much as the make and model of your motherboard. For example, older motherboards might offer you little or no upgrade path. This is especially so with certain proprietary 386 and early 486 models. Let me demonstrate why.

As depicted in the following figure, the typical legacy processor has pins that fit into holes on a processor carriage. There are two types of carriage: slotted and non-slotted. *Slotted* carriages are designed for convenience and enable you to swap processor chips (you simply pull out the old chip and insert a new one). Conversely, *non-slotted* carriages are not flexible—the chip is usually welded in—and, therefore, prohibit processor upgrades.

The typical legacy processor.

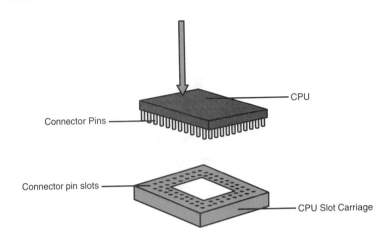

Before you decide to upgrade those old 386 and 486 boxes, open them up and take a close look. If your system has a non-slotted carriage, forget it. The only way you'll upgrade that processor is to replace not only the processor but the entire motherboard, too. (Of course, if you only want a modest upgrade—to 166MHz, for example—this is still a pretty economical move.) If your system *is* slotted, there are still other considerations. For example, many system boards support only Pentium—and not Pentium II—processors; worse still, they'll only handle up to 200MHz.

Since there are so many different motherboards and so many different processors, it is difficult to describe a generic procedure for processor upgrades (other than to suggest replacing the old chip with a new one). So, instead, here are some general tips that apply to all CPU upgrades:

➤ **Watch your voltage**   Different chips take different voltages; most modern motherboards support either 3.5 or 5 volts. If your chip requires 3.5 volts and your motherboard is set to 5, you might damage your processor. (You'll know if that happens: You'll see very strange results on the screen, such as characters broken in half and logos fragmented into fuzzy shapes.) To avoid accidentally frying your processor, consult your motherboard's manual. Invariably, you'll find that jumpers on the motherboard govern voltage. Really good motherboards provide visual notification of this. Typically, the voltage count is burned into the board, adjacent to the jumper. Also, in most cases, the chip's required voltage is visible on the chip's surface. Be certain to set your motherboard to the correct voltage prior to starting the machine.

➤ **Handle the chip with care**   Processor chips (like most computer components) are especially sensitive to static electricity. Older chips in particular (486, and early Pentium 100, 133, and 166MHz units) come with their pins embedded in an anti-static pad for this very reason. It's worth supporting your board with a rubber pad—or other non-static surface—while you perform the upgrade.

➤ **Provide the chip with adequate cooling facilities**   Most processors get pretty hot under extensive use. When you upgrade from an older chip to a new one, take this into account. Older chips (486 models and some early Pentiums) require only a small fan to keep them cool. However, newer chips often require more extensive measures (including heat synchs or, in the extreme, miniature internal refrigeration systems). Make certain that you employ the proper cooling procedure for your chip. If you don't, it overheats and burns out. (You'll know if your cooling system is inadequate; your system will chronically fail, reboot, or freeze at intervals ranging from 30 seconds to three minutes.)

➤ **If you don't have the original documentation on your current motherboard and processor, get it**   And certainly don't attempt an upgrade until you do. Here's why: Many proprietary systems—particularly from companies such as Acer, Compaq, and Packard Bell—tie key functionality of the processor to the system BIOS. Some systems are simply not compatible with certain chips (such as AMD's K6, for example). To prevent spending money that you might not recover, be absolutely certain that the upgrade processor you choose is compatible with your current motherboard.

Upgrading Communication and Networking Hardware

It's unlikely that you'll upgrade communication or networking hardware during your home network's first year of operation. As your network grows in size and scope, however, this might change. In particular, as you add more home computers you may need an additional hub. Since your home network's growth cannot be anticipated, only generalized tips and tricks can be offered in this regard:

➤ **Inquire vigorously**   For example, suppose a product advertises the fact that you can add as many home computers to your network as you like. Find out what additional hardware you're going to need to do this. How much will it cost?

➤ **Pay that extra dollar**   In networking, you often get precisely what you pay for. In other words, it's better paying a few extra dollars for quality equipment and guaranteed reliability. As your home network grows, reliability becomes a very serious issue. When many of your family members come to rely on your home network, you can't afford to have it go down.

➤ **Stick to a standard**   When purchasing hubs or adapters, buy them from the same vendor—or at least make certain that they offer very similar management features and functionality. By doing so, you'll avoid a new learning curve and you'll be less likely to encounter problems.

Software Upgrades

Upgrading software is rarely a necessity—avoid it if possible. Here's why: Software manufacturers (particularly in the Windows world) often radically change their software, which can introduce an entirely new learning curve. As a result, installing such software can sometimes hinder productivity.

A good example is Microsoft's migration from Windows 3.11 to 95. Windows 95 drastically differed from 3.11 not only in a superficial sense (the visual interface worked differently), but also in more profound ways (the new system used a Registry instead of simple configuration files). Many people didn't adjust well to that change and waited as long as possible before upgrading on a grand scale.

A good formula for determining whether you really need an upgrade is to weigh the following issues:

➤ Does the upgrade offer important functionality that was previously lacking?

➤ Does the upgrade fix problems that have plagued your system?

➤ Does the upgrade enhance your security?

➤ Is the upgrade a requirement to use new programs that you feel are essential?

Unless one of these four statements is true, you probably don't need the upgrade. Moreover, you need to assess the upgrade for negative points. For example, what if the upgrade *takes away* important functionality? Either way, whenever performing a software upgrade (or, for that matter, a hardware upgrade), test that upgrade first. The following section covers testing issues.

Windows Ninety-Ate My Drivers!

A good example is Microsoft's release of Windows 98. Because many older systems were incompatible with 98 (a fact not widely publicized), thousands of users upgraded only to have their computers malfunction. This led some large vendors (including Dell) to post advisories on their Web sites, warning users of possible dangers.

Testing Upgrades

As part of your upgrade strategy, you need to test proposed upgrades before implementing them. This prevents you from inadvertently propagating a faulty upgrade throughout the entire network. Remember that in a network, you want to try to preserve a stable computing environment. In this respect, maintaining a network is more structured than maintaining your own machine; you can't afford as many mistakes.

For testing purposes, always use the machine your family uses most infrequently. These needn't necessarily have the exact same hardware as your other home computers, but they should be configured as closely to other them as possible.

Oddly, your main concern (and the greatest chance for error) is with software upgrades. Although a rare occurrence, some software upgrades can cripple your existing configuration by damaging or replacing key system files with either newer or older versions.

By first testing such upgrades on a throwaway machine, you greatly increase your chances of identifying and eliminating potential hazards. To effectively perform this task, outfit your test machines with

➤ The same network operating system as your other home computers

➤ The same applications currently installed on your other home computers

➤ The same protocol support

➤ The same security settings

This guarantees that your test machines have a very similar (or identical) Registry and shared library configuration.

Each time you perform a test run, check that every application, all protocol support, and all security settings are still valid and operational. Only then should you institute that upgrade throughout your household.

The Least You Need to Know

Upgrades can lead to greater productivity or better game play, but they're also expensive and time consuming. Here are a few tips to help you maximize your potential and minimize cost:

➤ Always perform a test run on the home computer that you need the least to identify possible upgrade incompatibilities or problems.

➤ Always perform full backups before attempting any upgrade.

➤ Try to standardize as much as possible. Maintaining a consistent hardware set is as important as maintaining a consistent application set. For example, using an ethernet hub made by the same manufacturer who made your ethernet cards will reduce the time you spend configuring or upgrading them later.

➤ When performing a partial upgrade (where some existing hardware remains), make certain that the new and old components are compatible.

➤ When upgrading software, be certain that the new software reads old data flawlessly and that the learning curve is moderate.

➤ When upgrading home computers, do so judiciously by distributing your processor power and storage capacity where they're most needed.

Part 5

Enhancing the Digital Home

Using the home computer network as a base, this section reveals all the major highlights in the world of home area networking. First we show you how to get the most out of your home office. Whether you need to coordinate and communicate better with the head office or you just want to work more effectively at home, you learn it here. We also explore the fun side of the Internet with multiplayer games. If you need to relax, the chapters on audio and video show you how to access sights and sounds in ways you never imagined.

You learn to automate your household by remotely controlling lights, thermostats, or any other household appliance. Next, you can make your home safer and more secure by adding your security system to your home network.

In the final chapter, we show you some of the exciting products and technologies that companies are working to bring you. Faster networks, installed with fewer hassles, are just around the corner. Computers will become part of your home instead of being shuffled off to the basement. Every household device will join the home network.

Chapter 17

HAN SOHO: Networking Your Home Office

In This Chapter

➤ Communicating with voice and video

➤ Telecommuting made easy

➤ Software that helps you to work well with others

➤ An intranet for your home business

Working at home sounds great for the corporate worker. Every *Dilbert* cartoon depicts the daily trials of corporate life. This cubicle life-style has driven many thousands of people to flock to home-based businesses. What most of them have found, though, is that many of the things they took for granted at the office are nowhere to be found at home. Tasks such as faxing a document or holding a teleconference are less common at home than at work.

Fortunately, the home worker with an Internet-connected PC now has access to software that allows her to set up an office much easier and for far fewer dollars than in past years.

Using Microsoft NetMeeting for Long–Distance Calls

Communicating with others has always been essential for a thriving business; unfortunately, telecommunication costs have always been a large part of every business's budget. These days, however, you can save money through the use of Microsoft NetMeeting, a software application that lets you communicate using your Internet connection.

For example, suppose that Mary, who lives in West Virginia, wants to call a business associate, Jules, in France:

1. Mary emails Jules and asks him to send her his current IP address.
2. Jules find his IP address in Windows 98 by clicking the **Start** button, choosing **Run**, typing `winipcfg.exe` at the command line, and pressing **Enter**.
3. Jules should see the following dialog box; his IP address is `24.65.224.182`.

This dialog box allows you to view your IP address.

4. Jules emails this number back to Mary in West Virginia.
5. Mary opens Microsoft NetMeeting and clicks the **Call** button.
6. In the New Call dialog box, Mary must type Jules's IP address into the address line.

Place a new call by typing the correct IP address in this dialog box.

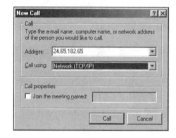

7. Mary selects **Network (TCPIP)** in the Call Using box and clicks **Call**.
8. Jules should accept Mary's call using NetMeeting; they will be able to talk to each other using their PC microphones. Instead of paying for long-distance calls, Mary and Jules incur only the cost of their Internet connections.

Jules now accepts Mary's call with this simple dialog box.

192

Using Microsoft NetMeeting for Videoconferencing

Even if you have all the technological benefits of a full-fledged office at home, one of the most important facets of business remains personal interaction. Although videoconferencing is not a replacement for a face-to-face meeting, it's the next-closest thing. Microsoft NetMeeting is set up to deliver videoconferencing capabilities from the desktop of your computer to the desktop of other computers anywhere in the world. If you each have a camera attached to your PCs (see Chapter 11, "Hardware for the Truly Digital Home," for details), you can transmit live video to each other to have a look at who is on the other end of the line.

Directory Servers

Although NetMeeting allows you to find people on directory servers, we don't recommend this. It's much easier to have one participant either send his or her IP address through email or ICQ (see Chapter 12, "Software to Tie It All Together"). The other participant can then call directly using NetMeeting.

You can use NetMeeting to videoconference in two ways:

➤ By placing a NetMeeting voice call to someone in the standard fashion (as described in the previous section) and clicking **Tools**, **Video**, **Send** to send video.

➤ By configuring NetMeeting to automatically send video. To do this, select **Tools**, **Options,** click the **Video** tab, and select the **Automatically send video at the start of each call** check box.

A person can send and receive audio and video with only one other person at a time. You can switch from one person to another, or several pairs of people in a meeting can talk to and see each other at the same time.

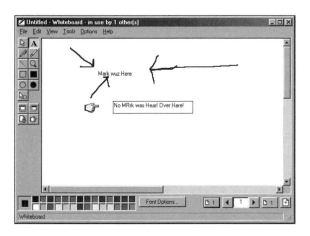

A NetMeeting call can display two participants.

Sharing Applications

Seeing and speaking with business partners may not be enough to convey an idea or a concept. You may want to share business applications with others. NetMeeting allows you to share any application on your desktop, such as Microsoft Word or Microsoft Excel. Simply do the following:

1. Start the application that you want to share.

2. After you are in a NetMeeting call, Select **Tools, Share Application**.

3. Select the application you want to share.

Any participant in the call can then control the application. Double-clicking the window gives the control over to another participant.

Sharing applications such as Microsoft Excel can make business presentations more effective.

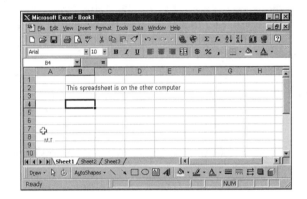

Using the Whiteboard

You may be used to walking up to your corporate whiteboard and illustrating an idea that is just too tough for words to describe. NetMeeting has a whiteboard that you can use to give everyone a chance to scribble his or her thoughts and ideas. To use the whiteboard, do the following:

1. In the NetMeeting window, select **Tools, Whiteboard**.

2. Use the tools on the left just as you would in Paint.

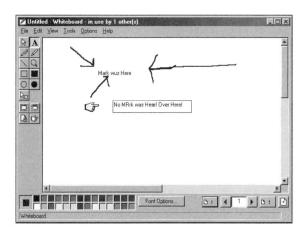

A whiteboard can enhance any presentation.

The Home Network Makes Telecommuting Simple and Painless

Whether you are fortunate enough to work from home some days or you have to work extra hours at your home, you need to have access to the files and applications that you use at your workplace. For example, imagine that it's budget time, and three or four people are working on the budget with you. You take a copy of what you think is the final version home on a floppy disk; in the meantime, one of your coworkers updates her numbers on your spreadsheet at work. You work all night on a budget that's out of date and head back in to the office in the morning to realize you just wasted an evening. Fortunately, software called pcTELECOMMUTE from Symantec solves this problem by allowing you to keep your home and office files in sync.

You access pcTELECOMMUTE by using the Telecommute Control Center. This gives you access to many of the applications you need to perform common tasks, including transferring and synchronizing your files between your home and work PCs.

The Control Center is a multipurpose control panel.

To synchronize your files, do the following:

1. Click the **File Sync** icon on the pcTELECOMMUTE Control Center.
2. Select **File**, **New** in the File Sync window.
3. Click **Next,** and type the name of the file on your home PC that you want to sync.
4. Click **Next** again, and type the name of the file on your work PC that you want to sync.

5. Click **Finish**. Your two files will now be displayed in one line in the File Sync window.

6. To begin the transfer, select the two files in the window and click the **Start** button.

Synchronizing files is easy with this dialog box.

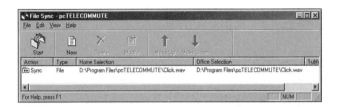

Your files will be synchronized, ensuring that the latest version of that crucial report is on both machines.

Overcoming Information Overload: Computer Telephony Integration

In a larger office setting, there is usually a dedicated fax machine, an officewide phone system with fully functional voice mail, and access to electronic mail through a corporate mail server. As you can imagine, this might be a little expensive to set up at home. Fortunately, you can have integrated fax, phone, voice mail, and email capability at home using your home PC and some dedicated software. TalkWorks Pro from Symantec is one of the leading products in this category; its Message Manager is shown in the following figure.

Message Manager organizes your communications.

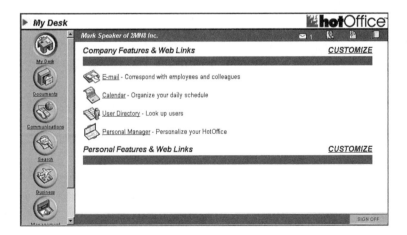

Its features include integrated voice mail, message notification, call tracking, and fax-on-demand capabilities, all designed to keep you in touch with customers. As an integrated application, it allows you to work faster and more effectively because you don't lose track of those crucial interactions with your suppliers and customers. TalkWorks can help you do the following:

➤ **Organize your voice mail**   With TalkWorks, you can use professionally pre-recorded greetings or create your own. You can even configure your system to automatically change the greeting after business hours. If more than one person is working at home, you can set up separate mailboxes for voice mail and fax on demand.

➤ **Keep track of who is contacting you**   TalkWorks PRO answers your phone and takes voice messages and faxes. It logs hangups and received items, as well as all the faxes and calls that you make. It even identifies who called if you have a caller ID service from your local telephone company.

➤ **Catch those important calls and faxes**   TalkWorks PRO can page or call you when you receive a voice message or a fax—it even relays the message to you. You can restrict notification by caller, date, and time. You can also call in at any time to retrieve your messages.

➤ **Set up a fax-on-demand service**   Customers can get information about your products or services 24 hours a day with a fax-on-demand service. They simply call and follow the instructions to select the documents they want faxed to them; TalkWorks instantly faxes the appropriate document.

➤ **Send high-quality faxes**   You can send laser-quality faxes right from your PC. You can also preview faxes before sending them, rearrange or remove pages from outgoing faxes, and merge documents from multiple applications into a single fax.

Create a Virtual Office

When you set up a company at home, it often means that certain employees are located elsewhere. Eventually, you'll probably decide that you need to keep track of key documents and communicate with each other just like you did in a traditional corporate environment. You like the freedom of working at home, but you need some structure when it comes to communication.

Providing Internet access, voice mail, email, and file sharing is an expensive undertaking in larger companies. A corporate headquarters may have to deal with 50 or more users and, as such, it is required to invest large amounts of money for phone, fax, and computer systems. On the other hand, as a home user, you can spend very little and outsource these functions using Web-enabled software.

hotOffice offers home businesses an affordable, secure solution at a fraction of the cost of purchasing and maintaining a traditional one. To use hotOffice, you pay a subscription of $12.95 per user per month, which allows you to use collaboration tools such as email, calendaring, documents, bulletin boards, online conference rooms, and so on. You can use hotOffice from any PC that has Internet access by accessing www.hotoffice.net. As shown in the following figure, hotOffice provides each user with a simple yet effective interface.

hotOffice is great for workers on the move.

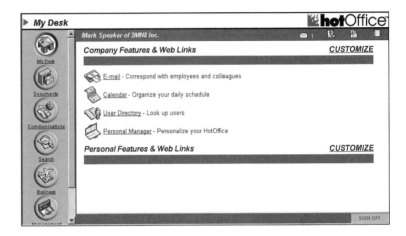

Selecting a button on the left provides you with different categories of options:

➤ Each user has her own customized section called My Desk, which contains her own email, calendar, corporate user directory, and personal manager. The email interface is easy to use and provides you with a corporate email directory that you can use to create groups of people for mailing lists. This comes in handy when you find yourself sending the same email to many people within your company.

➤ Possibly the most powerful function in this application, the Documents section enables you to do things like search for and browse corporate documents. These documents can be placed on your hotOffice intranet by your employees using an application called hotOffice Publisher, which comes free with the service. This allows you to keep company documents current and readily available to all employees.

➤ The Communications section gives you email, reminders, phone messages, access to NetMeeting, bulletin boards, and an online conference room where you can chat in real time. (You may be thinking that you can find similar applications for free elsewhere. The power of the hotOffice Communications section lies in the fact that these applications are all tied together in one common interface.)

➤ The Search section provides you with access to some of the most popular online search engines.

➤ The Business section directs you to online sites that can help you increase your business and save money. With applications like Package Tracking, you can perform routine business tasks more efficiently.

➤ The Management section allows you to set up departments and the users who work in them. As with all the sections, a user designated as management can grant or deny access privileges to each employee. This gives a manager complete control of information on the corporate intranet without the headaches of managing information technology employees.

The Least You Need to Know

➤ Working from home has never been as easy as it is today.

➤ Your PC can manage your calls, faxes, email, and files and can enable you to communicate with anyone in the world both cheaply and effectively.

➤ The home office worker need not be at a technological disadvantage when compared to the corporate office worker.

Chapter 18

All Work and No Play: Multiplayer Gaming

In This Chapter

➤ Discover the best places to buy games, both in the mall and on the Net

➤ Download a shareware or demo game

➤ Determine what types of games you might like to play

➤ Set up or join a multiplayer game of Quake II

You've just finished pounding through Chapter 17, "HAN SOHO: Networking Your Home Office." You're office is now a lean, mean efficiency machine. But, for some reason, you don't feel satisfied. Something is missing: You haven't blown anything up today!

Multiplayer games and game services have enjoyed incredible growth in the last few years. Although they have been around for more than a decade in one form or another, the release of one game in particular took the online world by storm. Overnight, a little game from ID Software called *Doom* ripped the world of single-player games apart. What arose from the ashes was a way to get together with friends and foes for the ultimate in interactive game play. No matter how intelligent the characters in a single-player game might be, they could never be as lifelike or as cunning as a *real* person.

A Gamer's Shopping List

Before you can begin your trip into the world of multiplayer gaming, there are a few basic provisions you should stuff into your pack.

➤ **A computer worthy of game playing** Games have long been known as the true test of a computer's mettle. Although there are exceptions, this trend continues today. Particularly in the realms of action, adventure, and simulation, the hardware requirements for a game computer can be intense. Be sure that you look closely at the hardware requirements for any game you are considering buying or downloading.

➤ **A reliable network connection** The lowest common denominator for a multiplayer game is, of course, a connection with another computer. There is no requirement for an Internet connection (see the next point) if you want to play games with another person. A simple home area network with two computers is all that is required.

➤ **An Internet connection** What's the fun of playing games with your roommate night after night when you can go online and team up with or against the millions of other online gamers?

➤ **A multiplayer game** Not all games that you buy, download, or play online are capable of multiplayer gaming, so make sure that you look before you leap into buying one if this is an important feature for you.

➤ **Somebody to play with** Although this might sound like a silly requirement, it is the point at which most people get tripped up when breaking into the world of multiplayer gaming. Software and services abound for helping people with the same games get together for fun or mayhem.

Save Some Cash: Compare Before You Buy

Although it sounds counterintuitive, shopping for a game at the game's own Web site may be the most expensive way to buy it. Instead, you might try checking out some impartial sites; for example, www.computershopper.com and www.shopping.com are both great places to look if you want to buy retail games online. These sites let you browse categories of games and compare prices before buying. Be careful when you visit these sites, though, because they sell just about everything under the sun. Those with low willpower and a high credit limit might want somebody else to hold the gold card for them when they're surfing these sites.

Retail Stores and E-Commerce Game Sites

Retail games are those you have to pay cash for before you can play. A quick trip down to your local computer store will show you thousands of retail games, many of which support multiplayer gaming.

Many of these titles are available directly over the Internet, either by downloading from the game manufacturer's Web site or by courier after you pay. Most game creators' sites let you type your credit card number into an online order form, making it quick and easy to order online. Some sites haven't gone quite that far yet, pointing you to an operator to place the order.

Download a Shareware or Demonstration Game

One of the most exciting trends in multiplayer gaming is the *demo version*. A demo version, often called *shareware*, can be downloaded over the Internet and tried out before you commit with cash. Because game quality and content can vary greatly, this is a great way to try before you buy. Most games available in retail stores are also available as demo versions from their creators' Web sites.

These versions are usually limited in some way, such as in the amount of time you are permitted to play them or in the number of levels that are available for play. These limitations are removed by registering the software on the game's Web site or by purchasing the retail version from a store.

A fast Internet connection will be greatly appreciated if you choose to evaluate video games using this method because they can be huge. Downloads of 20MB are common for demo versions of action and adventure games. Two Web sites—www.softseek.com and www.download.com—are excellent places to start if you are looking for downloadable games.

Games Worth Checking Out

Although the multiplaying gaming world is best known for its love of carnage and digital bloodletting, many different types of games are available. Here's a small sample of the games that support multiple players and where you can find them:

➤ **Old-style games**   These are the games that you used to play with your family at the kitchen table when you were a kid. Now you can play classic games such as Poker, Bridge, Scrabble, Hearts, and Spades with people all over the world:

   Scrabble   www.hasbro.com

   Spades   www.zone.com

   Poker   www.games.yahoo.com

   Bridge   www.games.yahoo.com

   Hearts   www.games.yahoo.com

➤ **Kids games**   The best places to find games for kids are the sites dedicated to children's games. One of the best ones around is www.bonus.com, a site designed specifically for kid-safe surfing. It has hundreds of browser-based games for kids to play in an *isolated* window. There are many different categories of games and diversions to let the little ones play, color, imagine, and explore. You'll find upon visiting these sites that there are far fewer multiplayer games in the kid category, but that number is growing every day.

Here are several other sites that have a good mixture of kids' games and not-so-violent adult games:

www.uproar.com

www.gamescene.com

www.macromedia.com

➤ **Action**   Every kind of blow 'em up, shoot 'em up, or slash 'em up you can imagine can be found online. Here are a few of the most popular titles:

Quake II   www.idsoftware.com

Unreal   www.unreal.com

Forsaken   www.forsaken.com

➤ **Strategy**   Although these games have a tendency toward destruction, they are focused mainly on winning battles through the proper application of wit and strategy:

Warcraft   www.blizzard.com

Mechcommander   www.fasainteractive.com

Total Annihilation   www.totalannihilation.com/

➤ **Simulation**   Flight simulators rule this game category, but a few others have sneaked in over the past few years:

Flight Simulator   www.microsoft.com/games

Viper   www.sierra.com/sierrasports

Motocross Madness   www.microsoft.com/games

➤ **Sports**   Every manner of sport an armchair athlete could possibly want is available for duking it out online. Many different football, baseball, and golf games are available for testing your skills:

Links 99   www.accesssoftware.com

Hardball 6   www.accolade.com

Madden NFL 99   www.easports.com

➤ **Role playing games**   Role playing games (RPGs) do their best to immerse you in another world. The name of the game in an RPG is a rich, full story line. If you like to play games that really draw you in, RPGs are for you. Here are some at the front of the pack:

Diablo   www.blizzard.com

Hexplore   www.hexplore.com

Setting Up a Multiplayer Game of Quake II

Regardless of which multiplayer game you want to play, the basics of starting a game for somebody else to join is the same. But just to make sure that you've been through at least one complete setup, let's configure a Quake II network server on your computer and then connect to it from your friend's computer.

1. Download or buy the game. To try it out, surf on over to www.idsoftware.com/quake2/demo.html and grab the current version of the Quake II demo.

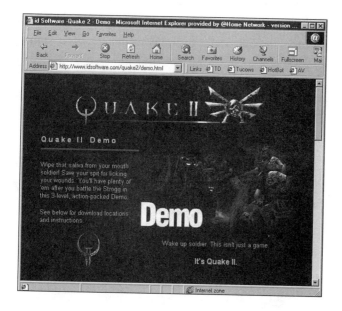

Gaming sites always have awesome graphics.

2. Determine your Internet Protocol (IP) address so that other gamers on the Internet can hook into your game server. If you're running a Windows 95/98 computer, the easiest way to figure out your IP address is to use the Winipcfg utility. To run Winipcfg, click the **Start** button and choose **Run** and then type **C:\WINDOWS\Winipcfg.exe** in the Run dialog box.

Run the Same Versions

All the people who are going to play the game need a copy of the software installed on their computers. Do yourself a big favor and make sure that everyone is running the exact same version of the game.

In-House Gamers

If you plan to play only with people in your home, you're in luck. Quake II automatically checks other computers in your home to see whether they are running a game server. So if your fellow gamers are on the same network as you, you can skip this step.

Dynamic Addressing

As a rule, you'll need to make sure that you are logged on to your ISP before you run Winipcfg because your computer isn't usually assigned an IP address until you log on (this is called dynamic addressing). Your ISP probably changes your IP address every time you log on, so you can expect to go through this little exercise every time you want to play.

3. Write down the IP address as it appears in the IP Configuration dialog box.

This dialog box allows you to see your computer's IP address.

4. Tell your friends via email or a chat utility what the address is. This way, they'll know where to go to join the game after you get it up and running.

5. Install the Quake II demo the same way as you would any other application you've downloaded.

6. Start Quake II by clicking the **Start** button and selecting **Programs**, **Quake II Demo**. When Quake II first starts, you are greeted with a scene from a recorded game. If you haven't played Quake II before, watch it to get a feel for what the game is all about.

7. When you've had enough of the recorded scene, press **Esc** and select **Multiplayer** from the Main menu.

8. Set the game to act as host for other gamers by selecting **start network server**.

Weighing In at 52 MB...

Make sure that the hard drive you install the game on has adequate free space. (The installed demo weighs in at around 52MB.)

Multiplayer games add a new level of tension to the gaming experience.

9. Configure the game server in the following screen. First, select the game environment, or *map*, in which you can play. Use the up- and down-arrow keys on your keyboard to select the **initial map** menu and use the left- and right-arrow keys to scroll through the options.

207

Selecting a map sets the stage for the game.

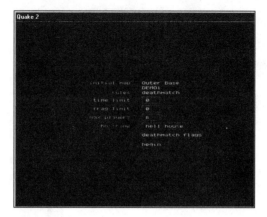

10. The Time Limit setting indicates how long it will be before the game advances to the next map in the series. Use your cursor keys to select a setting. (If it is set at 0, it will never automatically advance.) Setting the time limit to 30 is a reasonable number.

Cursor Keys

The up/down cursor movement and right/left choice selection methods hold throughout all the menus in Quake II.

11. Use the Frag Limit setting to indicate how many kills the best-ranked person in the room can get before the game automatically advances to the next map in the series. Like Time Limit, if it is set at 0, the map will never automatically advance.

12. Fix the Max Players setting to reflect the maximum number of players that the server will allow into the game.

13. In the Hostname box, you can enter a name for the game. This is the name that appears in the other gamers' screens when they point at your server. If you are the only game server on a network, this isn't a big deal, but if more than one person is hosting a game on your network, it can get confusing if you don't name your game.

14. Start the game by clicking on the **Begin** menu item and pressing **Enter**.

Joining a Game of Quake II in Progress

If you want to join a game of Quake II that is already being played (instead of setting up your own game server), do the following:

1. Start Quake II and press **Esc** to exit the game demo.
2. Select **Multiplayer** and then click **Player Setup**.

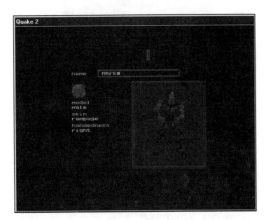

Customize your Quake II soldier to your liking.

3. Using the cursor keys, you can change the sex of your soldier, his or her skin color, and even whether he or she is right or left handed.
4. Press **Esc** to return to the Multiplayer menu.
5. Assuming that you already have the IP address of the game server to which you want to connect, click **Join Network Server**. (See the sidebar at the end of this section if you're joining a game that's being played on your home network.)
6. Select the **Address Book** option and enter the game server's IP address.
7. Press **Esc** to return to the Join Network Server menu. Click **Refresh Server List** to update the connection list with the entry you just made in the server address book. In this example, Big Dog is the name of the game server, DEMO1 is the name of the level being played, and there are currently two out of a maximum of eight players in the game.

Joining a game server is quick and easy.

209

Realistic graphics add excitement to the game.

Playing on Your HAN

If you are lucky enough to be playing a game with somebody in the same house as you are, you can skip step 6. The Quake II Join Network Server feature is smart enough to check all the nearby computers to see whether any are running a network server and automatically creates entries for all the servers it finds on the network. You can just select the game server you want and start playing.

Sooner or Later, That Horse Is Going to Buck You Off

It's a sad but true fact that game programmers, like all of us, occasionally make mistakes. These mistakes can result in little glitches that you learn to live with or big ones that you can't. Unfortunately, the big ones can make you completely reinstall your operating system!

Some people like to pretend that they'll never get bucked off a horse, but smart people realize that it's going to happen sooner or later and prepare for it. Whether it's a new video game or a lightning strike through the window, sooner or later your computer is going to buck and kick for all it's worth.

Religiously back up important information and play those games to your heart's content.

8. Using your up- and down-arrow keys, highlight the server to which you want to connect and press Enter. You're ready to rumble.

Multiplayer Game Services

The best way to break into multiplayer games is to register with one of the online services that specialize in them. These services have everything you need for a rich multiplayer game experience, including

- ➤ **A community** A gaming service's most important contribution to the Net is its capability to gather people together and help them form a community. Here, gamers can meet, play with, and learn from each other.

- ➤ **Game reviews** This can be particularly helpful for new users who might not be sure which games are worth trying. When you're staring down the barrel of a 30MB download, a review you trust can save you hours online.

- ➤ **Chat rooms** Talking about games and the people who play them is one of the biggest pastimes among people who visit game sites.

- ➤ **Automated software updates** One of the tricky things about playing multiplayer games is keeping everybody's version of the game at the same level. Most gaming software works only if all the people in the game are running the same software revision as everybody else.

- ➤ **Team and tournament scores** All the major game sites shown here let you set up and track teams that you form with other players. Watch out, though; this is one of the places where you have to stick your credit card in the slot. Most sites see this as a premium service, so you'll probably have to pay to take advantage of it.

- ➤ **Special games** These games are available for download from the service or sometimes run directly in a browser window, eliminating the need to download them. (See the section "Browser-Based Games.")

All the game sites listed here verify the version level of your game before you play and offer you automated downloads and installs to help make sure your games start and play properly. They also let you set up and track teams that you form with other players:

- ➤ **Heat (www.heat.net)** Heat offers both free and pay-to-play membership levels. The biggest thing that you sacrifice if you don't buy the premium membership is the ability to enter tournaments. Not a big deal if you're just looking to play a few games. On the other hand, if getting proper recognition for your carnage quotient is important, you may want to pay the $6 a month.

➤ **Kali** (www.kali.net)   Although Kali does not offer a free membership, it does have a limited version that you can test drive for 15 minutes of gaming at a time. Boasting more than 200,000 players, it's usually not too tough to find somebody to play a game with on Kali.

➤ **Microsoft Gaming Zone** (www.zone.com)   Although all the sites listed here support blow 'em up and role-playing games, Microsoft Gaming Zone also has a wide selection of classic games such as Backgammon, Bridge, Checkers, Scrabble, and so on. The site has recently added a free puzzle and mind bender section, called Mind Aerobics, that is sure to raise a bead of sweat on your furrowed brow. The Zone also offers a wide selection of browser-based games, which should help keep the impact of gaming on your computer to a minimum (see the section "Browser-Based Games").

➤ **Mplayer** (www.mplayer.com)   A well-rounded site, Mplayer has every type of game you could want. Check it out to dive into one of the largest multiplayer sites on the Net.

If online chat is your cup of tea, Mplayer also has well-developed chat rooms. In fact, Mplayer has taken the concept of the chat room one step further by adding voice capability. Using a CB radio–like interface, people in the chat rooms take turns clicking the Talk button to send their voices to everybody else in the room.

Heat.net's appealing graphics add to the excitement of online gaming.

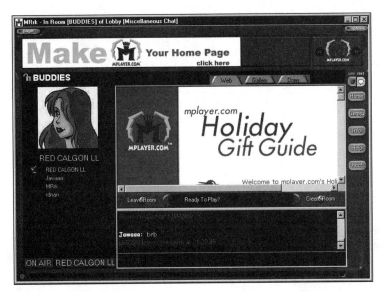

All types of games can be found at
`www.mplayer.com`.

Browser-Based Games

Modern video games can push a computer to its absolute limit. Incredible 3D graphics and surround sound will have your head spinning and your hard drive begging for more (space, that is). Thankfully, advances in Internet browsers, through technologies such as Java, JavaScript, and Shockwave, have given game developers the tools to build wonderful games that can run right in your Internet browser.

Browser-based games have several distinct advantages and disadvantages over traditional installable computer games:

➤ **No installation hassles** Most people find the process of downloading and installing games intimidating. The fear of a game wreaking havoc on their computer system keeps many people from trying them out.

Browser-based games enable you to avoid the download-install-play-delete cycle by letting you play the game directly within your browser. When you enter the game, you always get the current copy of the game to play, eliminating the version hassles described earlier. And when you leave the game's Web page, the game is gone, which minimizes its impact on your computer's hard drive.

➤ **You get to play them sooner** Because browser-based games tend to be much smaller than their installable brethren, they take much less time to download. This benefit can be a Godsend because nothing is more painful than waiting two hours to download a game that you don't like or, worse yet, one that doesn't install properly.

➤ **They're simpler to play** Some games have 20 or more commands or keys that you have to learn to play them effectively, whereas browser-based games typically have simple commands that you can learn in a few minutes. When you combine this with their fast download times, it's easy to try out four or five different browser-based games in a single surfing session.

➤ **Keep your browser and plug-ins current** To build the best games possible, developers of browser-based games take advantage of the best technology that the Internet has to offer. To see and hear the games the way their developers intended, try to keep your browser and associated plug-ins as current as possible.

To help you with this, most game sites tell you with which browser software their games work best. In addition to an up-to-date browser, you can expect browser-based game sites to call on your current version of Shockwave, RealPlayer, and Windows Media Player. These and other plug-ins greatly enhance your browser's capability to display multimedia games. (Chapter 12, "Software to Tie It All Together," discusses these applications in detail and tells you where to get them.)

The Least You Need to Know

➤ Multiplayer games are a great way to meet people and have fun online.

➤ To play an online game, you must either own a multiplayer game or have downloaded a demo version.

➤ After you have the game installed, you can connect to someone running a networked game server or set up a game server yourself for others to join.

➤ If you want to play games with people you don't know, multiplayer game services are a great way to meet other gamers. These services also provide software reviews and automatic software updates of games that you already own. In addition, many of these sites offer access to games that can run directly in your browser, making it fast and easy to try out new games.

Chapter 19

Get the Picture?: Adding Your TV to the Network

In This Chapter

➤ How to watch TV on your PC

➤ Surf the Web from your TV

➤ HDTV and DVD explained

➤ WebTV benefits

It's interesting to think of the evolution of television like we think of computers, in terms of hardware and software upgrades. On the hardware side, television has gone through three major revisions, all three requiring a complete hardware upgrade:

➤ Television version 1.0 was the black-and-white behemoth that your grandparents owned. It anchored their living room and brought them *Amos and Andy* once a week. It was a sign that grandpa had a real job.

➤ Television version 2.0 was color. (When was the last time you heard someone shout, "Holy smokes! Lucille Ball is a redhead?") As with any major upgrade, new hardware was required.

➤ Television version 3.0 is HDTV, or high-definition television. HDTV provides much better resolution. As with the change to TV 2.0, HDTV requires completely new hardware.

HDTV: High Definition Television

HDTV is expected to eventually replace NTSC, the current television signaling standard. The NTSC standard defines a composite video signal with a refresh rate of 60 half-frames per second. Each frame contains 525 lines and can contain 16 million different colors.

High-definition televisions offer five times more resolution than today's NTSC televisions, as well as screens that are one-third wider than today's sets. This makes them great for watching movies recorded on DVDs. And because it's digital, the picture is free of signal noise and artifacts that can distort the picture.

To fully utilize HDTV, your favorite programs will need to be broadcast in the correct format. True HDTV broadcasts offer up to twice the resolution, as well as a new wide-screen aspect ratio, especially advantageous to movie broadcasts and artistic producers.

The audio standard for HDTV is Dolby Digital 5.1 with channel surround sound. The Dolby Digital system transmits completely separate channels for left, right, center, left surround, and right surround speakers. This creates an awesome viewing and listening experience.

We can make a similar analogy on the software side:

➤ TV Content 1.0 was delivered through the TV's VHF antenna or, more technically, "rabbit ears." It may have been so fuzzy that grandma thought every show was filmed in a snowstorm, but that didn't matter. It was new and exciting, and it led to a number of great inventions, such as the TV table.

➤ TV Content 2.0 was cable. For a monthly fee, you got many extra channels that your country cousins couldn't have. Cable television featured a number of new channels—some dedicated to movies, and some to shows without the swear words bleeped out. It revolutionized the delivery of content because users could select packages of channels that suited their needs.

➤ The 2.0 plus-pack was pay-per-view, without which you might never have been able to watch Mike Tyson bite Evander Holyfield's ear in real-time. Pay-per-view has given even more control to content providers because it allows them to charge for each program, not just each channel.

➤ Version 2.5 is digital cable, providing better-quality sound and picture.

➤ Version 2.7 is the content available through digital satellite systems. Content providers can deliver to a huge number of people, regardless of where they live.

➤ Version 3.0 is the new digital programming provided by HDTV. It gives you complete surround sound and a crisp, clear picture.

Why, Oh Why, Would You Ever Want to Watch TV on Your Computer?

Everyone remembers something dramatic he watched on TV, such as the first lunar landing or maybe a gold medal performance at the Olympic games. Chances are you weren't watching television through your computer, and it's also not likely that you had access to the Internet through your television. All that has changed; today, you can watch TV on your PC's monitor or surf the Web through your TV.

There are a few reasons you might want to watch TV on your PC monitor:

➤ If you spend a lot of time on your PC, whether you're surfing the Net or working on your home finances, it's nice to have the news (or the latest episode of *South Park*) playing in a corner of your monitor. That way, you can keep working and still be kept up to date.

➤ Instead of purchasing another television for your office, you can save some money and some space by adding TV to your PC. It might be easier to justify buying a larger monitor for your PC if you know you can watch TV on it.

➤ If you have a DVD player in your home computer, you can use it to watch movies. DVDs let you view movies with higher resolution and better sound. They also let you hop to any part of the movie and provide you with a lot of good information, such as subtitles, directors' commentaries, or background on the movie.

What You Need

Your computer is going to need a little hardware for you to watch TV on it. First and foremost, it'll need a tuner card, which enables your computer monitor to do double duty as a television screen. The card contains a TV tuner, for selecting channels and for processing your TV or video signal and passing it to the video decoder chip, and circuitry to convert the TV's video standard to your computer's video standard.

With a TV window, you can place a mini-television screen in the corner of your screen while you use your computer for other tasks. Most television boards support windowed TVs, as well as full-screen viewing, and produce TV images that are comparable to normal televisions. (Many home computers now come with television boards preinstalled.)

Look Before You Leap

If you're wondering whether your PC can handle a TV tuner card, your best option is to consult a professional. She can ensure your PC is fully capable of using a tuner card.

Selecting a Tuner Card

There are two possibilities when it comes to selecting a tuner card. You may choose to buy a single card with both tuner and graphics capability. Alternatively, you can buy a separate card for tuning and another to drive your graphics. If you're seriously into playing games, you may want to have a high-end graphics card.

Watching TV on Your Computer: Customized Television with the ATI All-Wonder-Pro

The ATI All-Wonder-Pro is a video card that allows you to watch TV on your computer. Using the ATI-TV Tuner option, you can watch TV in small or large screen areas, capture video images, and play movie files. The Tuner option also allows you to see and record closed-captioned text.

As you can see, the control panel for the Tuner option has many of the controls you'd expect, such as channel up, channel down, and volume. But that's where the similarities between this software and your TV end.

The control panel gives familiar controls to the user.

The ATI-TV lets you do many extra things that you can't do with your TV:

➤ **Scheduling** Have your ATI-TV turn on at a preset time and to a preset channel. You'll never miss your favorite show if you're anywhere near your computer. Just name the event and set the time and the channel, and the ATI-TV delivers your show to you.

Scheduling your ATI player is easier than setting your VCR.

218

➤ **Hot Words**   The ATI-TV can sort through all the words on television and, when they appear, will open to display the text. Simply enable Hot Words and then minimize ATI-TV. When the specified words appear, ATI-TV opens. You can also have ATI-TV automatically transcribe the text when the specified words occur.

Hot Words allows for intelligent searching.

➤ **Take a snapshot**   If a picture truly is worth a thousand words, your ATI-TV can save you a lot of typing. By clicking one button, you can get a snapshot of whatever is on the screen. Take a picture of Uncle Herb missing his chair at the family reunion and then email it to the whole family.

➤ **Preview channels**   Let your ATI-TV take a snapshot of all your selected channels and give you a quick look at what's on and what's not.

See what's on using preview channels.

Turning Your Computer into a VCR

Your ATI card can also act as a VCR. The controls, shown in the following figure, are simple to use and resemble standard controls on common devices. Beware of storing too much video, though, because it consumes a great deal of hard drive space. Setting the recording quality rate to medium instead of the good or best quality saves space but still provides decent playback quality.

The ATI player can become your virtual VCR.

You can also purchase a new style of VCR that has a large hard drive in it and is dedicated to enhancing your TV viewing experience. Both Replay Networks and Tivo, Inc., have released products that store programming on hard drives. They can search out, record, and store programming for viewing at a time that's more convenient for the viewer.

Why, Oh Why, Would You Ever Want to Use Your TV as a Monitor?

Computer monitors are designed for RGB (red, green, and blue) signals. Luckily, devices such as digital cameras and game systems produce video in RGB format. This allows your computer to display them with much more clarity than your television can, because your television is not designed to use RGB.

Your TV may not have the resolution that your computer monitor does (or the capability to display RGB with the clarity of your monitor), but that doesn't mean you won't occasionally want to use your TV as a monitor. Here's why:

➤ **Comfort and convenience**   Your living room couch is a great substitute for the wooden chair that sits at your office desk.

➤ **Gaming**   Even though your TV uses RGB, it's probably larger than your monitor, and your TV speakers are probably of higher quality than your computer speakers. This makes it ideal for action games.

➤ **Surfing**   Adding the Internet experience to your TV viewing can give you many more options. Whether you're looking up football statistics or emailing a friend, accessing the Internet is definitely an option that adds to your TV experience.

➤ **The TV can be an interface to your computer**   The TV is in the place where you are most likely to be when you are using your home area network. That's why many companies are using the TV to let you select options for their systems. For example, the IBM Home Director Professional Edition uses the TV to let you select a number of configuration options for your networked home.

Don't forget: Your tuner card will not be able to send sound to your TV unless it's connected to your sound card. Make sure that either an internal or an external cable runs between the two cards. Check your tuner card manual for proper installation.

Connecting Your TV to Your Computer

Connecting your TV to your computer requires that your TV's video inputs be either composite video or S-Video. If your TV supports S-Video, use it instead of composite video because the video quality will be higher.

S-Video is short for Super-Video, a technology for transmitting video signals over a cable by dividing the video information into two separate signals—one for color and the other for brightness. When sent to a television, this produces sharper images than composite video, where the video information is transmitted as a single signal over one wire. This is because televisions are designed to display separate brightness and color signals.

If you use S-Video, you have to be sure that your video or graphics card also uses S-Video, and you must also have an S-Video cable running between the TV and the stereo.

A Quick PIP Talk

Today, hundreds of channels are available to television viewers through cable, satellite, and public networks. There will surely be times when you want to watch two programs that are being televised at the same time. This is when the picture-in-picture (PIP) feature comes in handy. PIP places a smaller picture inside the larger, enabling you to watch two (or more) programs at once.

The tricky part about PIP is that you need a tuner for each picture that you see on the screen. You may have picture-in-picture functionality on your TV already, but unless you have a newer TV with two-tuner PIP, it probably uses the tuner in your VCR as the second tuning device.

Adding the output of your computer to your television allows your TV to use your computer's tuner card as a second tuner. This allows you to view your computer's desktop in a PIP screen. When you want to surf the Internet, you simply switch the PIP screen to your main screen using your remote control. When you're finished, just flip the view of your desktop back to the PIP or remove it altogether.

Remote Control of the Future: Wireless Keyboards and Mice

If you want to surf using your TV, you need some way to use your keyboard and mouse. An obvious solution is a really long keyboard cable, but a better solution would be a wireless keyboard and mouse. These wireless devices use infrared signals to communicate with your computer. The good news is that they don't have to be attached to your computer; the bad news is that they can only be six or eight feet away from the infrared base station, which has to be attached to your computer with a cable.

221

No PC Required: WebTV

Are you looking for easy access to the Internet from the comfort of your favorite living room chair and without the hassle of buying a computer? Microsoft's WebTV might be for you. It comes with many features that cater to those who don't want to spend a lot of time using a computer but want email and Internet access.

➤ WebTV enhances your TV viewing experience by giving you quick access to the channels you like the most. It also lets you check out detailed program times and descriptions on every channel for the upcoming week.

➤ WebTV has the capability to notify you of any upcoming program you want to watch. It can tell your VCR to record that show so that you can watch it at a later time.

➤ WebTV adds picture-in-picture to your TV so that you can watch TV and browse the Internet at the same time.

➤ WebTV enhances your viewing experience by creating links to related content. If more information exists on a program you're watching, WebTV places a symbol on the screen to make you aware of it.

➤ WebTV allows you to get many of the benefits that the Internet offers, such as browsing the Web, sending and receiving email, searching, chatting, finding news and information, and more.

➤ WebTV has a function called Rich E-Mail, which lets you add sound and pictures to your emails.

➤ With WebTV Plus-based Internet Receiver, you get a built-in parallel port so that you can hook up a printer and print out emails or Internet pages.

DVD and You

With all the improvements in TVs and monitors, it's only fitting that the programming delivered to them is improved as well. Meeting this challenge is DVD.

DVD, which stands for Digital Video Disc or Digital Versatile Disc, is the latest in optical disc storage technology. It's essentially a great big CD that can hold computer, audio, and video data. It has the potential to replace a number of other formats, including audio CD, videotape, laserdisc, and CD-ROM. DVD is becoming a popular format and is supported by all major electronics companies, all major computer hardware companies, and many movie and music studios.

Much like the way in which audio CDs are related to CD-ROMs, there is a similar relationship between DVD-Video and DVD-ROM. DVD-Video, which is usually called DVD, holds video programs and is played in a DVD player connected to a TV. DVD-ROM, however, holds computer data and is read by a DVD-ROM drive hooked up to a computer. Most people expect DVD-ROM to be more successful than DVD-Video; most new computers with DVD-ROM drives can also play DVD-Videos, but devices that support DVD-Videos don't support DVD-ROM.

The Least You Need to Know

➤ Watching television will never be the same. Whether you watch TV on your computer's monitor or view your computer information on your TV, you clearly won't be the same style of couch potato you used to be.

➤ With new technologies such as DVD, HDTV, and wireless keyboards and mice, you can treat yourself to a high-quality entertainment system that meets your information needs.

Chapter 20

The Song Heard 'Round the World: Adding Your Stereo to the Network

In This Chapter

➤ Learn how to play audio CDs on a computer

➤ Connect your computer to your stereo

➤ Use a computerized CD player to get playlists and lyrics for your audio CDs

➤ Record audio CDs to your hard drive

➤ Download music from the Internet

➤ Listen to live radio stations on the Internet

Computerized sound started out coming from a 2-inch piece of cardboard and plastic that sat inside your computer. The dings and whistles emanating from this poor excuse for a speaker left much to be desired.

Although the quality of computerized sound has taken a turn for the better, the impact of computers on music specifically is nothing short of earth shattering. The introduction of compact disc players into computers in the early 1990s bridged the music world and the computer world. In this chapter, we look at the state of the music world from the perspective of your computer and all the benefits that using a computer to play music can bring.

What Your Computer Needs to Play Music

To be able to play music, your computer must be equipped with the following:

➤ Sound card

➤ Speakers

➤ CD-ROM or DVD-ROM player

Sound Cards

The heart of your computer-based sound system is a sound card, which provides the connection between your speakers and the music being played by the computer. Sound cards come in several quality levels, from $50 built-onto-your-motherboard models all the way up to several hundred dollar ones that are capable of producing better sound than most people's stereos.

Many sound cards can also connect directly to a stereo, allowing the use of traditional stereo speakers and remote control on the stereo to listen to the music or sounds generated by your computer. This is a big benefit to those who play sound-rich games, or who have made the leap to watching movies on the DVD (digital video disc) player in their computer.

Two of the best sound cards available today are

➤ Creative Labs Sound Blaster Live!

➤ Diamond Multimedia Monster MX300

Creative Labs Sound Blaster Live!

The SB Live! sound card, which can be purchased for as little as $175, is an excellent sound card for gamers, capable of 3D sound if used in combination with *four or more speakers* (see the section titled "Speakers" for more information). The SB Live! creates realistic 3D sounds, adding to the wonderful 3D graphics that are common in the newest action and simulation titles.

When used with a DVD-ROM movie system, the SB Live! understands Dolby AC-3, Dolby's method for encoding sound for six-speaker systems. This provides the same 3D sound experience that has previously been possible only in high-end home theater systems.

If you really want to push the envelope, the SB Live! also offers an extensive array of digital and analog outputs, allowing connection directly between the computer and a stereo receiver. With these connections in place, your computer can *play* the music, which is in turn carried to the stereo receiver, which controls the speakers. Because it's going through a receiver, the speakers connected to the stereo can make the sound. (Whether this combination produces better sound than that coming from a good set of computer-connected speakers depends on the quality of the stereo.)

Diamond Multimedia Monster MX300

The Monster MX300, which can be purchased for as little as $100, is another truly awesome sound card. Like the SB Live!, it offers 3D sound, although with a twist: The Monster is capable of creating 3D sounds with only two speakers! Appealing primarily to gamers and those who prefer top-flight music on their PC, this sound card should be on any audiophile's short list.

Speakers

Every computer that comes with a sound card should also come with speakers. Many bargain-basement computers come with tiny speakers that aren't much better than the one that shipped with the first PC. Even if you're really short on cash, you can get very good sounding computer speakers for $50 or less.

> **Check This Out**
>
> **MX 300 Versus SB Live!**
>
> Because of the limited number of inputs and outputs on the MX300, the SB Live! may work better for those who are interested in integrating their computer with the rest of their audio/visual equipment.

Check This Out

Avoiding Monitor Distortion

Computer speakers are different from the speakers used by a traditional stereo. The magnets in traditional speakers can be quite large, and these magnets are very bad for your monitor's health. Computer speakers use special *magnetic shielding* to prevent video distortion that will eventually damage a monitor.

Although it shouldn't happen with good computer speakers, keep an eye out for monitor distortion or discoloration if you keep speakers near your monitor. If the distortion changes when you move the speakers, move the speakers far enough away from the monitor for the discoloration to disappear.

If the distortion isn't related to the speaker location, look on the monitor's front or rear panel for a *degauss* button and press it. The degauss function attempts to remove unwanted magnetism. If your monitor doesn't have a degauss function, check with a computer repair shop to determine what's wrong and whether it can be fixed.

Subwoofers

Because they usually don't have monitor-saving magnetic shielding, subwoofers *should not* sit on your desk. (And besides, the deep bass sounds provided by a subwoofer are nondirectional.) The best place to put your subwoofer is against a wall or in the corner of a room. This makes it feel like the bass sounds are emanating from the room itself! If the bass sounds harsh and *booming*, try placing the subwoofer in different parts of the room.

Computer speakers come in three different configurations:

➤ **Two speakers**   These speakers usually hook together and then run into your sound card via a single cable. Two-speaker systems produce good sound quality but, because there is no subwoofer, sound weak when playing music with a lot of bass. Likewise, the lack of a subwoofer leaves Quake's explosive reverberations sounding a little tinny.

➤ **Three speakers**   These systems have two front speakers and a subwoofer. The front speakers typically sit on your desk, one on each side of the monitor. They should be evenly spaced and pointing directly at you. Proper positioning of the speakers ensures the best stereo effects possible.

➤ **Four and more speakers**   The highest-quality products from computer speaker manufacturers closely resemble those provided by traditional speaker manufacturers. Driven largely by the capabilities of the newest sound cards, computer speaker systems can now support home theater–quality sound. With four or more speakers, you can hear your friends sneaking up from behind in a multiplayer game of Unreal, or hear planes that seem to fly around the living room in a DVD movie.

➤ **Center channel speaker**   Although not all systems include them, a center channel is used to properly position the voices coming from the actors in a DVD movie. Because it would sound weird to hear a voice from a character in a DVD movie coming from the rear speakers, the center channel usually sits as close to the monitor as possible—in fact, it should sit right on top of it. Accordingly, the center channel speaker should be magnetically shielded.

CD-ROM Player/DVD-ROM Player

Because most software is now sold in CD-ROM format, you probably already have a CD-ROM drive for installing new applications and games.

CD-ROM players come in many different speeds. The speeds used to identify the CD-ROMs are made in reference to the speed of the original CD players. For example, a 12-speed CD-ROM can read data from a compact disc 12 times as fast as the original CD-ROMs could. Although the speed of your CD-ROM has an impact on how long it takes to install software, it has no effect on how well your audio CDs play.

DVD-ROM is a new format of optical disk, capable of storing many times as much information as a regular CD-ROM. Like a regular CD-ROM, they can also play music CDs. DVD-ROMs are discussed in detail in Chapter 19, "Get the Picture?: Adding Your TV to the Network."

Playing Audio Compact Discs on Your Computer

Most modern operating systems come with audio CD player software built in. For example, Microsoft Windows 95/98 includes software called, appropriately enough, CD Player. To open CD Player, click the **Start** button, choose **Programs**, and select **Accessories**. (Depending on your version of Windows, you may have to open the Entertainment folder in the Accessories menu.)

Although the Windows CD Player provides the basic requirements for a computerized CD player, it isn't Internet enabled. That is, CD Player doesn't take advantage of the fact that it's on a computer attached to the Internet! The two biggest benefits of using Internet-enabled CD players are

➤ **Access to playlists** Although there is a table of contents (commonly called a *playlist*) on an audio CD, the only information it contains is the number of songs on the CD and how long each of those songs is. Wouldn't it be great to see the artist and title of each song on the CD? That way, changing songs is as simple as clicking the name of the song you want, rather than wondering if, for instance, track 4 is the one with that special song on it.

Fortunately, most computerized CD players let you type all the track information for the CD in the player, but who wants to type in all those CD playlists? Thankfully, the Internet provides access to a world of incredibly smart people with too much time on their hands. Several years ago, a group of music mavens created an Internet database for the submission, storage, and retrieval of music playlists. This database, called the compact disc database (CDDB for short), can be queried for playlists by computerized CD players that support CDDB.

➤ **Lyric lists** The only thing worse than hearing somebody sing a song badly is hearing him sing the wrong lyrics badly. With an Internet-enabled CD player, downloading lyrics for songs is as simple as clicking a button.

CD Player Software: CDmax

If your operating system doesn't come with audio CD player software, or if you're not satisfied with the player you have, don't worry; you can probably find software available for download over the Internet.

Although hundreds of computer CD players are available for every operating system from the download section of `www.cddb.com`, CDmax is one of the best for users of Windows PCs (and did I mention that it's free?). To ensure that you get the most current copy, pick it up from the source at `http://www.mindspring.com/~clark_tisdale/CDmax`.

CDmax offers two simple methods for downloading playlists:

➤ On-demand queries

➤ Auto queries

To perform an on-demand query, do the following:

1. Connect to the Internet.
2. Insert the CD into the CD-ROM player.
3. Select **File**, **Retrieve from CDDB**.

CDmax connects to the CDDB and retrieves the playlist for the CD (this should take only about 30 seconds on a regular modem connection). After this is complete, the artist's name appears in the lower-left corner, the title of the CD appears at the bottom, and a complete playlist becomes available in a drop-down menu in the middle of the player. You can change music selections by clicking the drop-down menu.

If you are lucky enough to have a computer that is always connected to the Internet, you can use CDmax's auto query feature. This enables CDmax to automatically connect to the CDDB every time a CD is inserted into the player. To configure CDmax to use this function, choose **Edit**, **Options**, and select the **Auto Query CDDB** check box.

CDmax displays the artist's name and the CD name as well as the names of all the songs on an audio CD.

After the playlist has been downloaded, CDmax can be used to select and sort songs for playback. To edit the playlist, do the following:

1. Select **Edit**, **Contents**, and click the **Playlist** tab.
2. In the Tracks Available pane, click a song that you want to play in this session and then click the **Add** button to move it to the Playlist pane. Repeat this step until all the songs you want to hear are listed in the Playlist pane.
3. Change the order in which the songs will be played by left-clicking a song and dragging it to whichever position you prefer. When you're finished, click OK.

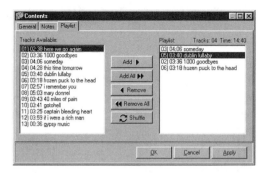

The CDmax Playlist editor lets you select which songs to play, in any order you want.

4. To get the lyrics for a song, choose **Help**, **Web Search**.

5. In the www.lyrics.ch tab of the Web Search dialog box, enter the artist, disc, and track name for the song whose lyrics you want and click **Search**.

CDmax lets you easily look up the lyrics in the Internet lyric database.

6. The `www.lyrics.ch` Web site opens, presenting the lyrics you requested.

MP3

CDs are great. The sound from them is crisp and clean. The size of a CD and the shape of the case make them easy to store, sort, and find. Right? Wrong!

Audio CD music is digital information, plain and simple—it just happens to be musical information. And because it's information, it can be saved, backed up, and downloaded just like any other information.

Think of it: If you could somehow store the songs in your CD collection on your hard drive, you could search and sort them the way you would any other type of file. Your music files could be organized by name, artist, or genre. And if you stored your music on your home area network, you could develop playlists that span your entire music collection.

Sound like a pipe dream? Guess again. In fact, several different methods were developed to do just this, but they all resulted in extremely large files—on the order of 50MB each. It doesn't take a rocket scientist to know that it's difficult to save many songs with sizes like these. So not only did somebody need to find a way to copy songs to a hard drive, but he would also need to find a way to *compress* songs into less space. And thus, MP3 was created.

231

Acronymania

Usually the expansion of an acronym tells you something about it, but not in this case. MP3 is short for MPEG1—Layer 3. Don't worry about going one level deeper because Motion Picture Expert Group 1—Layer 3 probably helps even less.

MP3 is the most common format for storing audio CDs on computers or other electronic devices. In response to the space problem, MP3 compresses sound files to around 12:1, reducing the size of an audio file from 50 or 60MB to 4 or 5MB each. Because a typical computer hard drive is now between 6 and 10GB, the MP3 format results in a much more tolerable file size.

Creating MP3s from Your Audio CD Collection: MusicMatch

To play music directly from a hard drive, your audio CD collection must first be converted from audio format to MP3 format. One of the best pieces of software for doing this is a shareware utility called MusicMatch. Available at www.musicmatch.com for only $29.99, it can be used to convert and catalog an entire audio CD collection on your home area network.

MusicMatch lets you record, play, and manage all your MP3 audio files.

After MusicMatch is installed, do the following to convert an audio CD to MP3:

1. Put a CD into your CD-ROM player.

2. Click the **Recorder** button on MusicMatch's screen.

3. To make it easier to choose which songs to *rip* (see the Check This Out), click the CDDB button to download the playlist for this CD. (Because you need to connect with the CDDB to do so, make sure that you are connected to the Internet first.)

Buzzword Watch: Ripping

Ripping is the Internet jargon used to describe the process of converting an audio CD to MP3. When you want to save an audio CD to your hard drive, you *rip* it.

4. After the playlist is downloaded, click the boxes to the left of the song titles to select which ones to rip.

5. Click the **Start** button in the Record From CD box in the upper-right corner.

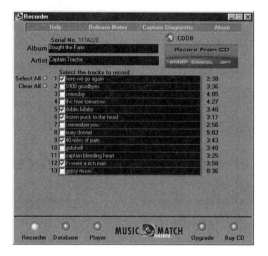

MusicMatch lets you rip select songs from your audio CDs.

6. After the ripping begins, you'll see progress indicators beside each song as it is being copied to your hard drive.

7. After the songs are ripped, click the **Database** button in the Recorder screen to see them. MusicMatch has excellent database listings for all songs stored, tracking title, genre, tempo, or mood and making it easier to select songs for playback later.

Song Storage

The default location for the storage of songs is the Music subfolder underneath the MusicMatch folder.

Not All CD-ROMS Support Ripping

If you're having problems ripping a CD, check out http://www.mp3.com/cdrom.html to see whether your CD-ROM supports ripping. Not all CD-ROMs do.

WinAmp: A Standalone MP3 Player

Nullsoft started the MP3 revolution in 1997 when it released a piece of software called WinAmp. Approximately 8 million copies of WinAmp have since been downloaded from its Web site, www.winamp.com, making it by far the most popular standalone MP3 player in the world. WinAmp is available for Windows 95/98/NT.

One big reason for WinAmp's unbelievable popularity is its attractive interface. It offers a wealth of visualization options, including a highly configurable graphics equalizer.

WinAmp lets you organize and play MP3 files that you've downloaded over the Internet.

Like MusicMatch, WinAmp can be used to create playlists from the MP3s you have stored on your hard drive. To organize a playlist, do the following:

1. Open the playlist editor by clicking the **PL** button in the lower-right corner of the WinAmp player.

2. After the playlist editor is open, you can click the **+File** button to add songs using a familiar Windows dialog box, or you can drag and drop files or folders into the playlist from Windows Explorer.

Credit Where Credit Is Due

If you want to see one of the hidden treasures of the Internet, take a look at the WinAmp credit screen. To do this, click the menu icon in the upper-left corner of the WinAmp player, select the WinAmp menu, and click the Credits tab. Make sure that you read the whole list. Trust me, you won't be disappointed.

Organize playlists by dragging and dropping MP3s into the WinAmp playlist editor.

Finding MP3 Files on the Internet

As you begin your first forays through the world of online MP3s, remember that they are still 5MB apiece. If you are using a regular modem, you'll be lucky to get four or five in a night.

The best place to start looking is the Links page in WinAmp. To view this page, click the menu icon in the upper-left corner of the WinAmp window, select the **WinAmp** menu, and click the **Links** tab. This page is periodically updated, so click the **Update Links** button to see whether there any new sites worth looking into.

Going Live: Streaming Internet Music

At this point, you're probably thinking you have two choices: You can either spend all night downloading MP3 files or all night ripping your CDs. If you are the kind of person who prefers to order in rather than make pizza yourself, you're probably wishing there was a way to play music without having to spend so much time getting ready to do so. You're in luck!

Fortunately, another side of the Internet entertainment scene is dedicated to listening to live songs, comedy, sports, and news. And by live, I mean just that. No downloads, no ripping, just click and crank up the speakers. Live Internet sound is known as *streaming*, because the sound *streams* directly to the computer without requiring a download. To listen to the majority of streaming sound available on the Internet, download and install any of the following sound software:

Are MP3s Legal?

All indications are that the creation of MP3s from a private CD collection is perfectly legal, as long as the music files aren't distributed to others. If they are used for your own personal listening enjoyment, everything should be okay.

On the other hand, it seems clear that people who swap MP3s for fun and profit over the Internet are bending copyright laws more than the Record Industry Association of America (RIAA) would like. The RIAA has threatened to file more than a few lawsuits against people deemed to be illegally distributing music over the Internet.

Don't take this to mean that it is illegal to download MP3s. It means that it's legal to download MP3s only from sites allowed to distribute them online. To get their music out, many artists and distribution companies give MP3 samples of music away for free. Others legally sell their own music on the Internet without going through a record distribution company.

➤ **WinAmp** In addition to being capable of playing locally stored MP3 files, WinAmp can also play MP3s that are *shoutcasted* over the Internet. Shoutcasting is the cool word that Nullsoft uses to describe streaming music. To get a list of shoutcast sites, go to www.shoutcast.com.

➤ **RealPlayer** Available for free from www.real.com, RealPlayer has a simple-to-use interface that includes a Presets menu loaded with almost every type of Internet radio station that you can imagine. Some of these radio stations are traditional stations that also transmit their programming over the Internet, whereas others transmit over the Internet exclusively. RealPlayer is available for Windows 95/98/NT, as well as for UNIX and Macintosh platforms.

RealPlayer gives you instant access to thousands of different radio stations on the Internet.

Find a Station

If you can't find the type of station you like, look no farther than www.broadcast.com. The collection and categorization of Internet sound sites is its sole mission in life.

➤ **Windows Media Player** Shipping as part of Microsoft Windows, the Windows Media Player also supports MP3s and RealPlayer files. If you're using Windows 98, you can access the Windows Media Player by clicking the **Start** button and choosing **Programs**, **Accessories**, **Entertainment**, **Windows Media Player**. (You'd think that something this important would be closer to the top of the menus.) Because it has been upgraded a few times since Windows 98 hit the shelves, make sure to get the most current copy of Windows Media Player from http://www.microsoft.com/windows/mediaplayer.

The Windows Media Player is another great streaming audio program.

Find Media Player Links

Point your browser back to www.broadcast.com. In addition to being a great site for RealPlayer, broadcast.com offers many links to sites created for Windows Media Player.

The Least You Need to Know

➤ Modern multimedia sound can sound as good as or better than a stereo.

➤ Some sound cards have outputs for connecting directly to a traditional stereo.

➤ A computer-based CD player can download playlists and lyrics while it plays audio CDs.

➤ Convert audio CDs to MP3 format for organized playback off a computer.

➤ Streaming Internet radio stations let you listen to music without having to download it first.

Ruling the Roost: Home Automation

John is a father of four active children. They constantly leave lights on around the house, not to mention the TV and the stereo. After John gets the troops to bed, he's exhausted. He stops by an LED panel on the wall on his way to bed and presses one button. All the basement and first floor lights go off, as do the TV and the stereo.

Bob and Brenda are always on the go. They love their dog Chico, even though they have to leave him at home once in awhile. Bob and Brenda have key chain remotes that open their garage door and control the outside lights. They have a motion sensor that turns on the TV for Chico as he passes by it. It keeps him entertained.

Mary is a senior citizen who lives on her own. She likes to have a clear, well-lit hallway when she wakes up at night. A remote control sits by Mary's bedside. With a lamp module attached to her bedroom lamp and a dimmer switch for the hallway, Mary can turn on the lights before she gets out of bed.

Home Automation: Making Life Easier

Home automation was dreamed up by a Scottish firm, Pico Electronics Ltd. It developed the first commercially available modules to control lights and appliances through existing electrical wiring in the late 1970s. Since then, many companies have come up with a wide array of devices that have lead to steady growth in the home automation industry.

Home automation appeals to the couch potato in all of us. Like the remote control for your TV, home automation tools let you handle routine chores with ease. They allow you to perform common, repetitive tasks more easily and on your own schedule. Home automation solves problems of inconvenience.

With home automation, you won't have to hike around the house to turn off every light, TV, and appliance at the end of the day. Wherever you are in your home, automation lets you control your environment with simple, easy to use devices. (And hey, wouldn't it be nice to turn off all the lights in the house and in the garage with one switch?)

Think of all the things you could do with home automation! Any device that is turned on or off with electricity can most likely be turned on or off on a schedule that you set.

➤ With home automation, you can start the coffeemaker, turn up the temperature, and maybe heat your towel rack to that oh-so-perfect temperature, all before your alarm clock goes off. This is great for people who want to take the difficult parts out of the morning.

➤ How about watering your lawn on a schedule, or even starting your car on those cold winter mornings?

➤ Swimming pools and hot tubs require a great deal of care and maintenance on a regular schedule. Your pool filter pumps can be scheduled to run during off-peak hours and after the water cycling is complete.

With home automation, you can set up your home appliances to respond to certain events:

➤ When motion is detected in a room, you may want the lights to turn on.

➤ When your smoke alarm detects a fire, you may want lighted paths to the exits.

➤ How about turning on your outdoor Christmas lights at dusk?

➤ Older folks could use an emergency button to get help fast.

If you're the only one at home, you may want to set the air conditioning, lighting, and music to your liking. Wouldn't it be great if you could adjust all of them with the touch of a single button?

Not only can you use home automation while you're at home, but you also can set up your house to respond to commands from afar. Running late? Call ahead and fire up your hot tub, turn on your PC, turn up the thermostat, or start the oven.

Home automation means many things to many people. You can completely automate your home with integrated audio, video, and security, or you can set up home automation to perform only simple tasks, such as turning on a few lights and appliances with a central controller.

The Home Automation Tools at Your Disposal

Most home automation devices utilize the electrical wiring that you already have in your house. A home automation device is an electrical unit into which you plug your lamp, TV, or stereo cord; this unit, in turn, is plugged into an electrical outlet. After a device is hooked up, you need only adjust a few settings to make it work. You can purchase multiple home automation devices individually, or you can buy a home automation kit that takes the guesswork out of automating your home.

What's It Going to Cost Me?

Some people have spent as much as $20,000 on fully automated homes, but don't let that intimidate you! For as little as $150, you can automate many of the routine functions in your house.

The basic tools used to automate your home networking arsenal include the following:

➤ **Transceiver**   The transceiver is the quarterback of your system, relaying commands to all your modules.

➤ **Lamp modules**   Setting lights to on, off, or dim is easy with lamp modules. You usually have a number of lamp modules in your home—one for each lamp—that are all controlled with one or more macros (groups of controls).

➤ **Appliance modules**   Similar to lamp modules, these devices let you control standard devices such as stereos or TVs.

➤ **Remote control**   A remote control is used to send commands to your transceiver and can often be used to control your TV and stereo (allowing you to use one remote instead of many).

➤ **Key chain remotes**   Often used from your car, a key chain remote enables you to do things such as turn on the lights in your home using a macro.

➤ **Motion sensor**   Usually used to turn your lights on and off, a motion sensor can add safety to your home.

➤ **Dimmer switches**   Used for controlling overhead lighting and fans, dimmer switches allow you local or remote control. They look exactly like standard dimmer switches, which makes your home automation less visible.

➤ **Computer interface**   Software has been created that allows you to perform many home tasks using your home computer.

X10 and Home Automation

Home automation devices talk and listen using a communications protocol called X10. X10 uses commands such as on, off, and dim to control appliances in your home. Your electrical system doesn't interfere with the commands because they are sent at a different frequency than the one used to power your appliances.

How It Works

A device called a transceiver sends signals through the electrical system to modules; these signals instruct lights, televisions, and so on to turn off or on. The transceiver plugs into an electrical outlet and is usually a box about the size of a Walkman. It can be controlled through the dials on its front, through commands coming from a remote control, or through your personal computer.

A module is named using two codes—its house code and its unit code. For example, a module used to control a lamp could have a network name of B2, where B is its house code and 2 is its unit number. The transceiver would send an off signal destined for B2, and the lamp would be turned off.

There are 16 possible house codes (A–P) and 16 unit codes (1–16). This gives you 256 possible modules to use on your home network. A macro, or group of commands, can be named with a house and unit code as well, allowing you control of a number of modules.

After you've taken the plunge and decided to automate your home, consider the following:

➤ Make sure that anything you implement is easy to use by any member of the family.

➤ You may not live in your house forever. Implement solutions that you can remove if you want to.

➤ Try to choose components that can run independently. For example, you don't want a motion sensor to be rendered inactive just because your computer crashes.

➤ Add a few components at a time. Home automation is perfect for those who want to add incrementally. You can test each device before assimilating it into your family's everyday life.

➤ Try changing the devices you already have to work in different configurations.

➤ Watch for new and innovative devices. A speaker that plays the sound of a dog barking is an easy addition to the automated home. In addition, voice-activated devices are becoming more popular all the time.

The PC at the Center of the Networked Home

With all the electrical appliances in your house, it only makes sense to control them from one central point. There are many reasons why your home computer is the natural choice:

➤ It has an operating system that can support software that can be constantly upgraded.

➤ You're used to working with it.

➤ It's already near an electrical outlet in your house.

➤ You don't need to buy another interface.

ActiveHome

Fortunately, any number of companies manufacture software for home automation. One of the leading suppliers in North America is X-10, Inc., which distributes software called ActiveHome.

ActiveHome, which can be downloaded as freeware from www.x-10.com, allows you to control all the devices in your home from your home PC. You can add as many devices as you want and then "model" them onscreen. For example, suppose that you've configured ActiveHome to control your outdoor lights, bathroom lamp, TV, and stereo. In this case, all these devices would be represented by a module on the screen. (Notice that the bottom box on each device module has a label that contains the house and unit code for that device. For example, the TV Set module is set to house code B and unit code 1.)

Notice the module labeled Goodnight. It is listed as a *macro* and is called VirtualWiring to let you know that it doesn't represent an actual device but instead represents a series of commands. To take a closer look at this macro, click **Macro** on the toolbar and then select **Edit Macro**. This presents you with all the macros that you currently have configured in your house. They can be run on a set schedule, by remote control, or even by a message from a sunlight sensor. You can see that whenever the macro is run, it accomplishes a number of things:

➤ The bathroom lamp, using code A2, is turned off (set to 0%).

➤ The outdoor lights, using code A1, are turned on.

➤ The TV set, on B1, is turned off.

➤ The stereo, on B2, is turned off.

ActiveHome devices are designed for ease of use.

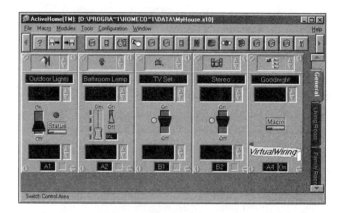

A macro allows you to do many things with just one click.

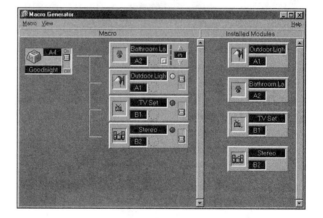

ActiveHome also allows you to see what codes are in use on your system. To do so, open the Housecode Test screen. A green light indicates that a device or a macro in your home uses a particular code, whereas a red light indicates that the code is in use elsewhere. Some codes may be affected by interference and are therefore codes to avoid (signified by a yellow light).

ActiveHome also allows you to view the times when the devices in your home are in use. To do this, select **Tools** on the toolbar and then select **Statistics**. This gives you the times and dates that your macros and timed events were activated. To plot usage, simply click the **Plot** button.

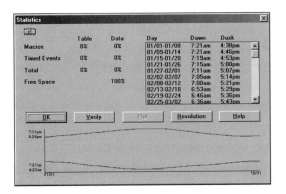

Measuring usage of your home appliances is now a snap.

Limitations of Home Automation Today

The biggest limitation of traditional home automation is caused by the lack of available commands. Your TV needs to know that you want to turn down the volume or change the channel. This is difficult when the only commands you have to work with are on, off, dim, and so on.

The second limitation of X-10 is that devices cannot communicate with each other. Modules are only meant to receive commands, not issue them. If the lamp could communicate with the central controller and pass along a note that said "My bulb is burnt out," the controller could notify you at work that you need to pick up a bulb on the way home. Hopefully, new products will allow this in the future.

X-10 networks also occasionally fail. A power surge in the home can cause the X-10 system to become useless, leaving you to (gasp!) turn off all your lights one at a time. (Unthinkable, I know.)

Your home automation project can also be affected by your neighbor's home automation project. For example, the power lines that connect your houses together might transmit your X-10 signals to your neighbor's home. If your neighbor has an X-10 system like yours, consider buying a X-10 signal filter to prevent you from turning off his TV in the middle of Jay Leno.

The Least You Need to Know

➤ Home automation can add convenience and control to your home life, letting you manage your household from a distance.

➤ Whether you're down the hallway or downtown, you can have complete control over your home.

➤ Home automation ensures that appliances like lights and televisions turn on when you want them to.

➤ Using home automation, you can specify that tasks be performed on a fixed schedule or in response to a household event.

➤ Using your PC to control your home has many advantages.

Chapter 22

Safe and Sound: Home Security

In This Chapter

➤ The home security tools available to you

➤ Safety is as important as security

➤ Your computer at the center of your home security network

➤ Securing your garage and your vehicles

Planning a home security network requires knowledge of how a burglar enters a home. The data collected from a Pennsylvania study as reported by the National Burglar and Fire Alarm Association gives the following numbers:

34% of burglars entered through the front door

23% through a first-floor window

22% through the back door

9% through the garage

4% through the basement

4% through an unlocked entrance

2% through a storage area

2% anywhere on the second floor

With this information in hand, you know that you should focus on the first-floor doors and windows, along with the garage. But in addition to threats from burglars, natural events such as fires, floods, and freezes can place you and your home in jeopardy. Thankfully, there are any number of tools on the market that can help keep you and yours safe and sound. And to keep you sane, you can set up your security system to utilize your home network!

The Home Safety Tools at Your Disposal

Like any network, a home security network utilizes the combined strength of many simple devices. Understanding how each device works gives you a basis for planning an effective network. Although some of the tools for a home security system are the same as you'd find in a home automation kit, they are usually wireless for added protection:

➤ **Central controller** The system's brain. It controls alarm, monitoring, and programming functions and communication. It could be your personal computer, or it could be a device that is attached to your personal computer. A discussion of the advantages of using your home PC can be found later in this chapter.

➤ **Door/window sensors** These are usually used to trigger alarms on doors and windows but can be mounted on anything that opens and closes. They consist of two components that protect your home from intruders: a magnet that detects the opening of the door/window and a transmitter that sends signals to the control panel. When the magnet is moved away from the transmitter, the transmitter sends a signal to the central controller, which sets off an alarm.

➤ **Glass break sensor** These add protection by detecting when a burglar has broken the glass of a door or a window. Glass break sensors are best used on windows with nonmovable panes or on glass cases that display valuable items (such as your home networking books).

➤ **Motion detector** These offer additional protection for large open spaces with unprotected hallways or multiple windows. You have probably seen motion detectors used outdoors, but they are probably more effective indoors because more false alarms occur outdoors. Remember to mount motion sensors on stable walls where they face a solid reference point. Don't aim them at heating vents or air conditioners because they may be triggered inadvertently.

➤ **Lamp/appliance modules** These receive signals to turn on and off lamps and appliances, which allows you to come home to a lighted house. As with home automation, you need to set the house and unit codes on these devices before they can be used. To use a lamp/appliance module, perform the following steps:

1. Turn on the lamp or appliance.

2. Unplug the lamp or appliance and plug the appliance into the module.

3. Plug the module into the wall socket.

4. Your central controller should now be able to turn on the light or appliance.

➤ **Remote controls**   Usually activated with a P.I.N. (personal identification number), a remote control is used to operate most of the functionality you have set up with your central controller. You can input the unit code numbers of the appliance modules in your home to turn them on and off. All programmed modules can be controlled as a group or individually.

➤ **Hand/keychain remotes**   These convenient devices perform some of the functions of your remote control. Keychain remotes usually control lamps and have panic, arm, and disarm buttons. They usually have a range of about 100 feet, which makes them useful for protecting you when you are walking from your car to your house.

➤ **Remote power sirens**   These can deliver a high-pitched blast or even a dog's bark. They are typically set up like appliance modules—you simply set the house and unit codes to the appropriate numbers and plug them into an electrical socket.

A burglar isn't the only threat to you and your family. Fires, floods, and freezing can be as dangerous as any intruder. Sensors provide an excellent way of notifying you of impending danger:

➤ **Carbon monoxide sensors**   These can be used to protect your family from the deadly effects of carbon monoxide. High levels of carbon monoxide can cause sickness and death if undetected. Faulty appliances and fires can produce carbon monoxide, which is difficult to detect because it is odorless; fatalities due to carbon monoxide poisoning frequently occur at night.

➤ **Flood sensors**   These are usually placed in the basement and are usually connected to your security system to activate an audible alarm on the control panel, which alerts you to rising water levels.

➤ **Freeze sensors**   Freezing conditions can burst pipes and cause a lot of damage to your home at times when help may not be able to reach you. Add freeze sensors to your security system to generate a control panel alarm if low temperatures threaten to damage your property. You can then adjust heating accordingly.

➤ **Smoke sensors**   Smoke sensors with self-contained siren alarms are essential for alerting you before a fire gets too large. A good smoke sensor should be able to signal your central controller, which can then create a lit path to safety.

All these home security products can be purchased from reputable home automation and home security companies. We recommend Honeywell Home Control products (see www.honeywell.com/HomeControl) and X-10 products (found at www.x-10.com/products).

Networked to the Outside World: Monitoring Services

Monitoring services can be critical to the success of your home security system. As with car alarms, people tend to ignore the sound of a home alarm. Likewise, if you are home but unable to call the police, you may not be able to receive police assistance in a dangerous situation.

Monitoring services give you 'round-the-clock monitoring, 365 days a year. A good example of a company that provides monitoring services is Protection One Alarm Monitoring, Inc. (www.protectionone.com). In addition to providing monitoring services, Protection One offers additional services such as Response One, which sends a Protection One officer to your home who can then alert the police if necessary.

Here's how the Response One system works:

1. When an alarm in your home is triggered, a signal is sent to a Protection One call center.
2. If you can't be reached, a Protection One armed officer is dispatched.
3. The officer arrives at your home and, if necessary, contacts the police.
4. When the police arrive, the Protection One officer informs the police of the situation and remains onsite until the situation is resolved.

Most monitoring services, including Protection One, call the police when the following things occur:

➤ No one answers when the home is called.
➤ No one gives the correct password.
➤ An answering machine answers the call.
➤ The line is busy.

After alerting the police, the central monitoring facility usually calls your office, your neighbor, a family member, your mobile phone, your pager, or any numbers that you specify on your call list.

24/7

Remember to use a monitoring service that provides 24-hour-a-day service.

The PC at the Center of Your Home Security System

A networked home security system that uses a PC as its central controller (or uses a central controller attached to the PC) has many advantages over traditional systems with simple control panels:

➤ You can control hundreds of lights and appliances as opposed to just a few.

➤ Lights and appliances can be turned on and off relative to sunrise and sunset.

➤ A PC can adjust for seasonal changes, such as daylight savings time.

➤ A PC can usually be configured to create protected areas inside or outside your home. For example, you may want the security system to be turned off inside your house but still have it working outside your home.

➤ A motion sensor aided by your home computer can signal your system to chime when you're home and blare when you're gone.

➤ Instead of spurring an alarm, you can configure a sensor to turn on your lights in particular rooms of the house when you enter them.

➤ How about capturing the moment with sound and video? When a burglar breaks your window, you could have your computer record video and sound in your home.

➤ Your PC can be used to enable your remote control and keychain remotes. Macros can be created that allow certain lighting configurations at the touch of a button.

To Attach or Not to Attach?

We advocate using a central controller that is attached to your PC (as opposed to relying solely on your PC). This allows the home security system to remain working when your house is without power.

Protecting Your Home: Honeywell Home Control

A good example of a central controller that you can use in conjunction with your computer is Honeywell Home Control. To use this system, you need at least a 486/66 PC running Windows 95, Windows NT 4.0, or higher. It should have a CD-ROM drive, VGA monitor, 20MB of disk space, at least 8MB of RAM, and a free serial port. You can find this product at your local Sears store, or on the Internet at www.honeywell.com/HomeControl.

The Honeywell Home Control system gives you any number of security options, including

➤ Comfort patterns

➤ A latchkey function

➤ Event scheduling

➤ Sensor activation or deactivation

This system does not come with a professional monitoring service, but it can accommodate four telephone numbers for delivery of voice messages to local phones, long distance phones, cell phones, or pagers. Two numbers are used to announce emergency alarms (intrusion, smoke, or pushbutton emergency), and two numbers are used for notifications (latchkey overdue situation, freeze or flood condition, and power failure).

The Honeywell Home Control has a simple, easy-to-use interface.

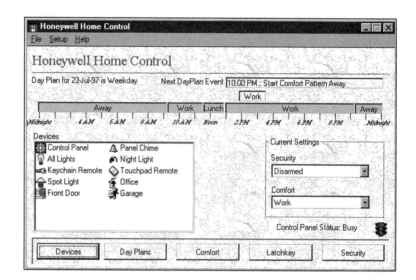

Comfort Patterns

You can use Honeywell Home Control's Comfort Patterns option to change the lighting configuration of your home. A *Comfort Pattern* contains a set of commands to turn lights on or off or to dim them to a certain level at a certain time or as a result of a sensor being tripped. For example, you could set your system to turn on lights just before you arrive home from work or when it's time for you to wake up.

To change the Comfort Pattern, do the following:

1. Click the **Comfort** button on the main Honeywell Home Control screen.

2. The Select Comfort Pattern dialog box appears, displaying a list of Comfort Patterns. Select **All Lights On** in the Comfort Pattern list, and then click the **Edit** button.

252

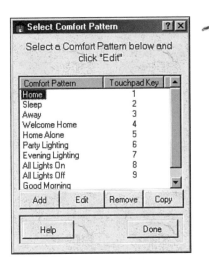

After a Comfort Pattern is set, you only have to spend a few moments to select it.

3. The Edit Comfort Pattern dialog box opens, showing the **All Lights On** Comfort Pattern. The bottom window shows the events that cause this Comfort Pattern to occur. As you can see, opening and closing the front and back doors causes all the lights in the house to come on.

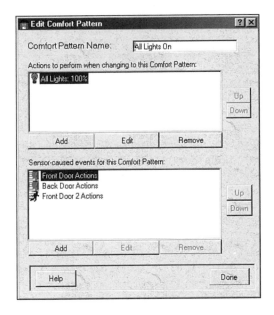

Editing the Comfort Pattern gives you control over the events that lead to an action in your home.

The Latchkey Function

When the Honeywell Home Control's Latchkey option is activated, the system automatically calls two preprogrammed phone numbers if it has not been disarmed by a specified time (no alarm or siren is sounded). This notifies you that your children have not arrived home from school as expected.

As you can see, adding names and numbers is easy:

1. Click the **Latchkey** button in the main Honeywell Home Control screen.

2. Add the appropriate names and telephone numbers.

3. Click OK.

The Latchkey system notifies friends or neighbors if your child hasn't come home.

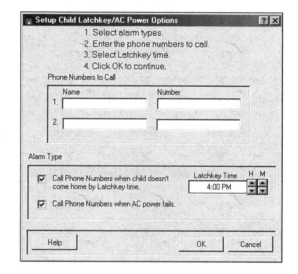

In addition to using the Latchkey function to keep track of your little ones, you can use it to notify you if your AC power fails. Simply check the **Call Phone Numbers when AC Power Fails** check box near the bottom of the dialog box.

Event Scheduling

In the Honeywell Home Control's main screen, you see a clock (it looks like a timeline) that can be used to turn a light, appliance, or Comfort Pattern on or off on a fixed schedule that is repeated each day.

If you don't want such a rigid schedule, click the **Day Plan** button and use the Edit Day Plans screen to

➤ Set different schedules for different days.

➤ Calculate the correct sunrise and sunset times for your area and schedule the activation or deactivation of lights or appliances relative to sunrise or sunset.

➤ Adjust for daylight savings time.

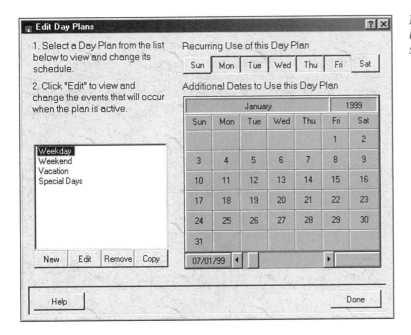

Now you can get your home working on your schedule.

Sensor Activation and Deactivation

All sensors fall into one of three alarm categories:

➤ Twenty-four-hour sensors go off whether Honeywell Home Control is armed or not. This sensor category is for safety sensors such as smoke, freeze, flood, and carbon monoxide sensors; these sensors always cause an alarm if they detect an unsafe condition.

➤ Perimeter sensors protect the outside of the house and are typically the sensors on the doors and windows.

➤ Interior sensors protect the inside of the house and are used to turn on lights when a person enters the room.

With Honeywell's Home Control system, you can specify whether your door/window and motion sensors fall under the Perimeter, Interior, or 24-Hour category. This allows for the selective arming of certain sensors, such as those that protect a shop or gun cabinet, while leaving other sensors unarmed. To selectively arm certain sensors, do the following:

1. Click the **Security** button in the Honeywell Home Control main screen.

255

2. Drag the icon for the sensor whose category you want to change to the category you want.

3. Click OK.

Allocating sensors to different locations allows for faster use.

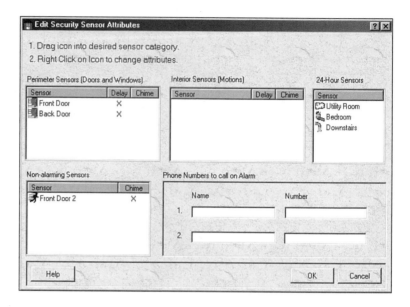

Check This Out

On PC Crashes and Power Outages

Most security systems are designed so that if the PC fails or power goes out, the system's capability to sound an alarm and make notification telephone calls will not be affected. However, all the PC-performed changes and Comfort Pattern changes will no longer operate.

Protecting Your Garage and Car

Thieves tend to like your garage. They want to get in there either to steal your car or, more likely, to access your house. If they park a van in your garage and shut the door, they can fill it with your belongings without being seen. Securing your garage and your vehicle inside it is a must.

Securing Your Garage

Although it's not directly connected to your PC, your garage door opener is, in effect, a part of your home network, to the extent that it is an electronic device that you use to secure your home. The part you hold in your hand is a transmitter, and the part in your garage is a receiver. Unfortunately, thieves can use this device against you. Using a radio receiver (such as a scanner), they record the transmission from your garage door opener when you leave in the morning or when you return in the afternoon. This gives them the "keys to your garage," and if your garage has a door opening to your house, they also have the "keys to your home."

With a simple device, you can create an effective barrier. Plug your garage door opener (the part inside your garage that physically opens the door) into a timer that controls power, similar to the one you may already use for your Christmas lights. Then set the timer to provide power during the times when you are likely to be leaving or entering your garage. The thieves won't be able to open the garage door during the times when it doesn't have power.

Alternatively, you could have an appliance module control the power for you. You could then put the appliance module on the same schedule as you did previously, but now using your home computer. Even better, have your keyless remote provide a signal to both the appliance module and the garage door opener. This would ensure that your system would receive power only when you are there.

Protecting Your Car

That keyless entry system that you use to open your doors and trunk is, in fact, a network. The handheld door opener sends a signal to a receiver in your car, which opens the door. But as with any network, it's not impenetrable.

3COM Palm Pilots, those nifty handheld devices that you can use to record appointments, have been found to serve another purpose: to copy the signal of infrared keys for cars. The Palm Pilot is then used to replay the signal when the owner of the car is not around, opening the doors instantly.

Fortunately, most cars that have a wireless key entry use a radio frequency to transmit the code, not an infrared signal. Check with your car manufacturer if you aren't sure whether your keyless entry system is susceptible to this type of attack.

The Least You Need to Know

➤ Whether for your house or your garage, many appliances are available for excellent protection.

➤ Whether security or safety is your primary concern, you're much better off having a home security network than standalone pieces.

➤ As the Honeywell Home Control security system illustrates, you have many more options available to you when you use a personal computer to assist you.

Chapter 23

Judy Jetson Eat Your Heart Out!: The Home Area Network of the Future

In This Chapter

➤ Why everyone will have his own computer

➤ How computer networks will show up in almost every home

➤ How networks add value to your home entertainment experience

➤ How smart homes learn what you need and give it to you before you ask for it

➤ Why the best home network is one that you don't even know is there

The preceding 22 chapters have looked at the *here and now* of home area networking. All the ideas, concepts, and products are tried and true, and the products discussed are available for sale.

This, the final chapter, discusses some uses for home networks that are not yet possible, and for which there are not yet products. Although these ideas may seem futuristic, all are under development by companies today.

Home Computers

Almost one half of all new computers sold go to homes that already have a computer. Look for this trend to continue as parents buy themselves and their children new computers over time. Although the cost of an entry-level computer is in the $750–$1200 range today, $500 computers will soon make it cost effective for every member of the home to have his or her own computer.

At the higher end, look for stereo-quality sound and movie-quality video to come directly to you from your PC. Monitors will get both larger and thinner as liquid crystal diode (LCD) technology makes it possible to hang a 21-inch monitor on your wall. If that isn't sexy enough, fashion-conscious computer manufacturers will make your current computer box look like an Edsel within a few years. Designer colors and cases, combined with the less obtrusive monitors, will prompt people to move computers out of offices and basements into the primary living area.

Software

As software manufacturers try to take advantage of networks wherever possible, connectivity will be the name of the game in all new software. Automatic updates and bug fixes, as well as notification of new software offerings, are but a few of the possibilities.

As more members of the household get their own computers, the growth of computer networks will be staggering. Because the average homebuyer will be far less tolerant than corporate network administrators, software to connect and manage home networks will become easier to install and use.

Home Computer Networks

Ethernet is a preferred method of wiring computer networks. Unfortunately, it is expensive to lay ethernet cable in an existing house. Look for ethernet networks to become a common option in middle and upper market houses. Rooms that can be used to support the cabling and hubs associated with the cable will of course be part of the package.

Phone line and wireless home networks are positioned to come on strong as the connection methods of choice in existing homes. Both are excellent options because they don't require any new cabling. Although there currently are limitations with the bandwidth available from phone line, wireless, and power line networks, these limitations will disappear as new technologies are introduced, upgrading them to full 10Mbps and beyond.

Connecting to the Outside World

As more services and products come to rely on networks, a connection between the home area network and the outside world will be essential. Even if your home doesn't have a computer, other devices in your home will want to take advantage of a connection. As more Web sites start specializing in high-bandwidth content (www.onbroadband.com for example), the average connection speed that people expect from their ISPs will continue to increase.

Deregulation in the telecommunications industry is driving every home network connection provider to try to take over your communications needs. Cable companies want to offer phone and Internet services, telephone companies will serve video, and power companies want to provide you with an Internet connection. Although there will be no shortage of choices, the combination of available bandwidth, market penetration, and a steady stream of content indicates that cable companies will be a major power in connecting homes to the Internet at high speed.

Television and Video

Don't think that computers and the Internet will be the only things to take advantage of home area networks. Wireless and wireline networks are being developed that will connect VCRs, DVDs, stereos, and TVs into a *home entertainment network*.

This will reduce not only clutter but also the number of copycat entertainment devices that homes tend to collect. For example, many homes have two or three TVs as well as two or three VCRs. Why shouldn't the VCR or DVD player down in the basement be able to play a movie on the TV upstairs?

Music

Tighter integration between the computer, the Internet, and the other components in your home network will make it much easier to store, catalog, search for, and play the music in your personal music collection. As for building that collection, music sold over the Internet will become commonplace. Once purchased, it will be easy to download and add that music to your collection, particularly if you have a high-speed connection to the Internet.

If you still feel attached to plastic CDs, you'll just *burn* the music files onto a rewritable CD or DVD on your home computer. Although CDs will continue to be created in raw audio format (the way they are today), traditional stereo CD player manufacturers will support MP3-formatted music as well.

Don't think you'll be cut out of the Internet sound revolution if downloading and paying for music isn't your cup of tea. In addition to traditional broadcasts, most radio stations will *webcast* their programs over the Internet as well. Although the majority of music will still be delivered over the airwaves, many radio stations will transmit their music and other content exclusively over the Internet.

Traditional broadcasting requires expensive equipment and many people to support it. This implies that the programming coming from traditional radio stations will continue to conform to what is expected of them by their sponsors. Webcasted radio stations, on the other hand, can be set up for a fraction of the cost, giving their programmers greater freedom to select their own content. This personal slant toward a specific type of programming will push people to the Internet to find radio stations that play exactly *what* they want to hear, *when* they want to hear it.

261

Webster's Update: Burn

The process of saving information onto a writable compact disc is known as *burning*. For instance, if you wanted to save 300MB of songs that you had purchased over the Internet, you'd say, "I need to *burn* these songs onto a CD."

Contrast this with *ripping*, which is the process of converting audio CD files to MP3 format. This lets you download music from the Internet, save the music onto a CD in MP3 format, and then play it on a regular music CD player.

Although it might sound silly to take music from the Internet and put it back onto a CD, don't forget that MP3-formatted music is about 1/10 the size of a raw audio file. This means that instead of fitting 10 or 15 songs on a CD, you could fit 100 or 150 songs on a single CD! Who would bother to buy a bulky CD changer if they could fit six hours of music onto a CD?

Home Offices

The line between home and office will continue to blur in the next millennium. In many cases, the technical capabilities of home offices will exceed those of corporate offices. This, as well as many other factors outside the scope of this book, will enable more people to work out of their homes than ever before—but with a twist. Integration of the home office with a well-laid-out home network will make home office life much better than life at the corporate office:

➤ Cable and ADSL modems give home workers more usable bandwidth than can be expected from corporate offices.

➤ Inexpensive teleconferencing and videoconferencing equipment will let home workers keep in touch with headquarters like never before.

➤ Corporations' increased use of the Internet as a communications tool will ensure that those outside the main office are seldom out of the loop.

Home Automation and Security

Home automation has been given a bad rap in the past few years—companies have provided solutions where problems didn't necessarily exist. Rows of switches on your countertop to replace all the light switches on your walls weren't always seen as particularly helpful.

Home automation will mature, as will the companies selling it. The focus will shift to doing things that make your life easier and more secure. As well, major networking initiatives from Microsoft (Universal Plug and Play) and Sun Microsystems (Jini) will make it simple for you to install networked devices in the home yourself:

➤ A 3 a.m. doorbell or phone ring does something to that part of your brain that knows where the light switch is. Hallways that light themselves at such times would provide a real service.

➤ Smart appliances that perform tasks on schedule or upon a certain event would add real value for homeowners. For instance, a stove that turns itself off if there is nothing in it for an hour would be wonderful. There's nothing worse than the terrified look on the face of someone who just realized that the oven has been on since last night's casserole came out.

➤ Thermostats and lights that know when somebody is at the office, puttering around the house, or lying in bed will save a great deal of money in heating and electrical bills.

Taken to its natural conclusion, every device in your house that has power will be capable of being a networked device. Whether you want it to be or, more importantly, whether you are willing to pay for it will depend on how much value that device being networked adds to your life.

Personal and Adaptable Living Spaces

As the intelligence of networked homes grows, so-called *smart homes* will do much more than acknowledge your passing. They will monitor not only that you came into the room but also what you did while you were there: which TV shows you watched, what type of music you liked to listen to, how you had the light and temperature set while you relaxed in certain chairs, as well as which Web sites you visited at certain times of day. All this information will be logged by your home network and used as the default settings for you while you are in the room.

The Incredible Disappearing Network

As a victim of its own success, the best home networks will not intrude into your life at all. There won't be any cables snaking across the floor or any bulky monitors cluttering up your desk. Whether the music you're listening to is coming from a CD, from an MP3 file on the family server, or across the Internet will seem like a silly question to ask—because it won't matter.

The computers and networks will disappear as they become embedded in everything electrical in your house and get ushered into back closets. Controlling them will be done with wireless keyboards, remote controls, or voice commands. Seeing what they do will be done on your HDTV or via wall-mounted monitors in every room.

The process of networking equipment will also become invisible to the homeowner as devices automatically report themselves to the home network when they get plugged into the wall. After a device is permitted by your home network, it will join in without a hitch.

A *Star Trek* world is still a few years away, but we're closing in fast. All the pieces are in place; all you need is a little motivation to make it happen.

Straight ahead, Mr. Sulu. Warp factor 2.

The Least You Need to Know

➤ Home networks don't have to be expensive.

➤ Home networks should be installable by the average computer owner.

➤ Home networks will eventually touch everything in your house that has power.

➤ Home networks should add value to your life.

Part 6

Just when you thought you knew all there was to know about home networking, here we go adding more! Here you'll find a glossary of home networking terms (so you can sound like a pro), a list of Internet resources that'll come in handy as you connect the machines in your house, and some info on high-speed Internet service providers.

Speak Like a Geek: Networking Words

10BASE-2   Coaxial (thinwire) ethernet capable of transmitting to distances of 600 feet.

100BASE-T   Fast (100Mbps) ethernet, supporting various cabling schemes and capable of transmitting a distance of some 205 meters.

active hub   An active hub is one that has intelligence built into it (for example, to make it error tolerant). See also *hub*.

adapter   A hardware device used to connect devices to a motherboard. In networking context, an ethernet adapter/card.

ADSL   See *Asymmetric Digital Subscriber Line*.

analog system   This term is generally used to describe the telephone system, which uses analog technology to convert voice to electronic signals. Many telephones in modern office systems are *digital*, which means that if you plug your modem into the jack, you risk damage to the modem.

application layer   Layer 7 of the OSI reference model, the highest layer of the model. The application layer defines how applications interact over the network. This is the layer of communication that occurs (and is conspicuous) at the user level. (For example, the File Transfer Protocol interfaces with the user at the application layer, but routing occurs at layer 3, the network layer.)

ARPAnet   Advanced Research Projects Agency Network. This was the original Internet, which, for many years, was controlled by the Department of Defense.

ASCII   American Standard Code for Information Interchange. ASCII is a common standard by which many operating systems treat simple text.

Asymmetric Digital Subscriber Line (ADSL)   A high-speed digital telephone technology that's fast when downloading (nearly 6Mbps) but much slower uploading (about 65Kbps). Unfortunately, ADSL is a new technology that's available only in major metropolitan areas.

attachment unit interface (AUI)   A 15-pin twisted-pair ethernet connection or connector.

attribute   The state of a given resource (whether file or directory), as well as whether that resource is readable, hidden, system, or other.

AUI   See *attachment unit interface*.

back door   A hidden program, left behind by an intruder (or perhaps a disgruntled employee), that allows him or her future access to a victim host. This term is synonymous with *trap door*.

back up   To preserve a file system or files, usually for disaster recovery. Generally, a backup is done to tape, floppy disk, or other portable media that can be safely stored for later use.

backbone   The fastest and most centralized feed on your network. The heart of your network to which all other systems are connected.

bandwidth   The transmission capacity of your network medium, measured in bits per second.

baseband   Audio and video signals sent over coaxial cable, typically used in cable television transmissions. In particular, the signals are sent without frequency shifting of the wave. (The *BASE* in 10BASE-T refers to this type of signal.)

broadband   A very high-speed data transmission system, capable of supporting large transfers of media such as sound, video, and other data. Unlike baseband, broadband can use several different frequencies.

broadcast/broadcasting   Any network message sent to all network hosts. Also, the practice of sending such a message.

Browser Cache   A feature of Internet Explorer and Netscape Navigator designed to make surfing the Internet faster. By storing snapshots of a Web page when it is first visited, subsequent visits to the Web page are able to load faster.

bug   A hole or weakness in a computer program. See also *vulnerability*.

burn   The process of copying files from a computer's hard drive to a compact disk. A read/write or rewritable CD player is required in order to burn a compact disk.

cable modem A modem that negotiates Internet access over cable television networks. (Cable modems provide blazing speeds.)

Cache See *Browser Cache*.

client Software designed to interact with a specific server application. For example, WWW browsers such as Netscape Communicator and Internet Explorer are WWW clients. They are specifically designed to interact with Web or HTTP servers.

COM port A serial communications port, sometimes used to connect modems (and even mice).

common gateway interface (CGI) A standard that specifies programming techniques through which you pass data from Web servers to Web clients. (CGI is language neutral. You can write CGI programs in Perl, C, C++, Python, Visual Basic, and many other programming languages.)

compression The technique of reducing data size for the purposes of maximizing resource utilization (for example, bandwidth or disk space). The smaller the data, the less bandwidth or disk space you need for it.

convergence See *Digital Convergence*.

cracker Someone who, with malicious intent, unlawfully breaches security of computer systems or software. Some folks say *hacker* when they actually mean *cracker*.

data link layer Layer 2 of the OSI reference model. This layer defines the rules for sending and receiving information between network devices.

Digital Convergence As radio, television, VCRs, DVDs, and other communications and information devices begin to transmit information in formats accessible to computers, a coming together or *convergence* of technologies will result. The addition of the computer will allow all of these technologies to be managed from a single interactive interface.

domain name service (DNS) A networked system that translates Internet host names (for example, `traderights.pacificnet.net`) into numeric IP addresses (for example, `207.171.0.111`).

encryption The process of scrambling data so that it's unreadable by unauthorized parties. In most encryption schemes, you must have a password to reassemble the data into readable form. Encryption is primarily used to enhance privacy or to protect classified, secret, or top-secret information. (For example, many military and satellite transmissions are encrypted to prevent spies or hostile nations from analyzing them.)

ethernet A local area network (LAN) networking technology that connects computers and transmits data between them. Data is packaged into frames and sent via wires.

fiber-optic cable   An extremely fast network cable that transmits data using light rather than electricity. Most commonly used for backbones.

file server   A computer that serves as a centralized source for files.

File Transfer Protocol (FTP)   A protocol used to transfer files from one TCP/IP host to another.

filtering   The process of examining network packets for integrity and security. Filtering is typically an automated process, performed by either firewalls, routers, or software.

firewall   A device that controls access between two networks according to source and destination addresses and ports.

FTP   See *File Transfer Protocol.*

full duplex transmission   Any transmission in which data is transmitted in both directions simultaneously.

Gigabit Ethernet   Very Fast (1000Mbps) Ethernet, supporting various cabling schemes. Typically used for backbone networks.

hacker   Someone interested in operating systems, software, security, and the Internet in general. This is the original (and correct) definition from the good old days when hackers were the good guys. Also called a *programmer.*

hardware address   The fixed physical address of a network adapter. Hardware addresses are just about always hard-coded into the network adapter.

hole   See *vulnerability.*

home area network   A collection of devices joined in such a way as to enhance education, entertainment, control, and security of the home.

home network   A collection of devices joined in such a way as to enhance education, entertainment, control and security of the home.

home PC network   Two or more home computers connected together by a computer network. Home PC networks form the heart of a home area network and are typically set up to share files, printers, and Internet connections.

host   A computer that offers services to users, especially on a TCP/IP network. Also refers to older mainframe computers.

hub   A hardware device that allows the sharing of a network segment by repeating signals between ports. (Like the spokes of a wheel, a hub allows many network wires to converge at one point.)

hypertext   A text display format commonly used on Web pages. Hypertext is distinct from regular text because it's interactive. In a hypertext document, when you click or choose any highlighted word, other associated text appears. This allows for powerful cross-referencing and permits users to navigate an entire set of documents easily.

Hypertext Markup Language (HTML)   The formatting commands and rules that define a hypertext document. Web pages are written in the HTML format.

Hypertext Transfer Protocol (HTTP)   The protocol used to traffic hypertext across the Internet. It's also the underlying protocol of the WWW.

ICQ   Pronounced "I Seek You," ICQ is one of the most popular instant messaging tools on the Internet. With the use of personally defined "buddy lists," ICQ can notify you when someone on your buddy list logs on or off of the Internet. Whether online or offline, ICQ lets you send them messages and more at your leisure.

Integrated Services Digital Network (ISDN)   Digital telephone service that offers data transfer rates upward of 128Kbps.

Interactive Mail Access Protocol (IMAP3)   A protocol that allows workstations to access Internet electronic mail from centralized servers.

Internet   Specifically, the conglomeration of interconnected computer networks—connected via fiber, leased lines, and dial-up—that support TCP/IP. Less generally, any computer network that supports TCP/IP and is interconnected, as in an *internet*. Usually, a local internet is referred to as an *intranet*.

Internet Protocol (IP)   The network layer of TCP/IP; the method of transporting data across the Internet.

Internetworking   The practice of using networks that run standard Internet protocols.

InterNIC   The Internet Network Information Center, located at www.internic.net.

Interrupt Request Line   A method used by Intel-based computers to allow peripherals prioritized access to the computer's CPU. There are 16 different interrupt levels on a modern computer, with the lowest IRQ number getting the highest priority access to the CPU. All IRQ numbers except 10, 11, 12, and 15 are preassigned.

intranet   A private network that utilizes Internet technologies.

intrusion detection   The practice of using automated systems to detect intrusion attempts. Intrusion detection typically involves intelligent systems or agents.

IP address   A numeric Internet address, such as 207.171.0.111.

IP spoofing   Any procedure where an attacker assumes another host's IP address to gain unauthorized access to the target.

IP   See *Internet Protocol.*

IRQ   See *Interrupt Request Line.*

ISDN   See *Integrated Services Digital Network.*

ISP   Internet service provider.

Java   A network programming language created by Sun Microsystems.

Jini   A technology developed by Sun Microsystems to make it easier to create network-aware devices. Jini-compliant devices can be added to a network simply by connecting it to the network.

LAN   See *local area network.*

Linux   A free UNIX clone that runs on widely disparate architecture, including *x*86 (Intel), Alpha, Sparc, Motorola, and PowerPC processors. Linux is becoming increasingly popular as a Web server platform.

local area network (LAN)   LANs are small, ethernet-based networks.

megabyte   1,048,576 bytes. (Abbreviated as *MB.*)

modem   A device that converts (modulates) signals that the computer understands into signals that can be accurately be transmitted over phone lines or other media. A modem can also convert the signals back (demodulate) into their original form.

MP3   MPEG 1 - Layer 3 is the most common format for transferring compressed music over the Internet. MP3 files are compressed between 10 and 12 times smaller than a CD audio file.

MPEG   Motion Picture Expert Group. A standard for compressing video images. MPEG compressed video can be viewed using either software or hardware MPEG decoders.

multiplayer game   A computer game that permits more than one person to take part in the game play. Depending on the game, players can compete against each other as individuals or join teams to play against other teams.

multiplayer game services   Web sites that make the process of setting up and joining multiplayer games easier. Some sites charge a fee for this service, while others are free.

network interface card (NIC)   An adapter card that lets the computer attach to a network cable.

network layer   Layer 3 of the OSI reference model. This layer provides the routing information for data, opens and closes paths for the data to travel, and ensures that the data reaches its destination.

Network News Transfer Protocol (NNTP) The protocol that controls the transmission of Usenet news messages.

network operating system (NOS) An operating system for networks, such as NetWare or Windows NT.

NIC See *network interface card.*

NNTP See *Network News Transfer Protocol.*

NOS See *network operating system.*

OSI reference model Open Systems Interconnection reference model. A seven-layer model of data communications protocols that make up the architecture of a network.

owner The person, username, or process with privileges to read, write, or otherwise access a given file, directory, or process.

packet Data sent over a network is broken into manageable chunks called *packets* or *frames*. The size is determined by the protocol used.

PALS See *Personal Adaptable Living Spaces.*

Parental Control Software Software designed to monitor and control the activities of children while using a computer. Primarily meant to control access to Web sites through the use of predefined or user-defined lists of objectionable sites.

Personal Adaptable Living Spaces Computerized agents that monitor and customize a living environment based upon the past use of that environment.

Personal Digital Assistant Small computers capable of being carried in a pocket or briefcase. Typically used for referring to address book and email without the hassle of a full size laptop or computer.

peripheral component interface (PCI) An interface used for expansion slots in PCs and Macintosh computers. PCI slots are where you plug in new adapter cards, including ethernet adapters, disk controller cards, and video cards (to name a few).

Phoneline Network A communications network that connects computers in a home over existing phonelines. The use of the phoneline network should not interfere with the use of telephones or ADSL modems.

physical layer Layer 1 of the OSI reference model. This layer deals with hardware connections and transmissions and is the only layer that involves the physical transfer of data from system to system.

Point-to-Point Protocol (PPP) A communications protocol used between machines that support serial interfaces, such as modems. PPP is commonly used to provide and access dial-up services to Internet service providers.

273

Post Office Protocol (POP3)   A protocol that allows workstations to download and upload Internet electronic mail from centralized servers.

powerline network   A communications network that connects computers in a home through standard power outlets. The use of the powerline network should not interfere with the use of electrical appliances.

PPP   See *Point-to-Point Protocol.*

presentation layer   Layer 6 of the OSI reference model. This layer manages the protocols of the operating system, formatting data for display, encryption, and translation of characters.

protocol   A standardized set of rules that govern communication or the way that data is transmitted.

protocol stack   A hierarchy of protocols used in data transport, usually arranged in a collection called a *suite* (such as the TCP/IP suite). The actual programs used to implement a protocol stack are colloquially called a "stack" as well (for example, the Microsoft TCP/IP stack).

proxy server   A server that makes application requests on behalf of a client and relays results back to the client. Often used for a simple firewall; routing domains are typically different. See also *application gateway.*

read access   When a user has read access, he or she has privileges to read a particular file.

RealPlayer   A popular browser plug-in that is used to listen to music and watch video played over the Internet. Available from www.real.com.

rip   The process of converting an audio CD to MP3 format and copying it onto a computer's hard drive.

router   A device that routes packets in and out of a network. Many routers are sophisticated and can serve as firewalls.

Scanner   A device similar to a photocopier that can create computer-readable files from paper-based text or graphics.

session layer   Layer 5 of the OSI reference model. This layer handles the coordination of communication between systems, maintains sessions for as long as needed, and handles security, logging, and administrative functions.

sharing   The process of allowing users on other machines to access files and directories on your own. File sharing is a fairly typical activity within local area networks and can sometimes be a security risk.

Shockwave   A popular browser plug-in that can be used to play animation, games, and music over the Internet. Available from www.macromedia.com.

Simple Mail Transfer Protocol (SMTP)   The Internet's most commonly used electronic mail protocol.

SMTP   See *Simple Mail Transfer Protocol.*

stack   See *protocol stack.*

suite   A term used to describe a collection of similar protocols. This term is used primarily when describing TCP- and IP-based protocols (when talking about the "TCP/IP suite").

TCP/IP   Transmission Control Protocol/Internet Protocol. The protocols used by the Internet.

terminator   A small plug that attaches to the end of a segment of coaxial ethernet cable. This plug provides a resistor to keep the signal within specifications.

topology   The method or systems by which your network is physically laid out. For example, ethernet and token-ring are both network topologies, as are "star" versus "bus" wiring. The former is a network topology; the latter is a physical topology.

transceiver   An essential part of a network interface card (NIC) that connects the network cable to the card. Most 10BASE-T cards have them built in.

transport layer   Layer 4 of the OSI reference model. This layer controls the movement of data between systems, defines the protocols for messages, and does error checking.

trojan horse   An application or code that, unbeknownst to the user, performs surreptitious and unauthorized tasks that can compromise system security. (Also referred to as a *Trojan.*)

Tuner Card   See *TV Tuner Card.*

twisted pair   A cable made up of one or more pairs of wires that are twisted to improve their electrical performance.

TV Tuner Card   An adapter card that allows cable TV and VCR signals to be viewed on a computer monitor.

Universal Plug and Play   An initiative under development by Microsoft for defining the interfaces and software drivers for easy to configure network devices.

UTP   Unshielded twisted pair. See also *10BASE-T.*

virus   A self-replicating or propagating program (sometimes malicious) that attaches itself to other executables, drivers, or document templates, thus "infecting" the target host or file.

vulnerability   This term refers to any weakness in any system (either hardware or software) that allows intruders to gain unauthorized access or deny service.

X10   A network protocol for communicating simple commands such as "on," "off," and "dim" over a household powerline network. X10 is typically used to control light switches, furnace thermostats and other common household devices connected to a home network.

Winamp   Software used to play MP3-formatted music. The most popular MP3 player on the Internet. Available from `www.winamp.com`.

Wireless Adapter   A network interface card that connects to a wireless base station. Used to create a home network that links computers using radio signals rather than wires.

Wireless Base Station   A radio transmitter and receiver that connects to a wireless adapter in a computer. Used to create a home network that links computers using radio signals rather than wires.

write access   When a user has write access, he or she has privileges to write to a particular file.

Online References for Home Area Networking

The world of home area networking is growing and changing at an alarming rate. This book is filled with the best information available at the time of printing. Unfortunately (or fortunately), developments in home networking hold still for no man, woman, beast, or book.

This appendix provides a list of Web sites to broaden and deepen your understanding of home networking and the companies that are driving its adoption.

Web Address	Company or Group
Home Networking Information	
www.2mn8.com	2MN8, Inc.
www.pcweek.com	ZDNet
www.pcmag.com	ZDNet
Phone Line Products	
www.tutsys.com	Tut Systems, Inc.
www.diamondmm.com	Diamond Multimedia, Inc.
www.actiontec.com	ActionTec Electronics, Inc.
www.epigram.com	Epigram
Wireless Products	
www.proxim.com	Proxim
www.webgear.com	WebGear, Inc.
www.diamondmm.com	Diamond Multimedia
www.intellon.com	Intellon Corporation
www.sharewave.com	Sharewave, Inc.

continues

Web Address	Company or Group
Power Line Networking	
www.intelogis.com	Intelogis
Component Manufacturers	
www.intel.com	Intel
www.national.com	National Semiconductor, Inc.
www.amd.com	Advanced Micro Devices
www.ti.com	Texas Instruments
Computer Manufacturers	
www.compaq.com/athome/homenetwork	Compaq
www.sony.com	Sony
Organizations	
www.cemacity.org	Consumer Electronics Manufacturers Association
www.homepna.org	Home Phoneline Networking Alliance
www.homerf.org	Home Radio Frequency Working Group
Ethernet Products	
www.cisco.com	Cisco
www.3com.com	3Com
www.pc.ibm.com/us/homedirector/	IBM
www.hp.com	Hewlett-Packard
Networking Software	
www.sun.com	Sun Microsystems
www.microsoft.com	Microsoft
www.netscape.com	Netscape
www.winproxy.com	Ositis Software
www.wingate.com	Deerfield Communications
www.applica.com	Concurrent Controls, Inc.
International ISPs	
www.compuserve.com	CompuServe
www.aol.com	America Online
Digital Cameras	
www.kodak.com	Kodak
www.olympus.com	Olympus

Web Address	Company or Group
Digital Cameras	
www.creativelabs.com	Creative Labs
www.logitech.com	Logitech
www.intel.com	Intel
www.connectix.com	Connectix
www.fonecam.com	FoneCam
www.alaris.com	Alaris
Speech Recognition	
www.dragonsystems.com	Dragon Systems
www.ibm.com	IBM
www.microsoft.com	Microsoft
Backups and Storage	
www.iomega.com	Iomega
www.sony.com	Sony
www.telebackup.com	Telebackup
Compression Utilities	
www.winzip.com	Winzip
Audio/Video/Graphics	
www.real.com	Real Networks
www.winamp.com	NullSoft
www.microsoft.com	Microsoft
www.macromedia.com	Macromedia
www.shockrave.com	Macromedia
www.musicmatch.com	MusicMatch
www.cddb.com	CDDB, Inc.
www.mp3.com	MP3.com, Inc.
www.diamondmm.com	Diamond Multimedia
www.replay.com	Replay Networks
www.tivo.com	TiVo, Inc.
www.onbroadband.com	Comcast
Online Chat and Collaboration	
www.icq.com	ICQ, Inc.
www.microsoft.com	Microsoft

continues

279

Web Address	Company or Group
File Transfer Utilities	
www.ftpserv-u.com	Deerfield Communications, Inc.
Antivirus Software	
www.mcafee.com	Network Associates
www.symantec.com	Symantec
Home Office	
www.microsoft.com	Microsoft
www.symantec.com	Symantec
www.hotoffice.com	HotOffice
Multiplayer Gaming	
www.computershopper.com	ZDNet
www.shopping.com	Shopping.com
www.softseek.com	SoftSeek, Inc.
www.download.com	Cnet
www.hasbro.com	Hasbro
www.zone.com	Microsoft
www.games.yahoo.com	Yahoo!
www.bonus.com	The Bonus Network
www.quake2.com	id Software
www.heat.net	SegaSoft
www.kali.net	Kali, Inc.
www.mplayer.com	Mpath Interactive
www.igl.net	IGL Enterprises
www.unreal.com	Epic MegaGames, Inc.
Home Automation and Security	
www.x-10.com	X-10, Inc.
www.ibm.com	IBM
www.homeautomatedliving.com	Home Automated Living, LLC
www.honeywell.com	Honeywell
www.leviton.com	Leviton Manufacturing Company, Inc.

High-Speed Internet Service Providers

Many Web sites are providing content that requires a high-speed connection. Multimegabyte home pages require much more speed than a 56KB modem can deliver. If you feel the need for speed, this appendix is for you. It provides a comprehensive list of Internet service providers (ISPs) that can handle truly high-speed connections.

To search for this information online, check out www.2mn8.com/highspeed for a graphical, up-to-the-minute list of high-speed ISPs.

Cable Modems

With speeds in the megabytes per second and available at only $30–$50 per month, cable modems are positioned as a premier contender for providing high-speed Internet access to the home in the next century. Table C.1, published in *Cable Datacom News* on February 1, 1999, by Kinetic Strategies, Inc., and found online at www.ispchannel.com, outlines cable modem providers.

Table C.1 Commercial Cable Modem Launches in North America

Cable MSO/ Telco	Location	Vendor/Service Provider	Deployment Notes
21st Century	Chicago, IL	Zenith	Two-way cable Internet service commercially available for $44.95/month, includes unlimited access and cable modem rental
Adelphia Cable	Coudersport, PA Plymouth, MA North Adams, MA Toms River, NJ Pittsburgh, PA Philadelphia, PA Buffalo, NY	Nortel Networks	Two-way Power Link Internet service commercially available for $39.95/month, includes unlimited access and cable modem rental
Adelphia Cable	Niagara, NY Western Reserve, Ohio South Dade, FL West Boca, FL Delray Beach, FL Wellington, FL Palm Beach Gardens, FL West Palm Beach, FL Stuart, FL Burlington, VT Charlottesville, VA Waynesboro, VA Staunton, VA Winchester, VA Blacksburg, VA Hilton Head, SC	General Instrument	Telco-return Power Link service available for $34.95/month
Advanced Cable Communications	Coral Springs, FL	Com21, ISP Channel	Residential Internet service $49/month

282

Cable MSO/ Telco	Location	Vendor/Service Provider	Deployment Notes
Armstrong Cable Services	Connellsville, PA	Nortel Networks	Residential Zoom Internet Service $39.95/month for 500 Kbps downstream and 256 Kbps upstream access
Avenue Cable TV	Ventura, CA	Hybrid Networks, Internet Ventures	Offering PeRKInet telco-return cable Internet service for $29.90 per month
BellSouth	Vestavia Hills, AL	Nortel Networks	High-speed Internet access, including cable modem rental, priced at $45/month
BellSouth	Chamblee, GA	Nortel Networks	High-speed Internet access, including cable modem rental, priced at $39.95/month
Bresnan Communications	Marquette, MI	Nortel Networks	Two-way BresnanLink Internet service commercially available for $39.95/month, includes unlimited access and cable modem rental
Cable Atlantic	St. John's, Newfoundland	Zenith	Offering Road Runner and Internet access, including cable modem rental, for C$49.95/month
Cable America	Mesa, AZ	Nortel and Tonna	Two-way cable Internet service with Nortel LANcity modem $44.95 per month; telco-return $39.95 with Tonna modem
Cablecomm	Johnstown, PA	Motorola, Road Runner	Offering Road Runner and Internet access, including cable modem rental, for $39.95/month
Cable Communications Co-op	Palo Alto, CA	Com21, ISP Channel	Cable Internet service starts at $49/month for 500-Kbps downstream, 100-Kbps upstream access

continues

Table C.1   Commercial Cable Modem Launches in North America Continued

Cable MSO/ Telco	Location	Vendor/Service Provider	Deployment Notes
Cable Regina	Regina, Saskatchewan	Zenith	Cable modem rental and Internet access with up to 2GB of data transfer for C$49.95/month
Cable TV Montgomery	Montgomery County, MD	Com21	Modem rental and unlimited Internet access is $64.95/month
Cable TV Arlington	Arlington, VA	Com21	Modem rental and unlimited Internet access $64.95/month
Cablevision of Lake Havasu	Lake Havasu, AZ	3Com, ISP Channel	Residential Internet service $49/month
Cablevision of Lake Travis	Lake Travis, TX	Com21, ISP Channel	Residential Internet service $49/month
Cablevision of Loudon	Loudon County, VA	General Instrument, Com21	Commercial deployment of Pulse high-speed Internet service
Cablevision Systems	Oyster Bay, NY Westport, CT	Nortel Networks, Terayon, @Home	Unlimited Internet access and cable modem rental $44.95/month
Cable York	York, PA	Nortel Networks, 3Com, BlazeNet	$49.95 per month for two-way BlazeNet Express Internet service, including cable modem rental; telco return service $29.95/ month with purchase of 3Com modem at retail
Capital Cable	Columbia and Boone County, MO	Com21, HSA Corp.	Commercial launch of two-way cable modem service
Century Communications	Norwich, NY	Motorola	Internet service available for $39.95/month ($49.95/month for non-cable subs), customer must purchase modem for $199

Cable MSO/ Telco	Location	Vendor/Service Provider	Deployment Notes
Chambers Cable	Chico, CA	Scientific-Atlanta	Telco-return Chambers Multimedia Connection Internet service $39.95/month with $299 modem purchase
Charter Communications	St. Louis, MO	3Com, Earthlink	Telco-return Charter Pipeline Internet service available for $34.95/month including modem rental, plus a one-time installation fee of $169.
Charter Communications	Riverside, CA	General Instrument, Earthlink	Telco-return Charter Pipeline Internet service available for $29.95/month including modem rental
Charter Communications	Pasadena, CA Newtown, CT	Com21, Earthlink	Two-way Charter Pipeline Internet 256 Kbps service $35 month including modem rental; 512 Kbps service $60/month
Coast Cablevision	San Mateo, CA	Com21, ISP Channel	Residential Internet service $49/month
Coaxial Communications	Columbus, OH	General Instrument, Frontier GlobalCenter	Telco-return Internet service available for $34.95/month with purchase of modem for $279
COGECO	Ontario, Canada	Nortel Networks, Cisco, Samsung, @Home	C$39.95 for unlimited Internet access and modem rental
COGECO	Quebec, Canada	Nortel Networks	C$54.95 for unlimited Internet access and modem rental
Comcast	Baltimore, MD Sarasota, FL Union County, NJ Detroit, MI Philadelphia, PA Orange County, CA	Motorola, @Home	Residential Internet service package offers modem rental and unlimited Internet access for $39.95/month ($59.95/ month for non-cable subs) with a $175 install fee

continues

285

Table C.1   Commercial Cable Modem Launches in North America Continued

Cable MSO/ Telco	Location	Vendor/Service Provider	Deployment Notes
Comcast	Chesterfield, VA Atlanta, GA	Cisco Systems, @Home	Internet service package offers modem rental and unlimited Internet access for $39.95/month ($59.95/month for non-cable subs)
Communi-Comm Services	Durant, OK	Zenith	Basic residential Presto Internet service $39.95/month for unlimited access and modem rental; Deluxe service $44.95/month
Conway Corp.	Conway, AR	Zenith	Cable Internet service $39.95/month for unlimited access and modem rental with a $20 install fee
Cox Communications	Orange County, CA Omaha, NB Newport News, VA Oklahoma City, OK Providence, RI	Motorola, @Home	Residential Internet service priced at $44.95 per month for unlimited access and modem rental ($54.95/month for non-cable subs) with a $149 installation fee
Cox Communications	San Diego, CA	Motorola, @Home	Residential Internet service priced at $39.95 per month ($49.95/month for non-cable subs) with a $149 install fee (including Ethernet NIC)
Cox Communications	Phoenix, AZ Meriden, CT	Nortel Networks, @Home	Residential Internet service priced at $44.95 per month for unlimited access and modem rental ($54.95/month for non-cable subs) with a $175 installation fee

Cable MSO/ Telco	Location	Vendor/Service Provider	Deployment Notes
Cox Communications	Kenner and Algiers, LA	Cisco Systems, @Home	Residential Internet service priced at $44.95 per month for unlimited access and modem rental ($54.95/month for non-cable subs)
Cox Communications	Las Vegas, NV *(acquired from Prime Cable)*	Com21	Commercial deployment of ATM-based cable modem service to homes and businesses
Cox Communications	Eureka, CA	Hybrid Networks, Internet Ventures	Offering PeRKInet telco-return cable Internet service for $29.90 per month
Daniels Cablevision	Encinitas, CA	General Instrument, Frontier GlobalCenter	Telco-return I-NET Express service available for $34.95/month with purchase of modem for $279
Frontier Vision	Camden and Rockland, ME	Terayon, Maine Internetworks	Quicksilver residential Internet service starts at $39.95 per month
Fundy Communications	Moncton, New Brunswick	Scientific-Atlanta	Telco-return cable Internet service; consumers purchase modem for C$279
GCI	Anchorage, AK	Com21.	256-Kbps Internet access is $69.95 per month with $399 modem purchase at CompUSA
Genesis Cable	Winder, GA	Com21, HAS Corp.	Commercial launch of two-way Genesis Online cable modem service
GTE	Clearwater, FL	Zenith	Modem rental and unlimited Internet access $43.90/month ($54.90/month for non-cable subs) with a $125 installation fee

continues

287

Table C.1   Commercial Cable Modem Launches in North America Continued

Cable MSO/ Telco	Location	Vendor/Service Provider	Deployment Notes
GTE	Ventura, CA	Nortel Networks	Modem rental $19.95/month and Internet access $44.95/month ($59.95/month for non-cable subs)
Halifax Cable	Halifax, Nova Scotia	Com21	High-speed Internet and remote LAN access
Helicon Corp.	Uniontown, PA Barre, VT	New Media	Telco-return cable Internet service $29.95 per month ($3 discount for Helicon cable subscribers)
Hibbing Cable TV	Hibbing, MN	Com21	"The Bridge" Internet service offered with Befera Interactive Cablenet; residential service $39.95/month and basic business $69.95/month
Horizon Cable	Central Michigan	Zenith and Nortel Networks	Residential Internet access $49.90/month for 500-Kbps link
Horizon Cable	Point Reyes, CA	3Com, ISP Channel	Residential Telco-return service $49/month
InterMedia Partners	Nashville, TN	Motorola, @Home	Commercial launch of @Home service
InterMedia Partners	Greenville and Spartanburg, SC	Motorola, @Home	Commercial launch of @Home service
InterMedia Partners	Kingsport, TN	General Instrument, Online System Services	Telco-return Internet service $39.95 per month with modem rental
Jones Intercable	Alexandria, VA	Nortel Networks, @Home	Internet service $43.90/month for unlimited access and modem rental with a $125 install fee

Cable MSO/ Telco	Location	Vendor/Service Provider	Deployment Notes
Jones Intercable	Prince William County, VA	Hybrid Networks, @Home	Telco-return cable modem service
Kingwood Cable	Kingwood, TX	3Com	Cable Internet service $54.95 per month for basic cable customers
Knology Holdings	Augusta, GA Columbus, GA Charleston, SC Montgomery, AL Panama City, FL	Hybrid Networks, MindSpring	OLOBahn cable Internet service $51 per month including modem rental
Limestone Cable	Maysville, KY	Terayon, HSA Corp.	Commercial launch of two-way cable modem service
Matrix Cable	Los Gatos, CA	3Com, ISP Channel	Telco-return service $49/month
Marcus Cable	Highland Park and University Park, TX	Nortel Networks, @Home	Residential Internet service $49.95/month; modem and installation package $499
Marcus Cable	Eau Claire and Rice Lake, WI	Com21, HSA Corp.	Commercial launch of two-way cable modem service
MediaOne	Greater Boston, MA	Nortel Networks	MediaOne Express $29.95 per month with $199 modem purchase at Circuit City; modem rental and unlimited Internet access $39.95/month
MediaOne	Detroit, MI Los Angeles, CA	Nortel Networks	MediaOne Express service with modem rental and unlimited Internet access $39.95/month ($49.95/month for non-cable subs) with a $99.95 install fee

continues

289

Table C.1   Commercial Cable Modem Launches in North America Continued

Cable MSO/ Telco	Location	Vendor/Service Provider	Deployment Notes
MediaOne	Atlanta, GA Chicago, IL	Motorola	Commercial launch of MediaOne Express service; modem rental and unlimited Internet access $39.95/month ($49.95/month for non-cable subs) with a $99.95 install fee
MediaOne	Chestnut Hill, MA	Nortel Networks	Commercial deployment of HFC video and data network at Boston College; provides connection to Boston College LAN plus Internet access
MediaOne	Jacksonville, FL Broward County, FL Dade County, FL Detroit, MI	General Instrument	Telco-return MediaOne Express service priced at $34.95/month for unlimited Internet access and modem rental with $99.95 install charge
MediaOne	Minneapolis, MN St. Paul, MN Avon Lake, OH Bay Village, OH	General Instrument	Telco-return MediaOne Express service priced at $39.95/month for unlimited Internet access and modem rental with $99.95 install charge
Media General Cable	Falls Church, Vienna, and Merrifield, VA	Motorola, Road Runner	Offering Road Runner and Internet access, including cable modem rental, for $49.99/month
Metro Cable	Philadelphia, PA	Cable Web Services	Telco-return HomeStream service priced at $19.95/month for downstream cable access, any dial-up ISP can be used for upstream link

Cable MSO/ Telco	Location	Vendor/Service Provider	Deployment Notes
Midcontinent Cable	South Dakota	Nortel Networks	Modem rental and unlimited Internet access at up to 1.5 Mbps $39/month
Midwest Communications	Bemidji and Cass Lake, MN	Com21, Befera Interactive Cablenet	Modem rental and Internet access at 512 Kbps $39.95/month
Mountain Cablevision	Hamilton, Ontario	Nortel Networks	WAVE service includes modem rental and unlimited Internet access for C$59.60/month
Northern Cable	Sudbury, Ontario	3Com	Telco-return Adesso service priced at C$39.95/month for unlimited Internet access
Prestige Cable	Forsyth County, GA	Hayes, Convergence.com	Telco-return Internet service $39.95/month
Prestige Cable	Forsyth County, GA	Cisco Systems, GI Convergence.com	Two-way residential Internet service $39.95/month
Prime Cable	Chicago, IL	Com21	512-Kbps Telco-return cable modem service $39.95 per month for basic cable subscribers
Ponderosa Cable	Danville, CA	Com21, ISP Channel	Internet service $49/month
Range TV Cable	Hibbing and Chisholm, MN	Com21, Befera Interactive Cablenet	Modem rental and Internet access at 512 Kbps $39.95/month
Rankin Cable	Rankin County, MS	3Com, BlazeNet	Telco return service $29.95 per month with purchase of 3Com modem
Rifkin & Associates	Miami Beach, FL Gwinnett County, GA	Com21, Convergence.com	Cable Internet service commercially available

continues

Table C.1 Commercial Cable Modem Launches in North America Continued

Cable MSO/ Telco	Location	Vendor/Service Provider	Deployment Notes
Rifkin & Associates	Bedford, VA Cookville, TN Columbia, TN Lebanon, TN	Nortel Networks, Convergence.com	Cable Internet service commercially available
Rogers Cablesystems	Metro Toronto Metro Vancouver Ottawa	Nortel Networks, @Home	Unlimited Internet access C$39.95/month
San Bruno Municipal Cable	San Bruno, CA	Com21, ISP Channel	Residential Internet service $49/month
Service Electric and Blue Ridge Cable	Eastern Pennsylvania	Zenith and Nortel Networks	Commercial deployment of Internet services through PenTeleData alliance
Shaw Communi-cations	Calgary Toronto	Motorola, @Home	Unlimited Internet access and modem rental C$39.95/month
Shaw Communi-cations	Victoria and Toronto, Canada	Terayon, @Home	Unlimited Internet access and modem rental C$39.95/month
Suburban Cable	New Castle, DE	3Com	Modem rental and unlimited Internet access $54.95/month for cable subscribers
Sun Country Cable	Los Altos, CA	3Com, ISP Channel	Telco-return service $49/month
Sun Country Cable	Spokane, WA	Hybrid Networks, Internet Ventures	Offering PeRKInet Telco-return cable Internet service for $29 per month
TCA	Amarillo, Bryant, and College Station, TX Lafayette, LA	Terayon	Modem rental and 128-Kbps unlimited Internet access $49.95/ month; 192 Kbps $84.95; 256 Kbps $124.95

Cable MSO/ Telco	Location	Vendor/Service Provider	Deployment Notes
TCI	Alameda, CA Antioch, CA Castro Valley, CA Dublin, CA Fremont, CA Hercules, CA Livermore, CA Petaluma, CA Pinole, CA Pittsburg, CA Pleasanton, CA San Ramon, CA	Nortel Networks, Motorola, @Home	Internet service priced at $39.95 per month for unlimited Internet access and cable modem rental
TCI	Hartford, CT	Nortel Networks, @Home	Internet service priced at $39.95 per month with cable modem rental
TCI	Aurora, CO McKeesport, PA	Com21, @Home	Internet service priced at $39.95 per month with cable modem rental
TCI	Garland, McKinney, and Stonebridge, TX Arlington Heights, IL Seattle, WA	Motorola, @Home	Internet service priced at $39.95 per month with cable modem rental
TCI	Spokane, WA	3Com, @Home	Internet service requires purchase of 3Com DOCSIS modem
TCI	East Lansing, MI	Zenith and Nortel Networks	Basic TCI-MET cable Internet service $49.95 per month
Time Warner Cable	Akron, Canton, Columbus, & Youngstown, OH Binghamton, Corning, & Elmira NY San Diego, CA Tampa Bay, FL Oahu, HI Memphis, TN Austin, TX	Motorola, Road Runner	Internet service priced at $39.95 per month for unlimited access, modem rental, specialized Time Warner and local content ($44.95 in Austin)

continues

Table C.1 Commercial Cable Modem Launches in North America Continued

Cable MSO/ Telco	Location	Vendor/Service Provider	Deployment Notes
Time Warner Cable	Portland, ME El Paso, TX Albany, Troy, & Saratoga, NY	Toshiba, Road Runner	Service $39.95 per month for unlimited home access and modem rental
TW Fanch	Altoona, PA Johnstown, PA	3Com, Zenith, Convergence.com	Cable Internet service commercially available
US West Communications	Omaha, NB	Nortel Networks	Service priced at $49.95/ month for Internet access and cable modem rental ($59.95/month for non-cable subs) with a $125 installation fee
Verto Communications	Duryea, PA	Hybrid Networks	Verto.Net cable Internet service $39.95 per month for basic cable subscribers
Videotron	Montreal, Alberta	Motorola	Commercial launch of high-speed Internet services; Montreal deployment includes InfiniT content service
Videon Cable TV	Winnipeg, Manitoba	Nortel Networks	WAVE service includes modem rental and unlimited Internet access for C$54.95/month
Western Coaxial	Hamilton, Ontario	Nortel Networks	WAVE service includes modem rental and unlimited Internet access for C$55/month
Western Shore Cable	St. Mary's County and King George's County, MD	Com21, HAS Corp.	Commercial launch of two-way cable modem service
Westman Communications	Brandon, Manitoba	Nortel Networks	WAVE service includes modem rental and unlimited Internet access for C$39.95/month
WestStar	Half Moon Bay and Monterey, CA	3Com, Zenith, Convergence.com	Cable Internet service commercially available

ADSL

The following tables, which were revised as recently as January 8, 1999, by ADSL Forum (see the source information at the end of this chapter if you want to contact this forum), can help you find an ADSL provider in your area.

Don't forget that the *A* in ADSL stands for *asymmetric*. As indicated by the *up* and *down* entries in the speed column, the upload speed (sending information to the Internet) will be different from the download speed (pulling information from the Internet).

Note

This table is compiled from information obtained or derived from sources believed to be accurate (for example, company press releases, executives' speeches, and news stories), but the ADSL Forum does not guarantee the accuracy or completeness of the information nor shall it be liable for any errors in or omissions from the information or actions taken in reliance thereon.

Table C.2   ADSL Providers in the United States

Company	Availability	Speed	Applications	Trial Dates	ATM Transport	Service Deployments
Advanced Corporate Solutions (NSP) (see entry for Transport Logic)	Pacific Northwest	Down: up to 2.5 Mbps; Up: up to 1 Mbps	Internet/LAN Access, Video Streaming, Desktop Video, E-Commerce, Telecommuting	N/A		Service rolled out April 1997
Ameritech Corp. (ILEC)	Ann Arbor and Royal Oak, MI	Down: up to 6.0Mbps; Up: 684Kbps	Internet/LAN Access	N/A	Yes	Limited rollout in Ann Arbor in Dec. 1997; to be expanded to
Ameritech and IBM	Wheaton, IL (Chicago)	Down: 1.5 Mbps; Up: 64Kbps	Internet/LAN Access	Concept Trial: Oct. 96 to Apr. 1997 (closed)		Chicago area mid-1998; plans to make ADSL available to 70% of customers by year 2000
AUSNet Services, Inc. (NSP/ISP)	Portland, OR	Down: 2.6-7; Up 92-972 Kbps or 972 in both directions	Internet/LAN Access			Feb. 1997

continues

Table C.2   ADSL Providers in the United States
Continued

Company	Availability	Speed	Applications	Trial Dates	ATM Transport	Service Deployments
Avalon Networks, Inc. (ISP)	Iowa City, IA	Down: Exceeding 1Mbps; Up: 64Kbps	Internet/ LAN Access	Market Trial: Nov 97- March 98		Began offering commercial service in March 1998
Bay Junction Technology, Inc. (ISP)	San Jose, CA	Down: 1.5 Mbps	Internet/ LAN Access	N/A		December 1997 rollout
Branch Internet Services (ISP)	Ann Arbor, MI	Down: Up to 2MB; Up: 1Mbps	Internet/ LAN Access, Desktop Videoconf.	June 1- July 15, 1997		Aug. 1997
Cincinnati Bell	Northern Kentucky and Southeastern Ohio	Down: 1.5; Up: 768Kbps	Internet/ LAN Access	N/A		Approximately one-half of Cincinnati Bell's one million access lines have been deployed. Goal is to deploy more than 85% of 1 million access lines by end of 1999.
Concentric Network Corp. (ISP)	10 Cities in Northern California	Down: 1.5; Up: 384KB or 384KB in both directions	Internet/ LAN Access	N/A	Yes, in various locations	Launched ADSL in 10 Northern California cities in November 1997
Covad Communications Inc. (CLEC)	San Francisco Bay Area and Silicon Valley, Boston, and New York	384Kbps in both directions; 1.1Mbps in both directions; or Down: 1.5Mbps/ Up:384Kbps	Internet/ LAN Access	N/A	Yes, in various locations	Launched ADSL service in Dec. 1997 available to 700,000 homes, businesses; plans to offer ADSL to 5 million more in Boston, New York, Washington DC, Los Angeles, and Seattle by March 1999
DNAI (ISP)	Danville, San Ramon, and Silicon Valley	Down: 1.5 Mbps; Up: 384Kbps, or 384 in both directions	Internet/ LAN Access	N/A		Launched ADSL service in Dec. 1997
Dakota Services Limited (CLEC/NSP)	Milwaukee, WI, Chicago, IL	Down: up to 2.5 Mbps; Up: 1Mbps in both directions	Internet/ LAN Access	N/A		ADSL service deployed in Milwaukee Wis., in July 1997 expanding to most cities and towns in the states by mid-1998. In August 1998, began offering ADSL in Chicago too.

Company	Availability	Speed	Applications	Trial Dates	ATM Transport	Service Deployments
eazy.net (ISP)	Denver, CO	Down: 640 Kbps-2.5 Mbps; 272-1 Mbps-1Mbps	Internet/ LAN Access, Multimedia, Telecomm., Distance Learning	N/A		August 18, 1997; speeds up to 7Mbps expected to be available soon.
Elkhart Telephone Company	Elkhart, KS	Down: Up to 2.5 Mbps; Up: up to 1 Mbps	Internet/ LAN Access			February 1998 rollout to business and residential customers. Will offer video conferencing in the near future.
Epoch Internet (ISP)	Northern California, San Francisco Bay Area	Down: Up to 1.5Mbps	Internet/ LAN Access			Rolled out ADSL service in March 1998
Flashcom	Northern & Southern CA, MA, New York, Connecticut, Illinois, New Jersey, & Washington, DC	Down: 144 Kbps Up: 1.566Mbps	Internet/ LAN Access			Nov. 98 will offer service in Detroit, Dallas, & Houston. By March 1999, will add Miami, Cleveland, Atlanta, Austin, Baltimore, Seattle, & Denver
FullWave Networks	Most of New York	Down: 144 Kbps Up: 1.5Mbps	Internet/ LAN Access			Additional coverage in New York City available by end of 1998, will include Long Island, Northern New Jersey, Westchester and Fairfield counties in early 1999
Global 2000 Communications (ISP)	Albany, Schenectady, Troy, Glens Falls, and Plattsburg, NY	Down: 256 Kbps-10Mbps: Up: 256 Kbps-1Mbps	Internet/ LAN Access			ADSL service deployed in April 1998.
GTE Communications Corp. (newly formed CLEC subsidiary)	Southern California (Marina del Ray, CA)	Business-Down: 1.5Mbps: up:384Kbps	Internet/ LAN Access			GTE Com. commercially deployed ADSL mid Nov. 1997 in So. Calif. and will offer ADSL
		Residential-Dwn:680Kbps; up 256Kpbs				In "numerous key markets" through the US in 1998; GTE

continues

Table C.2 ADSL Providers in the United States Continued

Company	Availability	Speed	Applications	Trial Dates	ATM Transport	Service Deployments
GTE Network Services	Irving, TX (Dallas)	Down: 1.5 Mbps; Up: 64Kbps Up: 256-384Kbps	Internet/ LAN Access	Feb. 1996		Network plans to convert its ADSL trials into broad-market deployments
GTE and Microsoft	Redmond, WA	Down: up to 6Mbps; 384Kbps	Tele-commuting/ Net Access	Feb. 1996-Ongoing		at downstream speeds up to 1.5Mbps in Redmond and Kirkland, WA; Durham, NC; W. Lafayette, Ind., and
GTE and Duke University	Durham, NC	Down: up to 6Mbps; 384Kbps	Internet/ Medical Imaging	Nov. 1996		Beverton, OR, by June 1998. During the second half of
GTE and Purdue University	Lafayette, IN	Down: up to 6Mbps; 384Kbps	Internet/ LAN Access	Nov. 1996		1998, GTE plans to offer ADSL in at least 30 additional market clusters in 16 states.
Hart Telephone Company	Hartwell and other parts of Hart County, Georgia		Cable over ADSL, providing 80 channels of cable TV programming	Began offering ADSL in September 1998		
ICG Communications, Inc. (CLEC)	Colorado, California, Ohio Valley, and parts of Southeastern U.S.		Internet/ LAN Access			March 1998 launch
Intelecom Data Systems (ISP)	Rhode Island	Down: 640 Kbps-2.5 Mbps; Up*: 275Kbps - 1.08Mbps	Internet/ LAN Access, Video Streaming, Desktop Video Confer-encing, Telemedicine	N/A		March 1997 in Rhode Island; plans to expand to other NE areas
Inter-Access (ISP)	Chicago, IL	Down: 1.5 Mbps; Up: 64Kbps	Internet Access	N/A		Sep. 1996
Interstate Telephone Co. (CLEC)	West Point, GA	Down: up to 7Mbps; Up: 1Mbps	Internet/ LAN Access w/VPN	N/A		4th Quarter 1997

Company	Availability	Speed	Applications	Trial Dates	ATM Transport	Service Deployments
ioNET, Inc. (NSP)	Oklahoma City and Tulsa	Down: up to 7Mbps Up: Up to 1Mbps	Internet/ LAN Access	N/A		Mid-Sum. 1997 in Oklahoma City & Tulsa; Kansas City, Little Rock, Austin, Dallas, Houston & San Antonio soon thereafter
LEACO Rural Telephone Cooperative	Schools in South-eastern New Mexico		Internet Access	N/A		Began providing ADSL service for SE New Mexico schools in late July 1997
Loretto Telephone Company	Middle Tennessee	Down: Up to 2.5Mbps Down: Up to 1Mbps	Internet/ LAN Access	N/A		Began offering ADSL in July 1998 for educational and business customers in Middle Tennessee
Lyceum Internet (ISP)	Available now in Buckhead	1.5-7Mbps	Internet/ LAN Access			Began offering ADSL in August 1998 in the Buckhead area; will expand to Dunwoody and Powers Ferry areas of Atlanta in October 1998
Network Access Solutions (CLEC)	Mid-Atlantic region	Down: up to 6Mbps	Services to ISPs			February 1997; rolling out to other regional markets throughout 97
New Hope Telephone Cooperative	New Hope, Owens Cross Roads & Grant, AL	Down:680 Kbps; Up: 270Mbps	Internet/ LAN Access	Market Trial: March 1998 in New Hope		Will begin offering ADSL services in June 1998 also in Owens Cross Roads & Grant
Northwest Link (ISP)	Downtown Bellevue and Seattle, WA	*1Mbps in both directions	Internet/ LAN Access	June-Dec. 1997		Began offering ADSL services in Jan. 1998 to businesses and schools
OneNet Communica-tions, Inc. (ISP)	Downtown Cincinnati, OH		Internet/ LAN Access			Service launched December 1997; plans to expand service to entire Greater Metropolitan area
Orconet (ISP)	Southern & Northern CA	Down: 384Kbps; Up: 4Kbps or Down: 1.5Mbps; Up: 384Kbps	Internet/ LAN Access	N/A		Began offering ADSL in California in June 1998

continues

299

Table C.2   ADSL Providers in the United States Continued

Company	Availability	Speed	Applications	Trial Dates	ATM Transport	Service Deployments
Rhythms NetConnections, Inc. (ISP)	San Diego, San Francisco Bay Area & Los Angeles, CA; Boston and Chicago	Down: Up to 7Mbps; Up: 192 Kbps or 1 Mbps in both directions	Internet/ LAN Access and Remote File Backup	July 1997- Jan 1998		Rolled out ADSL in April 1998 to San Diego area businesses; will extend to San Francisco Bay Area and Los Angeles in June 1998; intends to expand into 30 metro markets by year-end 2000
SBC Communications, Inc. (ILEC) (through telephone subsidiaries Pacific Bell and Southwestern Bell)	200 communities in So. CA, and including San Jose, San Francisco, Oakland, Anaheim, Los Angeles, San Diego, Sacramento	Res: Down: 384Kbps; Up: 128Kbps SOHO: 384 Kbps symmetrical Bus: 384 Kbps symmetrical or 1.5Mbps down and 384Kbps up	Internet/ LAN Access	See the two entries below	Yes	Limited rollout Nov. 1997 in San Francisco Bay Area, Calif. (Pacific Bell) and in Austin, Tex. (Southwestern Bell). In September 1998, the following ISPs partnered with Pacific Bell to begin offering ADSL services in certain areas
Pacific Bell	San Francisco, Bay Area, CA	Down: 6 Mbps; Up: 640Kbps	Internet Access/ Video on Demand	Aug. 1996- Ongoing	Yes	of Calif: 4Link, Argotech, Bay Area Internet Solutions,
SBC Comm. (ILEC) and Shell Oil	Houston, TX	Down: 6 Mbps; Up: 640Kbps	Internet Access/ Video on Demand	Tech.: May 1996- Ongoing; Market: 7/96	Yes	Channel Islands Internet, CTSnet, Data Depot, DSL Networks, EarthLink Networks, Flashcom, Worldcom Advanced Networks, ihighway, Millenia Net, ISP Network, NetConcept, Netease, PacificNet, PC Solutions, Sirius Connections, Softcomm, Sonic, Znet, Best Internet, Direct Network Access
Signet Partners Inc. (ISP)	Austin, TX	Down: Up to 6Mbps	Internet/ LAN Access			Austin in January 1997; Houston and San Antonio, Tex. By June 1997

Company	Availability	Speed	Applications	Trial Dates	ATM Transport	Service Deployments
Slip.Net (ISP)	Silicon Valley, CA	Down: 1.5 Mbps; Up: 384Kbps; also 384Kbps and 1.1 Mbps in both directions	Internet/ LAN Access	N/A		Launched Dec. 1997 in Silicon Valley; San Francisco slated for Jan. 1998 rollout, with rest of Bay Area by mid-1998
SourceNet Corp. (ISP)	Northern Nevada	Down: Up to 1.5 Mbps; Up: 384/640 Kbps	Internet/ LAN Access	Early 1997		Rolled out ADSL service in Feb. 1998
Supra Tele-communica-tions & Information Systems (CLEC)			Internet/ LAN Access			Began offering ADSL service in Florida in August 1998 to business and residential customers
Teleport Communica-tions Group (TCG) and DualStar Technologies	New York City, NY	Down:up to 7Mbps Up: Up to 1Mbps	Internet/ LAN Access, including multi-tenant buildings	Nov-97		Rolled out ADSL service to New York City residents in May 1998
Transport Logic (ISP)	Portland, OR	Down: 640 Kbps-2.5 Mbps; Up*: 275Kbps-1.08Mbps	Internet/ LAN Access	N/A		April 1997 for Portland, Ore.; 4 more cities in Ore. and Wash. by the end of May
US West !nterprise (ILEC)	Available now in select cities in Colorado, Idaho, Arizona, Minnesota, Utah, Nebraska, & North Dakota	Speed Options: 256Kbps for home users; 512Kbps for tele-commuters, small businesses; 768Kbps or 1-7Mbps for large firms and power users	Internet/ LAN Access	Technical trial ends Dec. 31, 1997		Plans to deploy ADSL services 40 cities in 14 states by July 1998 for 5 million customers
	VDSL will be available in Phoenix in summer 1998	Down**: Up to 52 Mbps	Integrated Digital TV, Cable Programs, & Internet access			Will deploy VDSL in Phoenix this summer & expand to other markets in 1999

continues

301

Table C.2 ADSL Providers in the United States Continued

Company	Availability	Speed	Applications	Trial Dates	ATM Transport	Service Deployments
Valley Telephone Cooperative	Remote ranching area between San Antonio, TX. & the Rio Grande Valley	*700Kbps in both directions	Internet/ LAN Access			Began deploying ADSL services for business, school, and residential customers in March 1998
Verio Northern California (ISP)	San Francisco, CA	384Kbps in both directions; 1.1Mbps in both directions; or Down: 1.5Mbps/ Up:384Kbps	Internet/ LAN Access			1998 rollout
Western Regional Networks (ISP)	Grand Junction, CO		Internet/ LAN Access			Limited deployment began May 1997
World Web Internet Service (ISP)	Birmingham, AL	Down: Up to 6Mbps; Up: Up to 640Kbps	Internet/ LAN Access	Market Trial: Began Jan. 98. Expanding to Ft. Lauderdale, Raleigh, Charlotte, Atlanta, New Orleans & Jacksonville	Yes	Began offering ADSL service in Jan 1998 as part of BellSouth's market trial

Table C.3 ADSL Providers in Canada

Company	Availability	Speed	Applications	Trial Dates	ATM Transport	Service Deployments
BC TELECOM and 12 ISPs: Sympatico, Internet Direct, Internet Gateway, Smartnet, BCnet, Island Internet, Pacific	Greater Vancouver, Victoria, Kamloops South, Nanaimo, Kelowna, Vernon, & Prince George, BC	Down: 1-4 Mbps; Up: 160-640 Kbps	Internet/ LAN Access, Video Conferencing, Telecommuting	Tech./ Market Trial: Nov. 1996- Nov. 1997 Market Trial: Sept. 1997		Commercial service launched Jan. 1998, in Vancouver, Oak Bay, and Southern Kamloops in partnership with 12 ISPs. Service will be expanded throughout 1998 and 1999.

Company	Availability	Speed	Applications	Trial Dates	ATM Transport	Service Deployments
Inter-connect, Ultranet, ABC Comm-unications, Paralynx, Okanagan Internet Junction & Radiant Communica-tions						
Bell Canada	Ottawa/Hull & Quebec City areas	Down: 2.2 Mbps; Up: 1Mbps	Internet/LAN Access	Customer Trial: Sept. 1996-Ongoing in Kanata, ON and St. Bruno, Quebec	Yes, in various markets	Oct. 1997 rollout in the Ottawa/Hull & Quebec City areas to ISP's; will offer to businesses in 1998 and expand to Montreal and Toronto markets
CADVision (ISP)	Calgary, Alberta	Down: 2.5 Mbps; Up: 1Mbps	Internet Access	N/A		Service launched Nov. 1996
City Tel	Prince Rupert, BC		Internet/LAN Access, Streaming Video, Distance Learning, Tele-medicine, and Video on Demand	N/A		Service rolled out November 1997 with 1,000 lines; plans to fully deploy the service by mid-1998
Echelon Internet Corp. (ISP)	Ottawa, Ontario		Internet/LAN Access	N/A		Began offering ADSL to businesses
Maritime Tel. & Tel. (MT&T)	Halifax, Nova Scotia	Down: Up to 7Mbps	Internet Access	Tech: April 1997-Ongoing		Nov. 1997 limited deployment; April 1998 full commercial deployment in Halifax. Will expand service throughout Nova Scotia in 1998-1999.
QuebecTel	Central and Eastern Quebec	Down: 640 Kbps-2.2 Mbps; Up: 272Kbps-1 Mbps	Internet/LAN Access, Video on Demand; Distance Learning			Service launched Sept. 1997
SaskTel (CLEC)	Weyburn & Regina, Saskatoon, & Prince Albert Sask.	Down: up to 7.1 Mbps; Up: 64Kbps	Internet Access	N/A	Yes	Limited service launched Nov. 1996 in Regina & Saskatoon. Prince Albert added in Jan 1998.

continues

303

Table C.3   ADSL Providers in Canada Continued

Company	Availability	Speed	Applications	Trial Dates	ATM Transport	Service Deployments
TELUS Advanced Communications and TELUS PLAnet	Edmonton, Calgary, St. Albert and Sherwood Park	Down: up to 2.5 Mbps; Up: 1.0Mbps	Internet Access	N/A		Launched DSL services in January 1998.

Table C.4   ADSL Providers in Europe

Company	Availability	Speed	Applications	Trial Dates	ATM Transport	Service Deployments
Helsinki Telephone Co. (Finland)	Helsinki	Down: 2 Mbps; Up: 9.6Kbps	Internet/ LAN Access, multimedia, 3D virtual city, 'Net phones and live video	Aug. 1995-March 1996		Began limited rollout Feb 1997 in Helsinki. There could be 20,000 xDSL users by the year 2000

Table C.5   ADSL Providers in Asia/Pacific

Company	Availability	Speed	Applications	Trial Dates	ATM Transport	Service Deployments
Hong Kong Telecom (Hong Kong)		Down**: 51Mbps; Up: 1.5 Mbps	Video on Demand	VoD: Summer 1996		Commercial rollout in July 1997; telco projects 250,000 users by year 2000.
Nippon Telegraph & Telephone (NTT)	Japan	Down: 1.5 Mbps; Up: 512Kbps	Internet Access	Testing Ended December 1998		NTT will start deploying ADSL in limited areas in the Fall of 1999. Nationwide deployment will take place in Fall 2000.
Singapore Telecom (Singapore)	5,000 homes there by year-end 1997	Down: 8 Mbps; Up: 1Mbps	Video on Demand, Internet access; nearly 100 applications available	Technical: Feb. 1996; Commercial trial began Jun-97	Yes	Expects 10,000 lines deployed in 1997; island-wide rollout by the end of 1998; projects 80,000 subscribers by then.

304

Table C.6 Multitenant Buildings and Other ADSL Installations

Company	Availability	Speed	Applications	Trial Dates	ATM Transport	Service Deployments
American Information Systems (ISP) & The John Buck Company	Evanston (Chicago), IL	Down:1.5 Mbps; Up: 64Kbps	Internet/ LAN Access	N/A		First deployed at luxury high-rise apartment building; other JBC properties to follow.
DualStar Comm. & TCG	Manhattan, NY	Down: 7 Mbps; Up: 1Mbps	Internet/ LAN Access	N/A		Rolled out in West End Towers.
GTE Communications Corp. (newly formed CLEC subsidiary)	Southern California (Marina del Ray, CA)	Business-Down:1.5 Mbps; Up: 384Kbps Residential-Down: 680 Kbps; Up: 256Kbps	Internet/ LAN Access	See GTE entry for trial information		GTE Com. Commercially deployed ADSL mid-Nov. 1997 in Southern Calif.
GTE Government Services		Down:1.5 Mbps; Up: 64Kbps Down*: 640-2.2 Mbps; Up: 272Kbps to 1.08	Internet/ LAN Access	N/A		Deployment August 1997 at U.S. military bases around the world.
ITT Sheraton Corporation	Sydney, Australia		Internet/ LAN Access, Video on Demand	N/A		Began service December 1 in Sydney, Australia, with a rollout throughout Asia-Pacific beginning Feb. 1998; other properties in Europe, the Americas, Middle East and Africa to follow
Televideo, Inc.	New York City		Video on Demand and other interactive multimedia	N/A		Rolled out in high-rise apartment building February 1997
Thorn Communications (ISP; filed for CLEC status) & Newmark Real Estate	Manhattan, New York "Silicon Alley"	Down: 2.56 Mbps	Internet/ LAN Access	N/A		Deployed in select office buildings in the downtown Manhattan financial district

continues

Table C.6 Multitenant Buildings and Other ADSL Installations Continued

Company	Availability	Speed	Applications	Trial Dates	ATM Transport	Service Deployments
Trump Organization & FreelinQ	Trump Tower in New York City	Down: 6 Mbps; Up: 640Kbps	Internet/ LAN Access, Audio & Video on Demand	N/A		Deployed Oct. 97 in Trump Tower

Legend

CLEC	Competitive Local Exchange Carrier
ISP	Internet Service Provider
NSP	Network Service Provider
VPN	Virtual Private Networking
ILEC	Incumbent Local Exchange Carrier
VDSL	Very High Digital Subscriber Line
IXC	Interexchange Carrier

Source

ADSL Forum

39355 California St., Ste. 307

Fremont, CA 94538-1447, USA

Phone: 510-608-5905

Fax: 510-608-5917

Email: ADSLForum@adsl.com

Web site: http://www.adsl.com

Satellite Services

Satellite Services are available from DirecPC in the following areas:

➤ North Asia

➤ Canada

➤ USA

➤ Europe

➤ Mexico

Although these areas may seem a little broad, consider that the satellites for Internet communication cut a wide swath as they orbit the earth.

Just in case you're thinking of high-speed net surfing via satellite from the top of Mount Rainier, don't forget that you also need a local ISP to carry your outbound clicks to the Internet. See Chapter 7, "You've Got the Whole World in Your HAN: Connecting to the Internet," for more information on how satellite Internet connections work.

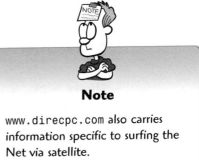

Note

`www.direcpc.com` also carries information specific to surfing the Net via satellite.

ISDN

Although nowhere near as speedy as cable modems, ADSL, or satellite, ISDN is still twice the speed of a 56KB modem, and as such should be considered a high-speed alternative.

Local carriers include

➤ Ameritech

> ➤ **Home page** `www.ameritech.com`

> ➤ **Ameritech ISDN Lookup** `www.ameritech.com/products/data/isdn/isdnfrm1.html`

> ➤ To order ISDN from Ameritech, call 1-800-832-6328

➤ Bell Atlantic

> ➤ **Home page** `www.bell-atl`

> ➤ To order residential ISDN, call 1-800-204-7332

> ➤ For ISDN sales and tech support, call 1-800-570-4736

➤ BellSouth

> ➤ **Home page** `www.bellsouth.com`

➤ Cincinnati Bell

> ➤ **Home page** `www.cinbelltel.com`

> ➤ For Cincinnati Bell's ISDN Service Center, call 513-566-3282

➤ GTE

> ➤ **Home page** `www.gte.com`

> ➤ For availability and orders, call 1-800-GTE-4WCN

➤ Nynex

  ➤ **Home page** www.bell-atl.com

  ➤ For availability and orders, call 1-800-GET-ISDN

➤ Pacific Bell

  ➤ **Home page** www.pacbell.com

  ➤ For availability and pricing, call 1-800-4PB-ISDN

➤ Southwestern Bell

  ➤ **Home page** www.sbc.com

  ➤ For availability and orders, call ISDN sales at 713-567-ISDN

➤ US West

  ➤ **Home page** www.uswest.com

  ➤ **ISDN page** www.uswest.com/isdn/index.html

  ➤ **US West ordering information** www.uswest.com/isdn/order.html

Long-distance ISDN carriers are fewer and farther between:

➤ AT&T Digital Long Distance Service

  ➤ **Home page** www.att.com/home64/

➤ Sprint_ISDN

  ➤ **Home page** csb.sprint.com:80/home/local/c.html

Index

313

N

X-Y-Z

Pronounced "to emanate," the 2mn8 name was chosen to describe the free flow of education that we wanted to provide.

The site was developed to continue our quest to provide the most up-to-date and informative source for the emerging field of home networking. We hope you enjoy reading it as much as we did contributing to it.

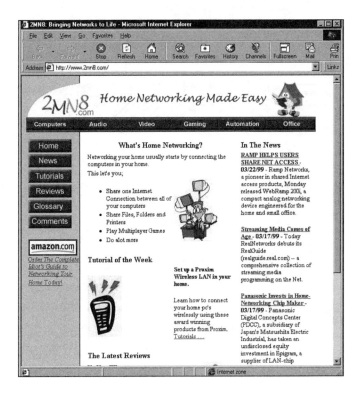

We wanted to continue to provide simple, fun, and effective tutorials on home networking. Please visit our comments area and let us know what tutorials you would like to see.

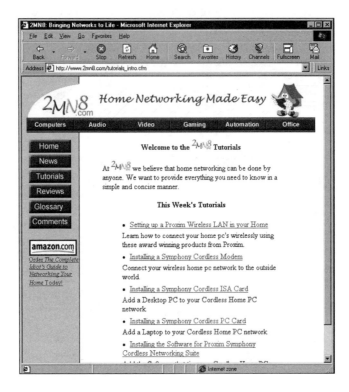

Many new home networking products are being released every week. We are providing reviews of the best products as they come to market.

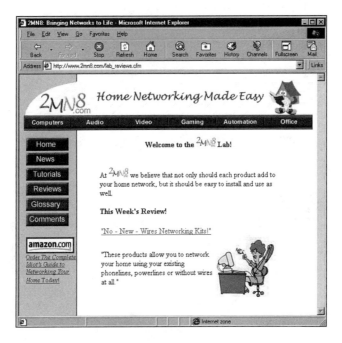

The technical terms used in this field can sometimes be baffling for readers. We have tried to simplify many of these with a straightforward definition and an even simpler 2MNaSHUN, pronounced "to emanation."

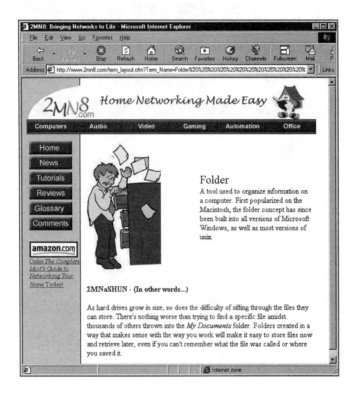

The home area network is something we have been envisioning for quite some time. We are happy to see that its time has come.